El Lissitzky

El Lissitzky

Beyond the *Abstract Cabinet*:
Photography, Design, Collaboration

Margarita Tupitsyn, with contributions
by Matthew Drutt and Ulrich Pohlmann

Yale University Press

New Haven and London

German edition ©1999 by Schirmer/Mosel, Munich,
and Margarita Tupitsyn.
A Schirmer/Mosel production. All rights reserved.
English edition ©1999 by Yale University and
Margarita Tupitsyn.

Illustrations by Josef Albers, Boris Ignatovich, El Lissitzky,
Man Ray, and Otto Umbehr (Umbo), ©1999 by VG Bild-Kunst,
Bonn.

Designed by Klaus E. Göltz, Halle

Front cover: El Lissitzky, *Self-Portrait* (Constructor), 1924.
Photomontage, gelatin silver print, collage. State Tretiakov
Gallery, Moscow.

Frontispiece: El Lissitzky, design for the *Abstract Cabinet*,
1927. Gouache, collage. Sprengel Museum Hannover.

Back cover: El Lissitzky, with Aleksandr Grigorovich and
Mikhail V. Nikolaev. *USSR: An Album Illustrating the State
Organization and National Economy of the USSR, 1939.*
Larry Zeman and Howard Garfinkel, Productive Arts, Brooklyn
Heights, Ohio.

Concept of the exhibition: Margarita Tupitsyn

Translations from the German:
Ulrich Pohlmann's essay, by Pauline Cumbers;
El Lissitzky's letters, by Kenneth Kronenburg.

Library of Congress Number 99−072781
ISBN 0−300−08170−7

A catalogue record for this book is available from the British
Library.
The paper in this book meets the guidelines for permanence
and durability of the Committee on Production Guidelines for
Book Longevity of the Council on Library Resources.
10 9 8 7 6 5 4 3 2 1

Contents

Acknowledgments

As a freelance curator I am particularly dependent on my colleagues in various museums. I wish to thank Ute Eskildsen of the Museum Folkwang, Essen, and Vicente Todolí, of the Fondação de Serralves, Porto, who from the beginning supported my intention to organize an exhibition of El Lissitzky's photographic work. I am also indebted to Ulrich Krempel of the Sprengel Museum Hannover, who invited me to realize the exhibition and provided me with extraordinary research opportunities that were further expanded by a grant from the International Research and Exchanges Board (IREX). I am grateful to Thomas Weski of the Sprengel Museum for his patience, encouragement, and professionalism during the project. Ulrike Schneider, who joined us during the last phase, oversaw many details that were essential for the completion of the book and exhibition.

Although I am indebted to all the lenders, Larry Zeman of Productive Arts, Brooklyn Heights, Ohio, and Priska Pasquer of Photographic Art Consulting, Cologne, were especially helpful in obtaining many loans. Nancy Perloff was most helpful during my research visit to the Getty Research Institute for the History of Art and the Humanities. El Lissitzky's son, Jen Lissitzky, shared valuable information about his late father and mother.

In Russia, Elena Gasparova of the Russian State Archive for Literature and Art exhibited dedication, professionalism, and knowledge. My thanks also go to Natalia Adaskina and Lidia Iovleva of the State Tretiakov Gallery for their continuous support and to Ekaterina Selezneva for organizing the loans and photographs for the State Tretiakov Gallery.

Vicente Todolí and Manuel J. Borja-Villel of the Museu d'Art Contemporani de Barcelona should be acknowledged as partners of the exhibition tour. Their participation in this project amply demonstrates that the three of us continue to share the same beliefs we advanced as Ph.D. students at the Graduate Center of the City University of New York in the 1980s.

I am grateful to Lothar Schirmer, Schirmer/Mosel Verlag, and to his highly professional staff, Birgit Mayer and Regine Kaiser in particular, for producing the striking catalogue that accompanied this exhibition. Judy Metro, senior editor at Yale University Press, provided enthusiastic support for the English edition of this publication. Karen Gangel, manuscript editor, provided excellent editing. The thoughtful and illuminating essays by Matthew Drutt of the Guggenheim Museum and Ulrich Pohlmann of Münchner Stadtmuseum Fotomuseum have greatly enhanced this volume.

Finally, my thanks go to my husband, Victor Tupitsyn, for providing me with inspiring conversations and necessary criticisms. The transformation of my daughter, Masha, from a teenager adapting to her mother's intense and rigorous work schedule into a young writer and helpful editor indicates how long I have been on the path of sorting through the turbulent history of the Soviet avant-garde.

Margarita Tupitsyn

Foreword

Ten years after the retrospective held on the occasion of El Lissitzky's one hundredth birthday at the Sprengel Museum Hannover, we are pleased to present, together with the Museu d'Art Contemporani de Barcelona, and the Fondação de Serralves, Porto, another large exhibition of photographs and designs by this important Soviet artist as well as his collaborative projects. *El Lissitzky: Beyond the Abstract Cabinet* illustrates for the first time the breadth and complexity of Lissitzky's career beyond his better-known abstract production. We owe the concept and suggestion for this exhibition to Margarita Tupitsyn, the guest curator. I wish to express my appreciation to her for a successful collaboration.

My particular gratitude goes to Preussag AG, whose interest and support made possible this outstanding exhibition. I would also like to thank the lenders for entrusting us with their valuable works. I am especially grateful to Jen Lissitzky, El Lissitzky's son; the Russian State Archive for Literature and Art; and the State Tretiakov Gallery in Moscow, who made available to the West for the first time many of the works by Lissitzky and his circle. I am also thankful to the directors of the cooperating institutions, Manuel J. Borja-Villel in Barcelona and Vicente Todolí in Porto, for their interest and commitment at an early stage of this exhibition as well as for their helpful and friendly collaboration.

Our valued association with the Munich publishing house Schirmer/Mosel continues with this catalogue. My thanks to Lothar Schirmer for his willingness to include it in his program.

The following colleagues were responsible for the exhibition at the Sprengel Museum Hannover: Thomas Weski, Curator of Photography and Media; Ulrike Schneider, who assisted in organizing the project, the catalogue, and the tour; Brigitte Nandingna, registrar for the processing of the loans; and Ria Heine and Martina Mogge-Auerswald, conservators.

I am pleased that through this project we have made a major contribution to the evaluation of El Lissitzky's photographic works and have presented one of those rare exhibitions of Soviet avant-garde art that goes beyond its first, abstract phase into the second, defined by the use of photography, photomontage, and film.

Ulrich Krempel
Director, Sprengel Museum Hannover

The auspices under which El Lissitzky traveled to Germany in late 1921 have never been firmly established. By some accounts, he went in an official capacity to help export Soviet culture abroad, which included assisting in the preparations for the Erste Russische Kunstaustellung (the First Russian Exhibition), a major art exhibition that was held the following year at the Van Diemen Gallery. Others surmise that he went independently, albeit as an "unofficial emissary," attracted by better working conditions and Germany's status as a crossroads for artistic activity.[1] Whatever the reasons, what resulted from his initial sojourn—which lasted barely two years and was characterized by frequent travel to various German cities and neighboring countries—was a series of collaborative and interdisciplinary projects that drew upon his explorations of painting, graphic design, and architecture combined with a burgeoning interest in photography, catapulting him into the limelight of the international avant-garde and transforming him into something of an ambassador for activities emerging both at home and abroad.

By the time Lissitzky arrived in Berlin, he was already an exemplary figure among the generation of vanguard artists who emerged in the wake of the Russian Revolution. Only a few years earlier, while he was teaching architecture and graphic design at the Khudozhestvenno-Praktichesky Institut (Artistic-Technical Institute) at the invitation of Marc Chagall, his work underwent a swift and fundamental shift from figuration to geometric abstraction. Under the tutelage of the Suprematist painter Kazimir Malevich, who joined Vitebsk's faculty several months after Lissitzky did, and formed the UNOVIS group (Affirmers of the New Art), Lissitzky began a body of work he would later call *Prouns* (an acronym for Project for the Affirmation of the New; fig. 1).[2] These dynamic compositions of abstract, geometric forms, lying somewhere between painting, design, and architecture, exemplified the modernist utopian vision of art as a means of social transformation that was emerging in a number of similar iterations throughout Europe. In an essay written in 1920, Lissitzky proclaimed: "The artist constructs a new symbol with his brush. This symbol is not a recognizable form of anything in the world—its is a symbol of the new world, which is being built upon and which exists by way of the people."[3] Lissitzky carried Suprematism beyond Malevich's original formulation of pure painting imbued with a spiritual aura. With their multiple references to real and abstract space, the *Prouns* became a system through which Lissitzky not only ruminated upon formal properties of transparency, opacity, color, shape, and line but began to dwell upon the deployment of these forms into socialized space, placing him into the path of the emergence of Constructivism, which, using a similarly reductive visual vocabulary, sought to merge art and life through mass production and industry.

That path came none too soon. Lissitzky moved to Moscow at the beginning of 1921 to teach painting and architecture at VKhUTEMAS (the Higher State Artistic-Technical Workshops), the Russian polytechnic comparable to Germany's Bauhaus. Its interdisciplinary environment, where painting, design, architecture, photography, and handcrafts were taught under a single roof, was radically opposed to the traditions of the academy and reflected the new persona of the artist as worker or engineer as it was evolving amid the rhetoric of Soviet culture. The collision between art for art's sake and art with a utilitarian purpose was settling there by the

Matthew Drutt

El Lissitzky in Germany 1922–1925

Art is the tool of universal progress.
—El Lissitzky, 1922

1 El Lissitzky: *Proun R.V.N. 2,* 1923. Mixed media on canvas. 99 x 99 cm. Sprengel Museum Hannover

1 Suggested by Peter Nisbet, "An Introduction to El Lissitzky," in *El Lissitzky: 1890–1941* (Cambridge: Harvard University Art Museums), 25.
2 Lissitzky called the *Proun* an "interchange station between painting and architecture." The acronym was formed from Pro + Unovis. Other meanings have been ascribed to it, but the interchange metaphor is the one that has endured. See Henk Puts, "El Lissitzky (1890–1941): His Life and Work," in *El Lissitzky, 1890–1941: Architect, Painter, Photographer, Typographer* (Eindhoven: Municipal Van Abbemuseum, 1990), 17.
3 El Lissitzky, "The Suprematism of the Creative Work," in S. Lissitzky-Küppers and J. Lissitzky, eds., *Proun und Wolkenbügel: Schriften, Briefe, Dokumente* (Dresden: VEB Verlag der Kunst, 1977), 15–20.

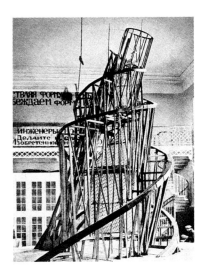

2 Vladimir Tatlin: Model of the *Monument to the Third International*, Moscow, 1920

3 El Lissitzky: Cover and typography for the magazine *Veshch-Gegenstand-Object*, vols. 1–2, Berlin, 1922. Collection Ann and Jürgen Wilde, Zülpich. Cat. 124

4 El Lissitzky, "New Russian Art: A Lecture (1922)," trans. in Sophie Lissitzky-Küppers, *El Lissitzky: Life, Letters, Text* (Greenwich: New York Graphic Society, 1968), 336.

time Lissitzky arrived. Leading figures at VKhUTEMAS included Aleksandr Rodchenko, who would declare the death of painting later that year, and Vladimir Tatlin, creator of the proto-Constructivist landmark *Monument to the Third International* (fig. 2). Lissitzky continued working on the *Proun* paintings and lecturing about them at VKhUTEMAS and INKhUK (the Institute of Artistic Culture), paying increasing attention to typographic projects that would be important points of departure for his work in Germany.

In spite of Lissitzky's affinities with Russian Constructivism at that time, his work remained somehow more idiosyncratic and privileged aesthetics above utility. In a lecture on Russian art given in 1922, he summed up these differences: "Two groups claimed constructivism, the OBMOKhU (the brothers Stenberg, Medunestky, Ioganson, and others) and the UNOVIS (Senkin, Klutsis, Ermolaeva, and others led by Malevich and Lissitzky). The former group worked in material and space, the latter in material and plane. Both strove to attain the same result, namely the creation of the real object and of architecture. They are opposed to each other in their concepts of the practicality and utility of creative things. Some members of the OBMOKhU group … went as far as a complete disavowal of art in their urge to be inventors, devoted their energies to pure technology. UNOVIS distinguished between the concept of functionality, meaning the necessity for the creation of new forms, and the question of direct serviceableness.[4]" Thus, for Lissitzky constructive art could be successful as art only if its aesthetic program remained dominant to technological considerations, a sentiment he would continue to assert in the ensuing years.

Despite the enormous vitality of Russia's contemporary art milieu, contact with Europe was severely limited. Thus when Lissitzky arrived in Berlin at the end of 1921, he was intent on building bridges with artists from abroad. Berlin of the 1920s was one of the great cultural capitals of Europe, surpassing Paris in both the diversity and density of artistic movements taking root there. After the war it became a fertile breeding ground for both Expressionism and Dada, the latter of which celebrated the "machine-art" of Tatlin at the Ersten Internationalen Dada-Messe (First International Dada Fair) of 1920, while gallerists such as Herwarth Walden and Alfred Flechtheim promoted vanguard art throughout Europe. Because of Berlin's geographic location, it was an obligatory stopover for artists traveling eastward, and vice versa, and developed into a kind of international way station, with people constantly coming and going. Moreover, its proximity to the Soviet Union nourished a large Russian community, composed both of émigrés who fled the country after the Revolution and those who went to promote the new Soviet state as part of the New Economic Policy of 1921. Berlin therefore became a strategic center for the promotion of Soviet politics and culture, and by 1920 more than one hundred thousand Russians of various persuasions had settled there.

Among them was a writer named Ilia Ehrenburg, who was affiliated with the Scythians, a group of intellectuals who supported the Revolution but opposed bolshevism. Ehrenburg became one of Lissitzky's close comrades in the early months of his stay. In the tradition of modernist journals proclaiming the arrival of new art forms to a broader audience, such as *L'Esprit Nouveau, de Stijl,* and *Valori Plastici,* Ehrenburg and Lissitzky published the periodical *Veshch-Gegenstand-Object* (fig. 3),

 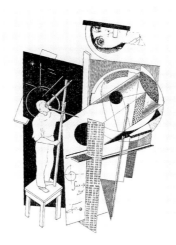  

which appeared only twice in 1922 but whose objective was to act as an international journal of contemporary culture, hence its trilingual title and content. It provided both a window to the West for artists back in Russia and a view for Western readers into the various cultural activities in the Soviet Union. The inaugural issue included notices of forthcoming exhibitions, artists' congresses, and announcements for other avant-garde periodicals, as well as interviews with such artists as Fernand Léger and Gino Severini, articles by Le Corbusier and Theo van Doesberg, and one by Nikolai Punin celebrating Tatlin's *Monument to the Third International,* which was fast becoming the symbol in Germany for Russia's artistic revolution.[5] In their editorial, entitled "The Blockade of Russia Is Reaching Its End," the editors declared: "From now on, art, while preserving all local characteristics and symptoms is international. … We consider the triumph of the constructive method to be essential for our present. 'Object' will champion constructive art, whose mission is not, after all, to embellish life but to organize it."[6] With this last remark, Lissitzky asserts his desire to forge a concrete relationship between ideas expressed through abstract form and the inhabited environment. Although such intentions would logically be played out in the realm of architecture, he would go through a series of intervening measures before arriving at that point, many of them photographic. Lissitzky's cover design for both issues of *Veshch* adapted the language of his *Prouns,* mediated by typographical treatments, though the rest of the layout was less dynamic; photography, for example, was used only for occasional illustrations.

Shortly thereafter, however, within a series of illustrations for Ehrenburg's *6 povestei o legkikh kontsakh* (*6 Tales with Easy Endings*; figs. 4.1–4.4, plates 3–5), Lissitzky created a number of photo collages that hinted at the role that design would play in his transition from painting and typography to photography. Using found photographs rather than images taken himself, Lissitzky used the human figure in abstract *Proun*-like compositions that anticipate Moholy-Nagy's photoplastiks, done shortly afterward (fig. 5). He was certainly not the first to work with photo collage. Several years earlier in Germany, George Grosz, Hannah Höch, John Heartfield, and Raoul Hausmann had used photo collage as a satirical device in their Dada compositions, while back in Russia, a closer parallel could be found in Gustav Klutsis's work, such as *Dynamic City* (ca. 1919), which blurs the distinctions between

4.1 El Lissitzky: Cover and illustrations for Ilia Ehrenburg's *6 Tales with Easy Endings*, Berlin, 1922. 20.2 x 13.8 cm. Stedelijk Van Abbemuseum, Eindhoven. Cat. 123

4.2–4.4 El Lissitzky: Cover and illustrations for *6 Tales with Easy Endings*, Berlin, 1922. Stedelijk Van Abbemuseum, Eindhoven. Cat. 123

5 For more on the issue of Tatlin and the influence of his work on art outside the Soviet Union, see Winfried Nerdinger, *Rudolf Belling und die Kunsttroemungen in Berlin, 1918–1923* (Berlin: Deutscher Verlag für Kunstwissenschaft, 1981), 75–82.
6 Lissitzky-Küppers, *Lissitzky,* 340–41.

5 László Moholy-Nagy: *Between Heaven and Earth,* 1923. Photoplastic. 65 x 50 cm. Collection Marzona

7 Lissitzky reports meeting Hausmann upon his arrival in Berlin and discussing photography with him (*El Lissitzky: Experiments in Photography* [New York: Houk Friedman Gallery, 1991], unpaginated; hereafter cited as Houk Friedman).
8 El Lissitzky, "PROUN: Not World Visions, BUT World Reality" (1920), in Lissitzky-Küppers, *Lissitzky,* 344.
9 Peter Nisbet, "Lissitzky and Photography," in Puts, *El Lissitzky,* 67.
10 "Statement by the International Faction of Constructivists," in Stephen Bann, ed., *The Tradition of Constructivism* (New York: Viking, 1974), 69.
11 El Lissitzky, "Exhibitions in Berlin," *Veshch,* no. 3 (May 1922); trans. in Lissitzky-Küppers, *Lissitzky,* 341–42.

representation and abstract form (fig. 6).[7] What is different about Lissitzky's convention is the implication that the incorporation of a photograph into an abstract space would have for his impending deployment of abstract space into real space. Again, theorizing these issues through the *Proun,* his primary preoccupation at the time, he wrote: "*Proun* begins as a level surface, turns into a model of three-dimensional space, and goes on to construct all the objects of everyday life."[8]

In the two illustrations for Ilia Ehrenburg's *6 Tales with Easy Endings* (plates 4–5), the human body weaves in and around geometric elements with a whimsicality found more often in Moholy-Nagy's works. Yet they also have the effect of making a two-dimensional environment feel three-dimensional, a strategy taken to its most complex level in another illustration, showing Vladimir Tatlin at work on his *Monument to the Third International* (plate 3). Here the double entendres of abstraction and objectivity resonate throughout the composition. Starting with a well-known photograph of Tatlin assembling his infamous "Tower" in his studio, Lissitzky redefines that composition as a series of abstract forms in dynamic relationship to one another, interjected by "real" objects with geometric parallels. The play of intersecting planes with alternating values of opacity and transparency further creates a sense of looking into a three-dimensional space, as do devices such as a hook of a planar form grabbing Tatlin's backdrop from behind. Thus, the studio of the constructive artist is transformed into one of Lissitzky's *Prouns.* Furthermore, a compass protrudes from Tatlin's eye, signifying the status of the constructive artist as an engineer whose rational creation of form results in the organization of space. Whether or not these strategies suggest Lissitzky's dissatisfaction with abstract painting, as some have suggested,[9] they mark an important step toward blending abstract space with real space and hint at developments in his art less than a year away.

Lissitzky's advocacy of international constructive art, begun in the pages of *Veshch,* continued throughout 1922. In May he was invited to participate in the Ersten Internationalen Kongress progressiver Kunstler (International Congress of Progressive Artists) held in Düsseldorf, a failed attempt at uniting artists under a common cause without regard to nationality. There he aligned himself with artists like Theo van Doesberg and Hans Richter to articulate universal form of visual expression and artistic practice. In their subsequent critique of the conference's proceedings, they proclaimed: "Art must stop being just a way of dreaming cosmic secrets. Art is a universal and real expression of creative energy, which can be used to organize the progress of mankind; it is the tool of universal progress."[10] This stance led to the curiously paired Dada-Constructivist summit that September in Weimar, where Lissitzky met Tristan Tzara and Hans Arp.

The success and visibility that these activities brought him eventually led Lissitzky to Hanover, where he had his first solo exhibition in January 1923 at the Kestner Society, a progressive arts organization in an otherwise provincial city. The plans for the exhibition were made with the assistance of Kurt Schwitters, Hanover's resident Dada artist, about whose work Lissitzky had written fondly the year before while still in Berlin: "Schwitters, with the brain of a writer, has eyes for color and hands for material. These attributes together produce a remarkable result."[11] The two became close associates in the ensuing months. As Peter Nisbet notes, the seemingly curious alliance between a Dada artist and one devoted to more "rational" forms of expression actually found common ground through a shared interest in reworking preexisting material and through the extension of art into the environment.[12] In October 1922, during Lissitzky's first trip to Hanover, Schwitters introduced him to Eckard von Sydow, president of the Kestner Society, and to Alexander Dorner, director of the Provinzialmuseum, who would become one of Lissitzky's great patrons. Through Schwitters, Lissitzky also met his future wife, Sophie Küppers, widow of the former president of the Kestner Society and an instrumental figure in planning his exhibition.[13] Lissitzky exhibited a group of *Proun* paintings made between 1919 and 1922, and by all accounts, the show was a great success. Several works sold to members of the society, who, according to Küppers's account, were accustomed to thinking of Russian culture in terms of dark expressionism and mysticism; Lissitzky's paintings, with their rational and precise composition, were therefore a revelation.

In March, one month after the exhibition closed, the Kestner Society invited Lissitzky back to Hanover to lecture on Russian art. His talk, entitled "New Russian Art," was based upon the important First Russian Exhibition, which had opened at the Van Diemen Gallery in Berlin in October 1922. Lissitzky's contributions to this exhibition included designing the catalogue cover and overseeing its move to Amsterdam the following year. Notable for its breadth and depth, this exhibition became the first occasion for Western audiences to see the full scope of Russian modernism, both pre- and post-Revolution.[14] In his talk, which he also gave later in Holland, Lissitzky provided a comprehensive overview of the events and movements that had shaped Soviet cultural expression. Lissitzky's understanding of the complexities of different groups and styles, coupled with his ability to identify and demystify important milestones, strengthened his reputation as an emissary of Soviet culture. Toward the end of his lecture, Lissitzky made a point of describing the relative isolation that many Russian artists felt from the West, a sentiment he and Ehrenburg had also expressed in their opening editorial in *Veshch*. He closed, however, with an optimistic outlook for potential international cooperation among different groups with shared interests, based no doubt on what he had experienced during his recent travels. "Then not only our achievements but also our unsuccessful experiments will bear fruit for those masters in every country who are consciously creating."[15]

Inspired by the positive reception of Lissitzky's exhibition and lecture, von Sydow and Dorner asked him to create a portfolio of lithographs to be offered to members of the Kestner Society as a means of raising money.[16] Known as the *First Kestnermappe* (*Kestner Portfolio* or *Proun Portfolio*; plates 2.1–2.2), it included six lithographs plus a cover and title page and was published in an edition of fifty in the summer of 1923. Printed in rich reds, blacks, and grays, the works reflect the diversity of approaches Lissitzky used in formulating the *Prouns,* from Suprematism to anthropomorphized abstractions. One sheet in particular, however, stands out: the *Proun* is turned into an axonometric architectural rendering. This image documents an installation Lissitzky had created that prior spring for the Grosse Berliner Kunstaustellung (Great Art Exhibition in Berlin), at the invitation of the Novembergruppe. Known as the "Proun Room," it gave Lissitzky the first opportunity to deploy his compositional thinking in real space. The installation was supposed to

6 Gustav Klutsis: *Dynamic City*, ca. 1919.
Gelatin silver print. 28.2 x 22.7. Private Collection

12 Nisbet, "Introduction to El Lissitzky," 28.
13 A rather romantic accounting of the proceedings is documented by Küppers in Lissitzky-Küppers, *Lissitzky,* 26–35.
14 See *The First Russian Show: A Commemoration of the Van Diemen Gallery Exhibition* (London: Annelay Juda Fine Art, 1983).
15 El Lissitzky, "New Russian Art," in Lissitzky-Küppers, *Lissitzky,* 340.
16 The ensuing success of this commission led to a series of other portfolios by leading modernists that today constitute an important body of modern graphic art.

contain an interlocking series of abstract forms, both painted and in relief, that unfolded counterclockwise on four walls, as well as across the ceiling and floor, but he was unable to implement the final element on the floor. By including this work within such a tightly indexed group of *Proun* types, Lissitzky makes clear the importance of working in real space while thinking in abstractions.

The project did not attempt a solution for practical space per se; rather, it suggested how exhibition space might be reorganized and reactivated through the intervention of abstract form. Its continuous progression emulates one's movement through an exhibition, though it was not intended as a new paradigm into which works could be inserted. In an essay explaining the project, written in May 1923, during his first visit to Holland, and published in July in the Dutch Constructivist journal *G,* Lissitzky states: "The new room neither needs nor desires pictures—it is not in fact a picture if it is transposed into flat surfaces. The equilibrium I seek to attain in the room must be elementary and capable of change, so that it cannot be disturbed by a telephone or a piece of standard office furniture. The room is there for the human being—not the human being for the room."[17]

The success of the *Proun* portfolio led to a private commission by a man named Chapmann, the owner of the printing press that produced the *Kestner Portfolio,* drawing Lissitzky back to Hanover for the latter half of 1923. He stayed at the home of Schwitters's dealer, Herbert von Garvens, but was provided with a studio at the Kestner Society.[18] In choosing the subject of the Russian Futurist opera *Pobeda nad solntsem* (*Victory over the Sun*) as the theme for this second portfolio, entitled *Figurinenmappe* (plate 1), Lissitzky reconnected with his roots—his mentor Malevich had done the original set and costume designs—and revived a project for which he had begun making watercolors before going to Germany. Throughout the portfolio, he demonstrates his facility for printmaking and illustration and his commanding sense of integrating the organic with the mechanical. The ten lithographs illustrate various characters in the opera as machinelike puppets, which in Lissitzky's hands become *Proun*-derived compositions with anthropomorphic features. The title page included a design for architectonic scaffolding of a hypothetical mechanical stage set. The character of the "Radio Announcer," the first print in the portfolio, was also used earlier by Lissitzky in his design for Mayakovsky's book of poems, *Dlia golosa* (*For the Voice*; plate 49), published in Berlin the prior year and still one of the masterpieces of Constructivist book design.[19]

During this same period, Lissitzky's engagement with photography evolved. These experiments—first with photograms and later with multiple exposures either in the imaging or printing process—augured an important shift in his practice, one that eventually would lead him to abandon painting and focus on projects that combined photographic and architectural concerns through exhibition design. The rapidity with which this shift occurred is remarkable, especially considering that only two years earlier Lissitzky had denied the visionary potential of photography. "The (painted) picture fell apart together with the old world in which it had created for itself. The new world will not need little pictures. If it needs a mirror, it has the photograph and cinema."[20] Exactly how and when Lissitzky began these experiments remains somewhat uncertain, since many are not signed or dated and only a few were published in his lifetime. The latter fact may account for why many of

17 El Lissitzky, "Proun Room, Great Berlin Art Exhibition (1923)," in Lissitzky-Küppers, *Lissitzky,* 361.
18 Lissitzky-Küppers, *Lissitzky,* 35.
19 See Lissitzky's essay "Topography of Typography," *Merz,* no. 4 (July 1923); trans. in Lissitzky-Küppers, *Lissitzky,* 355, who outlines his theories of design that are manifest in this book.
20 Nisbet, "Lissitzky and Photography," 66.

these works (as opposed to his better-known works of a few years later) have been generally overlooked in surveys of Soviet photography as well as in the general discourse on Lissitzky.[21] Certainly his encounter with other artists working across different mediums had something to do with his rapid conversion, and enough circumstantial evidence remains to at least contextualize the works and identify their pedigree.

Following his illustrations for Ehrenburg's *6 Tales with Easy Endings,* the first published photo-based work by Lissitzky to appear is a photogram created with Vilmos Huszar entitled *4 i Lampe* (Heliokonstruktion 125 Volt; fig. 7), which was published in the October 1923 issue of Shwitters's Dada periodical *Merz* and endearingly signed "El Huszar and Vilmos Lissitzky."[22] Huszar, with whom Lissitzky stayed while lecturing in The Hague that year, was one of the Dutch de Stijl artists whom Lissitzky met through Theo van Doesberg during the tour of the First Russian Exhibition. The picture, a Productivist statement *avant la lettre,* shows a Phillips lightbulb lying on its side and bracketed above and below by drinking glasses, one standing on end, the other upside down. What is possibly a glass mortar lies below and to the right, with another translucent but undecipherable object to the left and below the lightbulb. Finally, the entire composition rests on top of some kind of translucent sheets, whose outlines inscribe the background-like intersecting planes. The rendering is sophisticated, celebrating the aesthetic potential of both the industrial and everyday object. Moreover, its execution demonstrates a keen understanding of the transformative nature of the medium, since it is a positive print made from a negative paper original. A related work is the whimsical but no less sophisticated *Untitled* (Lissitzky and Huszar; plate 8), which combines photographic portraits of the two artists within a photogram whose elements (e.g., the lightbulb) refer to their collaboration in *Merz.* Lissitzky wears his signature checkered cap, in which he appears in numerous documentary images from the period.

Several other photograms known to be by, or attributed to, Lissitzky exist in both their positive and negative iterations. *Untitled* (Composition with Spoon; plate 45) shows an outlined hand underneath a lace mat with a spoon and glass on top. The subject matter is curious, in that it privileges the domestic object in a way that none of his other works do, unless one accepts the attribution to Lissitzky of two small untitled negative photograms (not included in this exhibition) whose compositions are related: one shows glasses, string, and lace, and the other a glass and string with opaque and translucent material.[23] The Lissitzky archive in RGALI in Moscow also contains three cyanotypes of household objects (tweezers, glass) and organic elements (chalk, flower) that are quite small in scale, but they seem less like formal compositions than didactic experiments in the medium (plates 47.1–47.3).

In 1929, Lissitzky published two photograms for which both positive and negative versions survive. *Untitled* (Compositions with Pliers and Wire; plates 43–44) shows a pair of pliers, wire mesh, and a glass or other translucent tubular object (but definitely not a spring as has been suggested elsewhere) standing on end. A related composition with pliers is identical in every way except for the absence of the tubular element, indicating that it was made at the same time as the other works. Other works show an artist's mannequin holding a film negative and racketlike object and leaping over a piece of mesh, thus combining photogram and photographic ele-

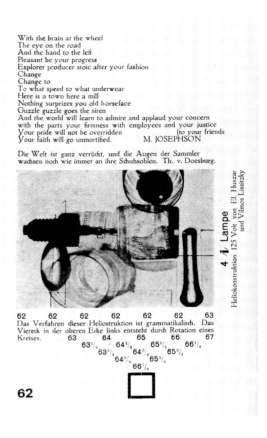

7 El Lissitzky and Vilmos Huszar: *4 i Lamp* (Heliokonstruktion 125 Volt), from *Merz,* no. 6. Merzverlag, Hanover, 1923. Kunsthaus, Zurich. Cat. 126

21 Schuldt was really the first to make this connection in his 1966 essay "El Lissitzky's Photographic Works," trans. in Lissitzky-Küppers, *Lissitzky,* 390–93. Though dated, it remains the most comprehensive study of Lissitzky's photo work. See also Nisbet, "El Lissitzky and Photography."
22 *Merz,* no. 6 (October 1923): 2.
23 Both photograms were formerly owned by the Prakapas Gallery, and both sold at Christie's New York: one on October 19, 1991 (lot 277), and the other on April 8, 1998 (lot 284). The absence of any inscriptions and the lack of solid provenance for these works suggest that they should be treated cautiously.

8 Christian Schad: *Amourette,* 1919. Photogram. 6.35 x 8.9 cm. The Museum of Modern Art, New York. Purchase. Copy Print. ©1999 The Museum of Modern Art

ments as in the aforementioned Huszar-Lissitzky portrait (see Tupitsyn, figs. 14–15).[24] Although at first glance these compositions suggest a sports subject, it has also been suggested that the racketlike object could be a magnifying glass and hence that the piece is an homage to the photographer at work.[25] The image in the negative has been identified as a photograph Lissitzky took in Paris, for it shows an image of the Eiffel Tower amid a vista of industrial buildings.[26]

The dating of these works remains highly problematic. Compositions with spoon and compositions with pliers and wire have both been dated to 1920 by their present owners, but there is no evidence whatsoever to support such an early date, especially given the absence of other photo works by Lissitzky that date that far back. Although the earliest reasonable date for any one of them could be 1923, it is just as likely that they were made as late as 1925–26, when Lissitzky was back in Moscow—especially the pincers and wire, which is a more Productivist composition than the other. Moreover, a larger negative version of the composition with a mannequin appeared in the 1929 Film und Foto exhibition and thus, along with its publication that same year, suggests that it was made around then (see Pohlmann, fig. 2).

All these works show Lissitzky exploring issues in abstract (as opposed to purely nonobjective) photography commensurate with his more sustained investigations of abstract painting and design. The transformation of real objects into abstract form is not unlike the devices explored in his collages for the Ehrenburg book. The contrasting values of translucency and opacity explored in the photograms are analogous to his *Proun* works, and both endeavors show him striving to achieve the ordering of space through the dynamic juxtaposition of colliding and intersecting forms. Although his use of the photogram does not constitute a major undertaking in the method, their contextual relationship to other forms of practice both preceding and following them should not be undervalued.

Lissitzky certainly did not invent the photogram, as some have zealously claimed in the past. The Huszar collaboration appearing in the context of a Dada periodical brings to mind the earlier works of the Dadaist Christian Schad, whose so-called Schadographs of 1919 were made by placing various forms of detritus on photosensitive paper, exposing them to light, and creating evocative compositions in the process (fig. 8). Schad's works probably reached Man Ray in Paris through their Dada colleague Tristan Tzara, for in 1922 Man Ray began experimenting with the process in a more sophisticated manner, thus earning him credit for inventing the photogram. His sustained exploration of the process, the product of which he called rayographs or rayograms, transformed all manner of objects, from organic matter to everyday items, into elegant or whimsical images. In his 1922 album of rayographs, *Champs délicieux* (Archive, figs. 1.1–1.5), with a preface by Tzara, Man Ray draws a parallel between his work in this medium and "automatic writing"— the stream-of-consciousness poetry published by André Breton and Philippe Soupault in their 1919 volume *Les champs magnétiques.* The fact that Lissitzky had five of the twelve rayographs from that volume in his archives is intriguing.[27] They present commonplace objects, some screened by mesh, and are generally reminiscent of Lissitzky's compositions with spoon and with pliers and wire. In a 1925 letter to Küppers, Lissitzky mentions having first heard about the *Champs délicieux*

24 A related negative version with the same dimensions as this example is in the RGALI archive in Moscow (f. 2361, op. 1, ed. khr. 21, l. 9).
25 Houk Friedman, 12.
26 This identification was made by Margarita Tupitsyn, who located an enlargement of the image in a private archive.
27 Margarita Tupitsyn was the first to bring these to my attention.

from Tzara at the Dada-Constructivist conference in Weimar in September 1922 and having seen subsequently a few of the pages from the album back in Berlin.[28] He goes on to both praise and critique Man Ray's work in the medium: "The *artistic merit* of the discovery [of photograms] is something completely discovered by Man Ray. He reaches the point of perversity in his complete abstraction of light. The underlying theme is both eccentric and American. There you have something of merit, and it has character too, even in its weakness, because it is alive."[29] But the fact that Man Ray ascribed his works to the effects of chance rather than to the deliberate study of organized formal values, as Lissitzky had, suggests that we should look to Moholy-Nagy's contemporary experiments in the medium for a closer parallel to Lissitzky's.

Certainly a work like Moholy's *Untitled* photogram from 1922 (fig. 9), with its use of mechanical objects juxtaposed with abstract geometric forms in an ordered composition, bears a stronger resemblance to Lissitzky's collaboration with Huszar than does anything by Man Ray. What's more, other photograms by Moholy show a use of similar objects—scissors, fabric, glasses, tweezers, and the like. Moreover, unlike Man Ray, Moholy was fond of making photograms and photographs in positive and negative pairs, just as Lissitzky had done, and of exploring the materiality and immateriality of opacity and transparency. Indeed, there are close formal parallels between the two artists in a variety of mediums, though the younger Moholy was usually a few steps behind. Moholy-Nagy's studio was among Lissitzky's first stops in Berlin, and indeed the two men visited often and stayed in contact on a range of subjects over the years.[30] In 1922, in a review of exhibitions in Berlin, Lissitzky spoke positively of his colleague's work: "Moholy-Nagy has prevailed over German expressionism and is striving to achieve an organized approach. Against the background of jellyfish-like German non-objective painting, the clear geometry of Moholy and [Laszlo] Peris stands out in relief."[31]

But three years later, in the letter quoted above, Lissitzky writes dismissively of Moholy-Nagy's "feigned achievement" with photograms, claiming that he introduced him to the whole idea of photography in 1921 and suggesting that the *Champs délicieux* was Moholy's source for experimenting with abstract photography. He continues: "What has Moholy contributed to it? Light? It has been left in the air. Painting? Moholy doesn't know the first thing about that. Theme? Where is that to be found? In order to concentrate, you've got to have a focal point. Character? That's the mask they always hide behind. It's idiotic of me to be taking this Moholy business so seriously, but this plagiarism is already getting to be too bare-faced."[32] In spite of this sweeping condemnation of Moholy's work, however, his approach to the photogram comes closest to Lissitzky's, and therefore justifies comparison.

Several years later, Lissitzky devoted an entire essay to the subject of photography; the title, "Fotopis," can be translated as either photo-writing or photo-painting.[33] Illustrated with only two photograms—one the positive of a composition with pliers and wire, the other a negative version of a composition with mannequin (see Tupitsyn, fig. 14)—he extols the expressive potential of the medium. "Without a camera, we use the varying degree of translucency of the object, and, most importantly, through the conscious organization of the light sources and the direction of their rays, we seek the construction of shadows which would render the object most

9 László Moholy-Nagy: *Untitled,* 1922. Photogram. 18.7x 13.6 cm. Centre Georges Pompidou, Paris

28 Letter from Lissitzky to Küppers, Moscow, September 15, 1925, in Lissitzky-Küppers, *Lissitzky,* 67.
29 Ibid.
30 These letters from Moholy-Nagy are in the Lissitzky archive at RGALI in Moscow.
31 El Lissitzky, "Exhibitions in Berlin," *Veshsch,* no. 3 (May 1922); trans. in Lissitzky-Küppers, *Lissitzky,* 341–42.
32 Margarita Tupitsyn was the first to bring these letters to my attention.
33 See Margarita Tupitsyn, "Between Fotopis' and Factography," in Houk Friedman, 5.

characteristically."[34] Photograms, however, were not Lissitzky's path into photography at this point. Two gelatin-silver prints have been dated to 1923, *In the Studio* (plate 7) and *Untitled* (plate 17). In both works, Lissitzky uses multiple exposures in printing to create images that speak to issues of dynamic motion, transparency, interlacing of form, and a lack of gravity. All these qualities can be found in his explorations of abstract form and space in the *Prouns,* some of which were meant to be rotated or hung in any direction.

The photographs also radiate a sense of simultaneous transmission of different moments in time, achieved through montage, thereby anticipating comparable techniques used in filmmaking, such as those in Dziga Vertov's *Man with a Movie Camera,* 1929 (Archive, figs. 12.1–12.4). *In the Studio* is clearly a very personal image, one that commemorates people close to the artist and that looks ahead to the portraits of Schwitters (plates 18–20) and Hans Arp (plates 22–23), as well as to his own self-portraits (plates 11–16), made in 1924. The date of the work seems secure; on the verso is an inscription that includes the phrase "in Berlin, okt. 1923." Yet despite the suggestion that the work is about his time in Hanover and was made there, a more careful examination would indicate that it documents his trip to Holland.[35] Although it is difficult to identify all the people in the picture, Sophie Küppers is unmistakably in the center. Whereas this might suggest the Hanover connection, the upside-down man at the top is the Dutch architect J. P. Oud, with whom Lissitzky had contact on a number of fronts at the time. Moreover, the fact that the photograph originates from the collection of Vilmos Huszar (whose stamp is also on the verso) reinforces the context for this work as growing out of Lissitzky's visit to Holland in 1923.[36] The Berlin reference in the inscription points not to the subject but to where the work was made.

Untitled is even more complexly crafted: it appears to be a combination of repeatedly printed negatives of industrial girders and wire mesh with a floral image at the center printed as a photogram, like the framing device that appears at the bottom and right side. The print has a solarized cast, with positive and negative values flowing seamlessly into and out of one another, giving the entire image an electrified feeling. Indeed, the entire composition emanates from a central vortex, as if we are witnessing an explosion of energy. The inscription at the bottom has often been miscopied or mistranslated, but it very clearly reads: "N^2ature + T^2echnology + A^2rt = $\sqrt{-1}$ = i." While the rendering of each first letter as an oversized capital has an affinity with Lissitzky's typographic experiments of 1922–23 (e.g., *For the Voice*), the underlying sentiment expressed by this cryptic inscription—whose last part ($\sqrt{-1} = i$) is a common convention for imaginary unity[37]—speaks to concerns that he was exploring in works from 1924–25, such as his collaboration with Kurt Schwitters and his 1925 essay "A and Pangeometry" (see below).[38] Less likely from 1923 than from 1924–25, the work is an affirmation of Lissitzky's commitment to a combination and balance of resources that add up to a harmonic existence.

This harmony was soon jeopardized, however, for toward the end of 1923 he became ill with tuberculosis. His condition worsened, and in February 1924 he left Hanover to recover in a sanatorium in Switzerland, where he remained until May 1925, when he was called back to Moscow. His treatments were costly, and in order to finance his medical bills an arrangement was made with Pelikan, a Hanover

34 El Lissitzky, "Fotopis'," *Sovetskoe Foto,* no. 10 (May 1929): 311; trans. in Puts, *El Lissitzky,* 70.
35 See, for instance, Nisbet, "Introduction to El Lissitzky," x.
36 My thanks to Malcolm Daniel of the Department of Photographs at the Metropolitan Museum of Art, New York, for supplying the inscription information.
37 My thanks to Victor Tupitsyn for supplying this information.
38 The vortex of imagery is curiously also like the composition of canceled proofs for the Pelikan posters he designed in 1924 (see below). Reproductions of these can be found in Lissitzky-Küppers and Lissitzky, *Proun.*

office-supply firm which paid him a monthly stipend in exchange for his designing their advertisements. Lissitzky turned hardship into opportunity; instead of being defeated by the necessity of working as a commercial artist for the first time, he embarked upon some of his most experimental works to date, in which he combined his design expertise with his recently acquired knowledge of photography. Moreover, the Pelikan designs (plates 24–35) point the way toward more ambitious projects, undertaken in the latter part of the twenties and thirties, that combined graphic design and photography.

Among the cleverest designs in the Pelikan group are those advertising carbon paper (plates 28–31, 33). Lissitzky uses the strategies of the photogram to play with issues of positive/negative and transparency. In two of the ads (plates 31 and 33), he extends this device to create a sense of dimensionality by simulating a shadow cast onto the background, as if a light source had passed through the Pelikan logo. Similar methods are used in several advertisements for Pelikan ink; one particularly dramatic design is composed exclusively with photograms (plates 24–25), the pen and inkwell rendered in mysterious shadow as if extracted from a German expressionist film.

Lissitzky also kept busy by writing articles on architecture and translating the writings of Malevich into German. Moholy-Nagy wrote to ask if he would write a book on typography as part of a series being published by the Bauhaus, but he replied indirectly through Küppers that, although interested, he was too busy at that moment.[39] Collaborating with his friend Schwitters, Lissitzky also designed and contributed an editorial to an issue of *Merz*. Entitled "Nasci," which is derived from the Latin word meaning "nature" or "everything which develops, moves and forms itself out of itself through its own strength,"[40] the journal opens with the following declaration: "We have had enough of perpetually hearing machine machine machine machine when it comes to modern art production." Typographically dynamic but conservative in its use of photographs, the project compared art and architecture with natural forms, not machines, reflecting the two artists' shared dislike of the hegemony of technology in art and solidifying their common interests in the organic.[41]

Lissitzky continued to experiment with photography as well, demonstrating a concern with montage and the multiplicity of time. In May he wrote to Küppers: "Please be sure to pack all my negatives, which are at the photographer's … so that I can make prints, if it should be necessary."[42] She subsequently arrived bearing her father's view camera, with which Lissitzky created some of his best-known works in any medium. He made three portraits of Schwitters (plates 18–20) or variations upon an original image, one of which is unique, the other existing in two known versions (these may have come from negatives made in Hanover). Both works show Schwitters in multiple exposure against a backdrop of *Merz,* a clear homage to their collaboration. In the more elaborate of the two works (plate 20), the *Merz* background is more disjointed, with typographical elements running in several directions, similar to the issue designed by Lissitzky. Superimposed on the left side is part of a Pelikan ribbon advertisement, apparently designed by Schwitters[43] and thus tying the two men closer together. The placement of a parrot in Schwitters's mouth, it has been suggested, is a reference both to his role as a spokesman for Dada and to his

39 This project never evolved. Lissitzky's reply is in Lissitzky-Küppers, *Lissitzky.*
40 From the title page of *Merz* 8–9 (July 1923).
41 For more on Lissitzky's interest in the organic, see Nisbet, "Introduction to El Lissitzky," 28–30.
42 Letter from Lissitzky to Küppers, May 31, 1924, in Lissitzky-Küppers, *Lissitzky,* 51.
43 Previously thought to be by Lissitzky, the Pelikan ad was reattributed to Schwitters in Houk Friedman, 16.

abstract *Ursonate* poems, which were composed of long combinations of seemingly meaningless words and sounds.

Another photographic portrait from this period is of Hans Arp (plate 23), also rendered in double exposure;[44] it portrays him against the background of the Dada periodical *391*, which includes the line "here comes the great Pra." This is a clue to Arp's identity, in that Lissitzky referred to Arp as the great Pra in a letter of February 1924.[45] He and Lissitzky collaborated on a major publication during the second half of 1924, *Die Kunstismen. Les Ismes de l'Art. The Isms of Art* (figs. 10.1–10.2), an idea that Lissitzky had originally proposed to Schwitters as the final volume of *Merz* in 1924, to be a "Last Parade of all the Isms from 1914–1924."[46] When Schwitters didn't take to the idea, Lissitzky found a willing collaborator in Arp, who came to visit him that summer, which is apparently when Lissitzky made several portraits of him.[47] Intended more as a closing out of the past with an eye toward new beginnings, *Isms* is a shorthand guide through the history of modernism, moving through Expressionism and Cubism and ending up with film, thereby assigning a privileged status to the mechanically reproduced image. Using one- to two-page spreads that illustrate exemplary works and seminal artists connected with a given movement (e.g., Mondrian and neoplasticism), the book also includes, in three languages, a series of key concepts or quotations about each art movement. The project apparently yielded some strain between the two artists, to which Lissitzky refers in a letter to Küppers of January 1925, while proofs were being finalized.[48] Nonetheless, the project was highly successful and provided yet another opportunity for him to strengthen contacts with artists throughout Europe, demonstrate his understanding of artistic issues beyond his own, and build another platform from which he could articulate an international agenda for modernism.

Included in the volume is a spread on the *Proun,* which includes a photomontage for a speaking rostrum entitled the *Lenin Tribune* (plate 37). This Suprematist composition, rendered in architectural terms, was actually the reworking of a design executed in 1920 by Ilia Chashnik, under Lissitzky's tutelage. To that original, Lissitzky added an animated photograph of Lenin speaking, the signboard above his head announcing "Proletariat." "Glad you like the Podium," he wrote to Küppers in May; "it's just what I wanted, the sweep of the structure emphasizing the gesture."[49] It is interesting that after being immersed so long in the neutral territory of abstract art, Lissitzky felt compelled to create such a powerful image of political propaganda. One explanation may lie in a letter he wrote to Küppers later that year, in which he regretted not having published the picture at the time that Tatlin's *Monument to the Third International* was becoming known, so that they might compete against each other.[50] The project certainly acquired iconic status as it became known, though it was never as ubiquitously recognized as Tatlin's tower. Lissitzky was also beginning to have visa problems, which would lead to his deportation from Switzerland and return to the Soviet Union. The *Lenin Tribune* may therefore signal his preparation for repatriation and a desire to engage art with politics, an arena that would give him the means and resources to apply his ideas to real situations.

In December 1924, Lissitzky produced one of his most celebrated works in any medium, a photographic self-portrait today known as Constructor (plate 14). Again resorting to montage to produce what he modestly referred to as his "great

44 The image was later published as part of a cover design for a book of poems: Il'ia Sel'vinskii, *Zapiski Poeta* (Moscow, 1928).
45 Letter from Lissitzky to Küppers, February 13, 1924, in Lissitzky-Küppers, *Lissitzky,* 38.
46 Letter from Lissitzky to Küppers, March 23, 1924, in Lissitzky-Küppers, *Lissitzky,* 48.
47 "Lissitzky took several photographs of Arp: a *profil en face* portrait and a photomontage, Arp with his Dada keyboard"; as cited in Lissitzky-Küppers, *Lissitzky,* 52.
48 Letter from Lissitzky to Küppers, January 25, 1925, in Lissitzky-Küppers, *Lissitzky,* 57.
49 Letter from Lissitzky to Küppers, May 26, 1924, in Lissitzky-Küppers, *Lissitzky,* 24.
50 Cited in Margarita Tupitsyn, "Fotopis' to Factography," in Houk Friedman, 2.

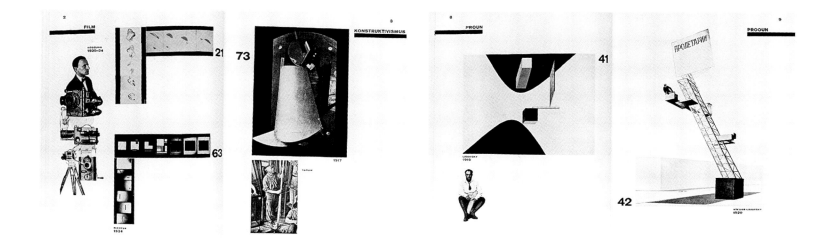

piece of nonsense," he made at least five surviving prints of the work, including a negative version and several related photographs (plates 10–13).[51] The image is a highly complex amalgam of references and techniques that not only refer to his own life and work but signify, more broadly, the status of the contemporary modern artist. Like his portraits of Schwitters and Arp, his image appears in the context of other objects that supplement his identity, a strategy that he expounds upon in his previously cited 1929 article on photography. Lissitzky emerges from a background of graph paper, the creative space of the designer-architect-engineer; a hand holding a compass, superimposed directly over his eye, seems to have just drawn a halo-like circle around his head. To the left is the letterhead he designed for himself around this time, printed as a photogram in reversed tones, with the stenciled letters XYZ overlaying it.[52] The stenciling has often been interpreted as a play on his past contributions to the architectural periodical *ABC,* but in an autobiographical typescript document from 1928, entitled "The Film of El's Life," Lissitzky makes the following entry: "My eyes. Lenses and eyepieces, precision instruments and reflex cameras, cinematographs which magnify or hold split seconds, Roentgen and X, Y, Z rays have all combined to place in my forehead 20, 2,000, 200,000 very sharp, polished searching eyes."[53] The self-portrait is therefore both a metaphor and an equation of the creative process as something rooted in the organic and the technological, an assertion made by Lissitzky earlier.

Lissitzky had linked the compass with the artist's creative consciousness in his collage with Tatlin while working on the *Monument to the Third International.* He used it again in another self-portrait (possibly made after *Constructor*), which shows him wearing a sanitorium cap and floating above typographical elements from his designs for Mayakovski's book of poems, *For the Voice* (plate 16). A strip of material montaged into his face resembles an illustration from his seminal article of 1925, "A. and Pangeometry," which signifies an object in a state of rest, thereby proclaiming his own condition. The hand and compass elements of the *Constructor,* an iconic composition in its own right, also appear as independent images: in a photographic print (plate 10), in an English-language design for a Pelikan ink advertisement (plate 35), and in a vertical orientation as the cover illustration for the 1927 yearbook of VKhUTEMAS (plate 36). But it was *Self-Portrait* (Constructor), which

51 Letter from Lissitzky to Küppers, December 12, 1924, in Lissitzky-Küppers, *Lissitzky,* 56.
52 See Nisbet, "Introduction to El Lissitzky," 190, 1924/17.
53 In Lissitzky-Küppers, *Lissitzky,* 325, and first mentioned in this connection in Houk Friedman, 26.

11　El Lissitzky: Design for *Room for Constructivist Art* (*Raum für konstruktivistische Kunst*) at the International Art Exhibition in Dresden, 1926. Gelatin silver print. 16.6 x 11.7 cm. Private Archive. Cat. 37

54 Will Grohmann, "El Lissitzky," *Der Cicerone* 17 (1925): 378; cited in Lissitzky-Küppers, *Lissitzky,* 62.
55 Kai-Uwe Hemken, "Pan-Europe Art and German Art: El Lissitzky and the 1926 Internationale Kunstausstellung in Dresden," in Puts, *El Lissitzky,* 46.
56 Letter from Lissitzky to Küppers, February 8, 1926, in Lissitzky-Küppers, *Lissitzky,* 74.

was widely reproduced in books and periodicals around the world (e.g., on the cover of Franz Roh and Jan Tschichold's *Foto-Auge*), that would become the symbol of the art of the 1920s, signifying the pursuit of creativity through a combination of modern technology and human intellect.

In May 1925, prompted by his visa problems and by the suicide of his sister, with whom he had been very close, Lissitzky returned to the Soviet Union. Once back in Moscow, he turned his attentions to architectural projects, which included a tribute to Lenin in the form of a cultural complex, his *Wolkenbügel* designs (plate 61), and two competitions, one for the "House of Textiles" and another for public housing, on which he collaborated with Nikolai Ladovski. He was not without a toehold in Germany, however. Küppers, who remained there with her two sons, shifted her home base to Dresden, with the assistance of Ida Bienert, a collector who had acquired a number of works by Lissitzky. There, in the winter of 1925, Küppers arranged an exhibition of his works at the Kuehl & Kuehn gallery, one of a number of modern art exhibitions she organized for them. A review in *Der Cicerone* attests to the success of the show and to Lissitzky's growing reputation: "Everywhere that the work of El Lissitzky has appeared, he has been convincing because of the incredible precision of his compositions. There can be no doubt that Lissitzky's work presents something of considerable value to the whole development of art."[54]

It didn't take long for Lissitzky to make his way back to Germany, however. Owing in large part to his desire to be reunited with Küppers, Lissitzky returned in the summer of 1926 to participate in the Internationale Kunstausstellung (International Art Exhibition) in Dresden, again supported by their mutual patron Ida Bienert. Although it had been intended as a pan-European exposition of achievements in the arts from the late nineteenth through the early twentieth centuries, the exhibition's organizers inadvertently turned the event into a contest among the participating nations.[55] Even before the invitation was extended, Lissitzky was making plans for a special exhibition room and a return to issues he had begun working out in his 1923 "Proun Room." This time, however, the space was to be an environment *for* art, not just an environment *of* art (fig. 11). In his words, it was to be a "kind of showcase, or a stage on which the pictures appear as the actors in a drama (or comedy). … Everything must be based not on colour but on the inherent properties of the material; then the colour of the pictures, of the painting, will shout out (or sing) without restraint."[56] With Küppers as his representative, his plans were brought to the attention of the exhibition's organizers. His innovative system for installing works of art, which included sliding panels, walls of various colors, and textured wood and metal surfaces, impressed Heinrich Tessenow, the architectural director. Lissitzky thus secured the commission to build a temporary exhibition room that would house works by Mondrian, Léger, Picabia, Moholy-Nagy, and Gabo, as well as some of his own pieces. This room, the only one in which different nationalities were represented together, exemplified Lissitzky's mission of promulgating the international character of modern art.

The Dresden room, completed in 1927, became the basis for a permanent gallery in the Provinzialmuseum in the Hannover Museum, commissioned by its director, Alexander Dorner. In the *Abstract Cabinet* (fig. 12 and frontispiece), as it

12 El Lissitzky: *The Abstract Cabinet*.
Installation at the Provinzialmuseum, Hannover, ca. 1930

came to be known, Lissitzky successfully placed abstract forms in space and created a dynamic environment for the presentation of constructive art. The positioning of the works, hung at different heights and on different types of surfaces, forced the viewer to confront objects in an altogether new way, the architectural context having become as much a part of the viewing experience as the objects on view. Some of the features of the *Abstract Cabinet* are reminiscent of ideas explored in his photographs. For instance, the effect of the open-mesh panels that partially obscure some works is not unlike that created in photograms where lace occludes other items. The introduction of movement in space through sliding panels recalls the movement expressed through multiply exposed images. And Lissitzky's intention to have differing light conditions periodically alter the character of the art and environment is not unlike his use of contrasting positive and negative values in photograms to explore the different effects of light on objects. Thus, the *Abstract Cabinet* provided a resolution to a host of experiments begun as far back as Vitebsk, in a sense closing one chapter of his career while opening another, providing a point of departure for his next role as designer of large-scale exhibitions celebrating the Soviet state.

Lissitzky's frayed address book, safely deposited in the archival boxes of the Getty Research Institute, immediately conveys the doubleness of his artistic footing. Progressing alphabetically, one encounters a harmonious blend of Russian and European names that include Vasily Elkin, Sergei Eisenstein, Le Corbusier, Albert Gleizes, Aleksei Gan, Raul Hausmann, Adolf Loos, Kazimir Malevich, Piet Mondrian, Mies Van de Rohe, Aleksandr Rodchenko, and Sergei Senkin. This list of designers, filmmakers, painters, architects, and photographers also attests to Lissitzky's professional multimedia commitments, which by the time of his return to Moscow in 1925, had equally grown. Lissitzky went to Berlin at the end of 1921 to disseminate fully articulated theories of Suprematism and Constructivism and to boost Soviet-German cultural contacts; he returned to Moscow in 1925 owing to public and private circumstances. These included problems with the Swiss authorities, who asked him to leave Switzerland following his recuperation from tuberculosis in the winter of 1924, as well as the shock of his sister's suicide in Vitebsk.[1] His return also had much to do with a growing dissatisfaction with his Western colleagues and the West itself, which he referred to as a "society which [was] destroying itself."[2] Another reason for his homecoming may have been that having had his health restored, he felt a full commitment to architecture, his true passion, was now possible and would be most realizable in a country involved in massive reconstruction.[3]

Settling in Moscow at the zenith of the New Economic Policy (Novaia ekonomicheskaia politika, or NEP), Lissitzky addressed a series of letters to his wife, a German named Sophie Küppers.[4] These letters reveal that his "faith and hope [lay] in architecture"[5] and attest to his firm belief that his "concentrating on architecture [was] right."[6] Lissitzky's anticipation of a productive architectural career, however, was disturbed soon after he settled in Moscow. The vast gap between Soviet architects' technologically advanced projects and the state's grossly limited means to realize them did away with any sense of financial security within the profession. As a result, Lissitzky promptly returned to graphic design, a field in which he achieved so much success in Germany, though he assessed the move as a withdrawal from more important projects. Less than five months after his return, he informed Küppers that "in order to make some money, I have to devote myself once again to book covers and posters, then maybe I can bring my earnings up to 500 roubles a month, but that means ruining myself physically and artistically."[7] The notion of typographic work as a practice of the past, to which he often turned merely to resolve financial problems, is emphasized in another letter. Informing Küppers about receiving *Typographische Mitteilungen,* the magazine of the German designer Jan Tschichold, Lissitzky noted: "Now that my typographic period has become past history, it is a good thing that a balance-sheet of it is to be found in this magazine."[8] The late Soviet critic Nikolai Khardzhiev, one of the first to examine Lissitzky's career as a graphic designer, challenges the seriousness of Lissitzky's derogatory and dismissive comments concerning this domain by insisting that Lissitzky "did not belong to those masters who divided their works into major and minor."[9] Khardzhiev therefore provokes us to take Lissitzky's return to graphic design, and later to photography, not merely as a source for survival but ultimately as a serious commitment.

Margarita Tupitsyn

Back to Moscow

The position is this: the ecstatic period of the Revolution is over. Now it's the working day.
—El Lissitzky, 1925

Now it is made clear to every communist that at this hour revolutionary work does not signify conflict or civil war, but rather electrification, canal construction, creation of factories.
—Walter Benjamin, *Moscow Diary,* 1926–27

1 Lissitzky had been diagnosed with tuberculosis in Hanover a few months earlier.
2 See the letters of October 16 and November 1, 1924, and Sophie Küppers's quote of one of Lissitzky's letters, in Sophie Lissitzky-Küppers, *El Lissitzky: Life, Letters, Texts* (London: Thames and Hudson, 1968), 53–54, 60.
3 An architect by education, Lissitzky often turned to other media because of his weak health, which kept him from projects that demanded high energy and physical endurance.
4 The New Economic Policy (NEP), inaugurated by Lenin in 1921, reintroduced in a limited way the capitalist market system.
5 Quoted in Lissitzky-Küppers, *Lissitzky,* 70, letter of November 5, 1925.
6 Ibid., 60, letter of May 25, 1925.
7 Ibid., 70, letter of November 5, 1925. In the beginning of 1926, Lissitzky's appointment at VKhUTEMAS as an instructor for interior design and furniture, in the department of wood and metal, was confirmed and guaranteed him a salary.
8 Ibid., undated letter written in 1925. I am not suggesting that Lissitzky did not invest all his energy and skills in his typographic work. Rather, I believe that at this point in his career he was anxious to move on to large-scale projects involving more-complex theoretical ideas.
9 Nikolai Khardzhiev, "El Lisitskii—konstruktor knigi," in *Iskusstvo knigi* (Moscow: *Iskusstvo,* 1962), 145.

The All-Union Printing Trades Exhibition

Lissitzky's marriage to Küppers, who arrived in Moscow in the winter of 1927, a year before Stalin's inauguration of the first Five Year Plan, did not reorient him toward Europe. On the contrary, Küppers, who had witnessed early fascist aggression toward artists and intellectuals, saw little future in Germany for herself and for Hans and Kurt, her two sons from a previous marriage. She was happy to be in Moscow, and her original impressions include an infatuation with architecture, observing joyful children at play, and a "superabundance" of "Russian food and drink."[10] Küppers's determination to enjoy her new home extended as far as her stalwart acceptance of Soviet *byt* (everyday life), which included a honeymoon in a communal apartment with four other families. Küppers was immediately introduced to Lissitzky's circle of friends, predictably a diverse community from a variety of fields, and again confirmed his interdisciplinary approach to art. By then, however, it was clear that he had a better chance of practicing Constructivism not in architecture but rather in exhibition and graphic design. With a layout for *Das Abstrakte Kabinett* (*Abstract Cabinet*; frontispiece), which he completed that same year for the Provinzialmuseum in Hanover, Lissitzky concluded his nearly ten-year involvement in abstract art and agreed to become the "architect" of Vsesouznaia Poligraficheskaia Vystavka (the All-Union Printing Trades Exhibition), scheduled to open in Moscow in 1927 (figs. 1, 2).

Sanctioned and controlled by high-ranking government committees, this exhibition summarized the decade-long accomplishments of the Soviet printing industry and featured advanced equipment from other countries.[11] Charged with planning the layout of this vast survey of printing and design techniques, Lissitzky became involved in a project whose eclecticism stood in explicit contrast to the stylistic homogeneity and intellectual clarity of his *Abstract Cabinet*. His own work was featured in the section of "Productivist Graphics" and in the exhibition guide designed with Solomon Telingater. Lissitzky's objects were catalogued in various sections, including "Avtolitografia" (Autolithography) and "Fotopis."[12] In addition to three figurines from the *Pobeda nad solntsem* (*Victory over the Sun*) portfolio (plate 1), printed earlier in Germany, the listing of lithographic work included several abstract compositions known as *Prouns* and the poster from the Vitebsk period, *Krasnym klinom bei belykh* (*Beat the Whites with the Red Wedge*), titled in the guide *Na Polsky front* (*To the Polish Front*, fig. 2).

The items catalogued under "Fotopis" include photographic images executed by a variety of techniques, among them multiple exposures, photomontage, and photogram. In "Artist in Production," the text that Lissitzky wrote for the exhibition guide, he defined *fotopis* as the technique that "unlike painting 'paints' its image with light directly on a photographic paper, using, depending on the task, negatives, obtained by means of a camera or through the direct impact of a light ray, which on its way to photographic paper encounters objects of different transparency and obtains direct reflections of them."[13] Of the titles found under "Fotopis," some are puzzling and others are easy to relate to Lissitzky's known photgraphic works. The more identifiable ones are *V lampe* (*In the Lamp*, 1923; plate 8), a portrait of Lissitzky and Vilmos Huszar; *Portret Arp* (*Hans Arp,* 1924; plates 22–23); *Avto-portret* (*Self-Portrait,* 1924; plates 14–15);[14] and *Rekord* (*Record,* 1926; plates 39–

10 Lissitzky-Küppers, *Lissitzky*, 83.
11 The exhibition bulletin mentions the arrival of sixty printing machines from Germany, which were not available for the opening because of electrical problems and poorly reinforced floors.
12 *Fotopis* is a neologism based on the Russian word *zhivopis*, meaning "painting" and is formed from two roots: *zhivo*, which means "live," and *pis*, "a root of writing." Lissitzky replaced *zhivo* by *foto*, indicating the nonmechanical origin of the photogram. He then added *pis*, thus creating a word that can be translated literally as "photo-writing" or "photo-scribing."
13 El Lisitskii, "Khudozhnik v proizvodstve," *Vsesouznaia Poligraficheskaia Vystavka: Putevoditel'* (Moscow, 1927), 7.

41), a photomontage with runners that Lissitzky made in Moscow for a water-sports and yacht club. More uncertain titles include *Portret "Meru,"* (*Portrait "Meru,"* 1924), which makes no sense in Russian but most likely refers to one of the portraits of Kurt Schwitters (plates 18–20), which Lissitzky, to avoid the articulation of a long German name, predictably submitted as *Portrait "Merz,"* the name of Schwitters's periodical). It is likely that the printers mistook the Russian letter *ts* for *u*, which looks similar.

Further down the list, and under the subtitle "Photograms," are *Snariad arkhitektora* (*Architect's Equipment*) and *Snariad naborshchika* (*Type-Setter's Equipment*). To these two listings, Lissitzky adds the Western term *photogram* in order to distinguish it from his newly coined neologism *fotopis*. Although it is not clear which work stands for *Type-Setter's Equipment, Architect's Equipment* almost certainly refers to the image of Lissitzky's hand with a compass (one of *Self-Portrait*'s elements; plate 10). This work, which was also used that year on the cover of *VKhUTEMAS Architecture* (*Arkhitektura VKhUTEMAS,* 1927; plate 36), is discernible from a photograph documenting the "Fotopis" section of the exhibition. The entry *"negativ-pozitiv"* (*"negative-positive"*) can stand for a number of pairs that Lissitzky has been credited with making in this dual format. Several compositions with pliers and wire (plates 43–44), those with a spoon (plate 45), and his *Self-Portrait* (Constructor) exist in negative-positive versions (plates 13–14). I would claim, however, that in the exhibition guide the title *"negative-positive"* most likely refers to the two identical compositions with pliers and wire rather than to those with a spoon. I say this because in the photograms with pliers and wire one finds the tendency, akin to that in *Type-Setter's Equipment* and *Architect's Equipment*, to depict professional tools. In this case the represented objects—pliers, wire, and pieces of fabric (perhaps canvas)—fit into the arsenal of objects that Lissitzky and his students could use for their interior and furniture production at VKhUTEMAS (the Higher State Artistic-Technical Workshops) that year.

The title *Teatralny proekt* (*Theater Project*), yet another work found in the exhibition guide under "Fotopis," has no apparent relation to the domain of printing or photogram technique, and no immediate clue to its identification. Judging,

1 Anonymous: View of the stands of the All-Union Printing Trades Exhibition, Moscow, 1927. Gelatin silver print. 11.4 x 17.4 cm. RGALI, Moscow, f. 2361, op. 1, ed. khr. 9, l. 4

2 Gustav Klutsis: View of the All-Union Printing Trades Exhibition, Moscow, 1927. Upper right: El Lissitzky's *Beat the Whites with the Red Wedge;* lower right: Gustav Klutsis and Sergei Senkin's *To the Memory of the Fallen Leaders*

14 The lithographic version of Lissitzky's *Self-Portrait* might have been made to test one of the foreign printing machines installed in the exhibition. That this portrait is reversed suggests that the Soviet printmakers could have overlooked the reversal of Lissitzky's logo, which is in Latin.

3 Anonymous: El Lissitzky working on a stage design of Sergei Tretiakov's play *I Want a Child* in the Meyerhold Theater, 1926−28. Gelatin silver prints. 8.6 x 12.8 cm. Private Archive. Cat. 238

4 Anonymous: El Lissitzky working on a stage design of Sergei Tretiakov's play *I Want a Child* in the Meyerhold Theater, 1926−28. Gelatin silver print. 8.4 x 9.5 cm. Private Archive. Cat. 239

15 Peter Nisbet, *El Lissitzky, 1890−1941* (Cambridge, Mass.: Busch-Reisinger Museum, 1987), 40.
16 It is interesting to compare Lissitzky's composition with a spoon with Láslzó Moholy-Nagy's 1926 photogram of a hand and a spatula. Similarly, a comparison can be made between Lissitzky's compositions with pliers and wire and Man Ray's 1922 rayograph with a spring. Both Man Ray's and Moholy-Nagy's works are at the Metropolitan Museum of Art.

however, from related projects that Lissitzky undertook prior to the opening of the All-Union Printing Trades Exhibition, *Theater Project* may be one of the photographs of Lissitzky at work on his set designs for Vsevolod Meyerhold's production of Sergei Tretiakov's play *Khochu rebenka* (*I Want a Child;* figs. 3−4). Until now, these photographs have been dated as 1928−29, but as Peter Nisbet suggests, considering that Lissitzky "initially (in 1926) … designed just sets for … [this] ultimately never realized production," and based on Lissitzky's younger appearance here than in portraits known to have been taken in 1928 (fig. 5), it is conceivable that *Theater Project* is a portrait of Lissitzky working on a small model of a set design for Tretiakov's play.[15]

Moving beyond the All-Union Printing Trades Exhibition, what is left to be dated of photograms commonly attributed to Lissitzky is a negative-positive pair of a composition with spoon (plate 45) and three cyanotypes from the Russian State Archive of Art and Literature (RGALI; plates 47.1−47.3). All these works are credited to Lissitzky based solely on the fact that they came from his family estate. Unlike the photograms with pliers and wire, which in accordance with the engineering climate of VKhUTEMAS are populated with practical tools and materials, the two photograms with spoon are composed of traditional still-life elements: a table, a drinking glass, a spoon, and a silhouette of a hand—all of which are crowded together on a lace tablecloth. Similar contrasts exist between the voluminous, three-dimensional shapes rendered in compositions with pliers and wire (in tune with the Constructivists' departure from the two-dimensional properties of painting) and compositions with emphasis on the spoon's flatness and inverted perspective, associated with the objectives of early modernism.[16] In view of these formal and thematic gaps between the photograms mentioned, I believe that compositions with a spoon were made at a different time from those with pliers and wire. Furthermore, because the Lissitzky estate recently revealed its possession of the reproductions of Man Ray's rayographs from the *Champs délicieux* album series (Archive, figs. 1.1−1.5), one might also assume that still more of other artists' works might have accumulated in Lissitzky's archive, leading to a possibility that compositions with a spoon could have been made by someone else.

As with the spoon compositions, one can only speculate on the dates and authorship of the three cyanotypes, two with amorphous and cylindrical shapes and one with tweezers, all floating in a plasmatic-like substance. Observing them together brings to mind Lissitzky's letter from the Swiss sanitarium: "[Dr. Steinitz] took X-rays," Lissitzky wrote to Küppers, "and showed me some interesting things. I have a pleurisy, which I hadn't detected, and this has separated the upper lobe of the right lung. There were also two spots in the left one which have healed by themselves, consequently the left one is sound. But the right one looks too much like a work of art."[17] Lissitzky's interest in the negative image as well as his emphasis on the manipulation of the negative in the creation of *fotopisnye* works may therefore have come out of his medical experience. In the 1929 article "Fotopis," Lissitzky summarized the photogram's properties as a technique without a camera, noting: "The following stage in the expansion of photography's possibilities is the exclusion of the negative from the automatic contact process. From one and the same negative it is possible to achieve various impressions—depending on the angle of its placement in relation to the paper, on the direction, strength and number of light sources."[18]

The three cyanotypes, visually vague and roughly cut as they are, could very well have been made by Lissitzky as playful exercises based on other artists' photograms.[19] This hypothesis is conceivable, because around 1927 his colleague Sergei Senkin—who exhibited in the All-Union Printing Trades Exhibition and later became a major collaborator with Lissitzky on the designs for the Internationale Presse-Ausstellung Pressa in Cologne—practiced the cyanotype technique in his experiments with photo portraits. Senkin's photo portraits are found in the poet Aleksei Kruchenykh's album dedicated to the Constructivists, which he compiled in order to accommodate the artwork he received from various artists as presents (Archive, figs. 4–6). Since Lissitzky was a close friend of Kruchenykh, one is able to find a number of images with his inscriptions in the poet's album (fig. 7; plate 22). Thus, it is reasonable to reflect on the possibility that when Lissitzky saw Senkin's images at Kruchenykh's apartment, he was inspired to contribute something similar to the album and made the three cyanotypes.[20]

On the Road to Pressa

The All-Union Printing Trades Exhibition represented a genealogy of Lissitzky's career since the Revolution. The work he exhibited attests to his lasting belief in the functional capacities of abstract form (as applied in both architecture and graphic design) and provides an overview of his experiments in photography, which generally took place within a rather limited cultural context. While Lissitzky was away, however, the Constructivists, some of whose works were hung next to Lissitzky's in the All-Union Printing Trades Exhibition, repudiated abstract form and proceeded to apply their skills to the representation of concrete subject matter. In their designs of books, posters, and postcards, intended for mass distribution, they relied particularly on documentary material derived from public archives and on the technique of photomontage, which served as an adequate tool for responding to the changes in contemporary life. One such example, the collaborative dust jacket *Pamiati pogibshikh vozhdei* (*To the Memory of the Fallen*

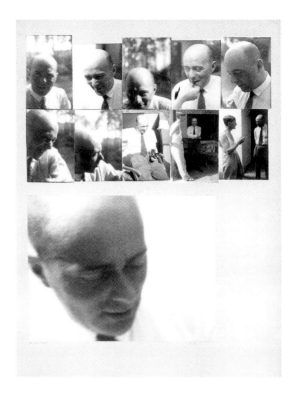

5 Josef Albers: *El Lissitzky*, Bauhaus, 1928–30. Photomontage. 41.8 x 29.7 cm. Metropolitan Museum of Art, New York, Ford Motor Company Collection. Cat. 242

17 Letter of February 23, 1924, quoted in Lissitzky-Küppers, *Lissitzky*, 39,
18 El Lisitskii, "Fotopis," *Sovetskoe foto*, no. 10 (1929): 311; trans. and rpt. in *El Lissitzky: Architect, Painter, Photographer, Typographer, 1890–1941*, ed. Jan Debbaut (Eindhoven: Municipal Van Abbemuseum, 1990), 70.
19 For example, Man Ray's rayograph of a gyroscope from 1922 consists of similar floating shapes.
20 Also in this album I have located several photograms that I believe were made by Georgy Zimin. Like Lissitzky, he was an architect and probably became interested in the photogram technique after the All-Union Printing Trades Exhibition. Lissitzky's photograms shown at this exhibition and his discussion of fotopis in the exhibition guide prompted various commercial designers to use this technique. See my fig. 8 and Archive, figs. 2–3.

6 Anonymous: Aleksei Kruchenykh with El Lissitzky's figurine portfolio for Kruchenykh's *Victory over the Sun.* N.d. Gelatin silver print. 20 × 29 cm. RGALI, Moscow, f. 1334, op. 1, ed. khr. 290, l. 4

7 Page with Lissitzky's *Self-Portrait* (Constructor), from the magazine *Production Graphics*, December 1928, Berlin-New York. RGALI, Moscow. Cat. 131

21 In a letter to his wife, Valentina Kulagina, of July 4, 1927, Klutsis made a drawing of this cover with an indication of his and Senkin's authorship (Private Archive).
22 El Lisitskii, "Khudozhnik v proizvodstve," 7.
23 Ibid.
24 Ibid.
25 Ibid.
26 Ibid.
27 See Lissitzky's letter of September 29, 1932, Letters, this vol., 203–4.
28 Quoted in Khardzhiev, "El Lisitskii—konstruktor knigi," 148.

Leaders, 1927; Archive, fig. 6), was the product of two formerly nonobjective artists, Senkin and Gustav Klutsis. Hung next to Lissitzky's Suprematist poster *Beat the Whites with the Red Wedge* (fig. 2), the dust jacket, in full spread, shows Lenin's mausoleum pierced by a zigzag line of workers (Klutsis's design) and two hands firmly holding a triple red flag (Senkin's design).[21] When Lissitzky returned to VKhUTEMAS in 1926, these and other Productivist artists guided the school's policy to some degree, and they, together with critics and filmmakers, would ultimately have a major influence on Lissitzky's photographic practices.

At the time of the All-Union Printing Trades Exhibition, however, Lissitzky embraced the current Productivist rhetoric only partially, as revealed in the "Artist in Production," mentioned earlier. In it he writes that after the October Revolution "it became necessary to transfer the experience of working in an individual studio and the experience of working with easel painting, to the context of the factory and the machine."[22] In his view "a single painting had devolved into a kind of luxury because it reflected a visible gap between energy that was invested into the painting and the scope of its function."[23] Furthermore, painting "was increasingly being annihilated by the printed page."[24] Evaluating various forms of typography, Lissitzky states that photomontage "was born and blossomed" in the Soviet Union in the revolutionary years as a response to the "social requirements of our epoch and the artist's mastering of new technology."[25] "Only in our country," he concludes, "was it cast into a clear social art form."[26] He goes on to define *fotopis* as "the next stage of development" along the same road, revealing his reluctance to designate photomontage, based on the cutting and pasting of readymade documentary material, as the ultimate tool of the Soviet design industry.

It is important to trace the degree to which Lissitzky embraced this form of photomontage (in a letter written to Jan Tschichold in 1932, he proudly reported making "400 montages in about 8 months") and what influenced him along the way.[27] Just before Lissitzky left for Berlin, he gave a lecture at the Moscow Dom Pechati (House of Press), in which he evoked a militant ardor for radical cultural aesthetics and called for the "burning of … cryptlike offices … a move toward unification with workers and thinkers, and technicians and inventors for collective constructions."[28] The general rhetoric of his speech conformed to the position of his colleagues within INKhUK (the Institute of Artistic Culture), who, in 1921, the year he left for Germany, formed the First Working Group of Constructivists. Founded by Aleksandr Rodchenko, Varvara Stepanova, and Aleksei Gan, INKhUK was engaged in radically rethinking the role of the aesthetic object, its subject matter, and the methods of its execution and distribution. Its members promptly advanced from painterly to laboratory Constructivism and then, just as quickly, moved on to Productivism by condemning the creation of spatial objects or three-dimensional abstract constructions with no predetermined plan of application. Had Lissitzky remained in the Soviet Union, he most likely would have followed this far-Left course of cultural politics and joined the camp of the Productivists. Arriving in the West, however, with its more moderate political atmosphere, Lissitzky could not afford to promote Productivist rhetoric. Consequently, his concept of a new aesthetic object, as outlined in *Veshch,* the magazine he edited upon arrival with the writer Ilia Ehrenburg, was instantly pacified (see Drutt, fig. 3). Betraying transnational aspirations, the section entitled "The Blockade of Russia Moves Toward Its End" explained the editors' objectives: "We have named our periodical 'Object' because to us art means nothing other than the creation of new 'objects.' … However, one should not think for that reason that by objects we mean explicitly useful objects. … Every organized piece of work—whether it be a house, a poem, a painting—a practical 'object,' not intended to estrange people from life, but on the contrary to call upon them to take part in its organization. Thus we have nothing in common with … painters who use the picture as a means of publicizing their renunciation of painting. Basic utilitarianism is far from our thoughts. 'Object' regards poetry, plastic form, drama, as essential 'objects.'"[29] From this text it is evident that Lissitzky's object was rather distanced from the political or practical function preached by the Productivists and was supposed to be executed in legitimized media and released into familiar cultural contexts.

Back in Moscow, Gan, the future participant of the All-Union Printing Trades Exhibition, published his pivotal book *Konstruktivism (Constructivism)*. An anti-art narrative with extensive references to Marxist writings and materialist philosophy,[30] Gan's publication has been read primarily by scholars of Soviet art as a source for definitions of, and elaborations on, such essential Constructivist terminology as *faktura* (the process of working material), *tektonika* (tectonics, which is based on the expedient use of industrial materials and which unites the ideological and formal), and *konstruktsia* (the actual process of putting things together).[31] The relation of these terms to the formal properties discussed in *Constructivism* overshadowed other aspects of Gan's text, which marked the beginning of concretization of Constructivist objects in both form and content. For example, in *Constructivism* one finds the earliest attempt to distinguish between *veshch* (object) and *obshchestvennaia veshch* (social object), which "take[s] the meaning of a 'public being,' enter[s] human society as a technical system, which forms its [society's] *veshchestvennyi* [object-oriented] labor apparatus."[32] Unlike Lissitzky, Gan denounced painting and wanted to replace it with *svetopis*, or photography. Gan also criticized traditional theater, which he believed had to be pushed aside by "mass actions," and he repudiated architecture as it had developed before Constructivism. Envisioning documentary film and photography as a logical replacement for earlier Constructivist inquiries into abstraction, Gan, in the same year he published *Constructivism*, launched the magazine *Kino-fot (Cine-Photo)*—a small weekly on cinematography and photography that lasted only one year; the first issue of *Kino-fot* explicitly demonstrated the difference between "prostranstvennaia veshch," represented by Rodchenko's three-dimensional abstract constructions, and "obshchestvennaia veshch," illustrated by documentary film stills from Dziga Vertov's *Kino-Pravda (Cine-Pravda)*.

Gan's long essay *Da zdrastvuet demonstratstia byta! (Long Live the Demonstration of Everyday Life!)* followed the publication of *Constructivism* and was also printed in a small book format. It was entirely illustrated with Vertov's film and photo stills, positioning his *Cine-Pravda* as an example of the new *kino-forma* (cine-form). The latter was to replace the Constructivist concept of *prostranstvennaia forma* (spatial form) and was a way to construct on a screen the sensation of

8 Solomon Telingater: Cover for the magazine
Aid to a Metalworker of Hardware Industry, no. 1, 1930.
Lithography. Private Collection

29 Quoted in Lissitzky-Küppers, *Lissitzky*, 344–45.
30 Significantly, as early as 1918 Malevich collaborated with Gan on the article "Zadachi iskustva i rol' dushitelei iskusstva" (The Tasks of Art and the Role of Art's Stranglers), written for the newspaper *Anarkhiia*; rpt. in Kazimir Malevich, *Stat'i, manifesty, teoreticheskie sochineniia i drugie raboty, 1913–1919*, 2 vols., ed. A. S. Shatskikh (Moscow: Gileia, 1996), 1:293.
31 On further explanations of these terms, see Christina Lodder, *Russian Constructivism* (New Haven: Yale University Press, 1983), 98–99.
32 Aleksei Gan, *Konstruktivism* (Tver, 1922), 47.

byt, which Gan defined as "an object-oriented and material form of life in human society."[33] With the establishment of this change, spatial objects of Constructivism were to be replaced by the social objects which, according to Gan, would be drawn from a painstaking following of byt's "diversifying aspects, [where] upon every step one comes across 'unfamiliar' forms of phenomena, and meets an endless line of the new *byt* expressions."[34] "One perceives," Gan concluded, "a tempestuous and incessant flow of people as an uninterrupted moving form of never stopping content."[35] If spatial objects were created through an abstract rendering of concrete materials such as wood, metal, plastic, and the like, the social objects, whose material was reality itself, were obtained by having that reality organized and articulated through the structures of cine-forms. The deliverance of this new representational instrument laid the grounds for the emergence of the second Soviet avant-garde, one that manifested itself through film, photography, and photomontage.

At the time of the publication of *Long Live the Demonstration of Everyday Life!* Lissitzky chose not to concern himself artistically with the transition from the spatial to the social object as prescribed by Gan. This refusal is confirmed in Lissitzky's introduction to *Veshch* and by his inclusion in that magazine of the installation at the 1921 exhibition of OBMOKhU (The Society of Young Artists), which features three-dimensional abstract constructions with no utilitarian aim. Nevertheless, one cannot ignore that as early as 1920 Lissitzky had attempted to adapt abstract forms (as they were developed in painting) to three-dimensional constructions of a practical nature. Henk Puts informs us that during that year Lissitzky encouraged his students who were part of UNOVIS (Utverditeli novogo iskusstva, or Affirmers of the New Art) in Vitebsk to apply Suprematist methods to the demands of real life and to design "a podium on which leaders of the revolution could speak to the people."[36] Puts goes on to say that Lissitzky also drew sketches of the project for his students, though "it is almost impossible to see that they involve plans for a podium."[37] Lissitzky's reluctance to endow abstract forms with specific context is similarly noticeable in his 1924 designs for the Pelikan company (plates 24–35). Although his decision to put the photogram technique to practical use was radical, he often sacrificed the content of the Pelikan designs in order to experiment with the spontaneous formation of an abstract form that the medium allowed. While working on the Pelikan commission in a Swiss health resort, however, Lissitzky, in an unexpected gesture, added the figure of Lenin to Ilia Chashnik's version of the Vitebsk podium, thereby specifying both the context and the content of its function (plate 37). Serving as the foundation for his later activities in the Soviet Union, Lissitzky's decision to corrupt the visual sterility of the objectless podium with an iconic, political image was probably triggered by two simultaneous projects he was developing. One, significantly, had to do with Kazimir Malevich, the high priest of abstraction himself: Lissitzky was translating Malevich's writings, which included *Lenin*, a new text. He wrote to Küppers on the subject: "I am translating [Malevich's texts] more or less like poetry, because otherwise I would have to raise a lot of objections. But even when I am restraining myself, such a fantastic force beats against me that I give up the struggle. I do not see anything that excites feeling in Germany any more."[38] The

33 Aleksei Gan, *Da zdrastvuet demonstratsiia byta!* 3
34 Ibid., 11.
35 Ibid.
36 Henk Puts, "El Lissitzky (1890–1941), His Life and Work," in *El Lissitzky: Architect, Painter, Photographer, Typographer, 1890–1941*, 17.
37 Ibid. Significantly, Nina Kogan, one of the students in Vitebsk's art academy, referred to Ilia Chashnik's drawings of a podium as "Novyi realism" (New Realism).

book was never published, but *Lenin*, which Lissitzky recommended to a German magazine, was.[39]

Written in 1924, the year of Lenin's death, Malevich's article dealt with the absence of portraits of the leader, with the exception of those found in films. "Later," Malevich wrote, "Lenin's portrait will be created in a way that communists will be able to support, and his artistic image will be received as a reliable fact. His teachings will spread with the artistic portrait. He, in the image transformed from material being into a holy one, becomes omnipotent in comparison to the material plane of the matter. The image would be elevated higher than the material matter. And it would be towards what the eyes would rise higher."[40] A devoted painter, Malevich in 1925 began to refer to films as the sphere capable of freeing an image from layers of false meanings. He referred specifically to Vertov's films, which "show object 'as such' and force society to see objects not lipstick-covered but real, authentic, and independent from the ideational order. [These objects] present a picture so much more powerful and interesting than all the faces [in paintings] and their 'contents.'"[41] Lissitzky, who could not ignore his teacher's references, added Lenin's portrait to the podium as an elevated image looming over material domains, attempting to bridge, via Malevich, current Soviet cultural politics.

A similar conversion of the abstract into the concrete occurred in Lissitzky's typographic work. A drawing from the RGALI holdings demonstrates how abstract *Proun* space acquired the configuration of an object such as a book (plate 48). Here the book, visually close to Lissitzky's *Prouns* (particularly to *Proun 30,* 1920) and constructed out of intersecting planes, is conceptualized as a nonreferential and nonfunctional "spatial book." Lissitzky then proceeded to design what he later called the "constructive book," which consisted of "black lines, circles, squares, photographs."[42] For his 1923 design of Vladimir Mayakovsky's *Dlia golosa* (*For the Voice*; plate 49), for example, Lissitzky introduced a thumb-index system that turned this book into an "active" object comparable with Constructivist mobile sculptures, specifically Rodchenko's *Spatial Construction No. 12.* Defined by Khardzhiev as the new type of "business publication," *For the Voice* invited the reader to actively respond to the book by taking advantage of its clever formal arrangement.[43] Lissitzky's layout for the "Prounen" book, made in 1924 (or shortly thereafter), was designed to begin with a photograph of the *Self-Portrait* (Constructor) and thus, as with the podium, brought a photographic image into his hitherto "objectless" typographic designs (plate 9).[44]

As early as 1925, and less than five months after his return to Moscow, Lissitzky wrote to Küppers: "I should like so much to carry out various photographic projects, but it's almost impossible here."[45] Devoted primarily to architectural designs at the time, Lissitzky conceived his first post-European photographic work while collaborating with his colleagues in Asnova (the Association of New Architects) on a water-sports and yacht club (plates 39–41).[46] This photomontage frieze, entitled *Record*, is composed of superimposed negatives, a technique that offers a visual complexity hard to achieve through the cutting and pasting of ready-made material. Made around 1926, this image exists in variations of one and two hurdlers running fiercely against the background of a city at night.

38 Quoted in Lissitzky-Küppers, *Lissitzky*, 46.
39 See *Das Kunstblatt*, no. 10, 1924.
40 Kazimir Malevich, "Lenin," in *Stat'i i teoreticheskie sochineniia, opublikovannye v Germanii, Pol'she i na Ukraine, 1924–1930*, 2 vols., ed. G. L. Demosfenova and A. S. Shatskikh (Moscow: Gileia, 1998), 2:26. The book, which Lissitzky translated, was never published. Another relevant project in which Lissitzky was involved was the design of a movie theater dedicated to Lenin and to be called "The Lenin Building."
41 Kazimir Malevich, "I likuut liki na ekranakh," in *Stat'i, manifesty, teoreticheskie sochineniia i drugie raboty*, 1:293.
42 El Lissitzky, "Do Not Separate Form from Content!" (1931); rpt. in Nisbet, *El Lissitzky*, 61.
43 Khardzhiev, "El Lisitskii—konstruktor knigi," 156.
44 Most likely this layout was made while Lissitzky was in Switzerland. The book was never published.
45 Lissitzky-Küppers, *Lissitzky*, 70.
46 In a letter of August 13, 1925, Lissitzky describes in detail his design for this sports complex on *Leninskie gory* (the Lenin Hills). Quoted in Lissitzky-Küppers, *Lissitzky*, 65–66.

Planned for Moscow, Lissitzky's unrealized frieze adopted Erich Mendelsohn's nighttime image of New York's Times Square.[47] This choice may be interpreted as a sign of Lissitzky's fascination with America—an alternative to Europe, which, as I pointed out earlier, had disappointed him. Equally, this example may signify his effort to internationalize Soviet photographic imagery by using images from foreign magazines sent to him by Küppers.[48] In the version of *Record* with the two runners, Lissitzky succeeded in endowing his frieze with cinematic qualities, accomplished by the rendering of high-energy running, a doubling of the city image, and the spreading of white vertical strips across the whole photomontage in an imitation of changing film stills.[49]

On the Margins of Pressa

After the success of the All-Union Printing Trades Exhibition, the Soviet government acknowledged Lissitzky as a designer capable of promptly and adequately planning the country's ambitious exhibitions at home and abroad. On top of Lissitzky's professionalism, the Soviets recognized that his name was well known in the West, which proved an invaluable asset given their interest in reporting abroad the success of the first Five Year Plan (1928–32). This new reputation defined Lissitzky's subsequent activities, steering him toward exhibition and eventually magazine and book design. The Soviet pavilion at the Pressa was the first such project, and predictably Lissitzky was asked to be chief designer. Unlike the All-Union Printing Trades Exhibition, whose elements, already in existence, simply had to be effectively laid out by the designer, Pressa had to be created from scratch. As a result, Lissitzky had to depend fully on his Soviet colleagues, not only because of the enormous number of exhibits to be constructed and the variety of themes to be covered but because, perhaps more important, up until that point Lissitzky had not been accustomed to, or particularly interested in, working with Soviet propaganda material.[50] In this respect, Pressa designs, which have been routinely associated with Lissitzky's name, present a much more complex web of collaborative efforts and can hardly be evaluated within a traditional methodology of an autonomous authorship.

Although most members of the large preparatory group mentioned in the Pressa catalogue were little-known artists, some names were familiar both as acclaimed Constructivists and as pioneer adherents to political and documentary photomontage. Given this background, two artists are of particular relevance: Senkin, who is known as the coauthor of the Pressa frieze, and Klutsis, the recognized founder of photomontage in the Soviet Union. Pressa granted to these artists a unique opportunity to advertise their artistic radicalism to Western colleagues and, owing to exceptional government subsidies, provided them an abundance of materials whose lack of availability had hitherto prevented the realization of many Constructivist projects. Elena Semenova, a participant designer, recalls the exciting aspects of this new opportunity: "This was the first time that we laid hands on plexiglass or that we used good-quality, colored paper, good-quality paints which didn't alter their colors and gray, factory-dyed pasteboard which could take oil, tempera or whatever. This was the first time that we were able to concentrate on objects (for the exhibition) which would revolve and move: to involve ourselves

47 *Amerika, Bilderbuch eines Architekten* (Picture Book for Architects) was published in Berlin in 1926. Mendelsohn came to Moscow in the end of 1925 and probably brought this book to Lissitzky, who then used this image. One of the reasons why Lissitzky appropriated this picture of New York was because the project was defined as "International stadium."

48 In a letter of November 6, 1925, Lissitzky thanks Küppers for sending her "beautiful cuttings." Küppers, *Lissitzky,* 70. Lissitzky's tendency to utilize cuttings from foreign publications to make Soviet photomontages can be compared with Rodchenko's similar strategy applied to his photomontages for *Pro Eto* (About This, 1923).

49 The strips also remind one of Lissitzky's wall designs for his 1926 "Room for Constructivist Art," made in Dresden. This presents an interesting connection between this last ambitious abstract project executed in the West and the first photographic one made in the Soviet Union. It is possible that Lissitzky did preliminary versions of the frieze with runners before he went to Germany and then added strips after he returned.

50 This is not to suggest that Lissitzky was not devoted to Soviet political causes. He was simply away long enough to lose a grip on most of the current political events. Lissitzky's early biographical data attest to his immediate involvement in the activities instigated by the Soviet regime. He joined *Izofront* after the Revolution and called himself and his contemporaries "draftees of the new beginning of human history." He made the first banner of VTSIK (the All-Union Central Executive Committee), which the members of Soviet government took to Red Square on May 1, 1918. See Nikolai Khardzhiev, "Pamiati khudozhnika Lisitskogo," *Dekorativnoe Iskusstvo SSSR,* no. 2 (1961): 29.

not with a dead spectacle but with dynamics. Because of the general conditions of those days we were unable to complete the mechanical aspect of the exhibition, and Lissitzky did it in Cologne."[51]

As the few surviving photographs reveal, various Pressa designs were preinstalled in the State Universal Store, known as GUM (fig. 9, this essay; Archive, fig. 7). With its high ceilings and wide corridors, GUM was a convenient space to assemble and test certain exhibition stands before they were shipped to Cologne. Later synthesized into Pressa's eclectic and abundant imagery, in the GUM photos single designs are set in a generous space and, like traditional sculptures, invite individual examination. Lissitzky's *Jubiläumsschau eines Dorfes* (*Anniversary Show of a Village*, plate 57) is seen in one such photograph before it was combined in the final Pressa installations with Lenin's death mask (plate 58) and with a female peasant holding a newspaper and topping the reading-room hut (plate 56). As observed in the GUM view, *Anniversary Show of a Village* is notably reminiscent of Lissitzky's figurine *Novyi* (*The New*, plate 1), which he made in 1920–21 as part of a portfolio of illustrations for *Victory over the Sun*. Although in the Pressa figurine Lissitzky preserved the pronounced rectilinear edges and extended hand gesture of *The New*, he also noticeably anthropomorphized it. In response to Pressa's orientation toward iconographic specificity, Lissitzky substituted the black flying object held by *The New* with a small model of a reading-room hut, a Soviet symbol devised for the peasants' literacy campaign. In this new capacity, the Pressa figurine exemplifies possibly Lissitzky's last effort to implant the same images into incompatible contexts (another example was his inclusion of the picture of New York in the frieze with runners) and to continue his attempt to transcend Soviet cultural borders.[52]

Pressa's frieze, which subsequently became the exhibition's emblem and the main image in the catalogue, was assembled in Cologne (fig. 10). Incorporating a wealth of political and everyday images rendered with visual immediacy, the frieze bares no apparent connection to the subject matter or optical complexity of Lissitzky's frieze with runners. Instead, there is a pronounced affinity here with concurrent photomontages by Senkin and Klutsis, which are similarly organized by

9 Gustav Klutsis: View of Pressa designs preinstalled in GUM (the State Universal Store), Moscow, 1928. Gelatin silver print. Private Collection

10 Anonymous: Installation of the photofrieze at the Soviet pavilion at Pressa, 1928. RGALI, Moscow. Cat. 190

11 Anonymous: Installation of the Soviet pavilion at Pressa, 1928. RGALI, Moscow. Cat. 191

51 Elena Semenova, "From My Reminiscences of Lissitzky," in *El Lissitzky* (Cologne: Galerie Gmurzynska, 1976), 23.
52 A different set of meanings evolves from another design installed at GUM and authored by Klutsis's wife, Valentina Kulagina. Contrary to Lissitzky's geometricized man, Kulagina's *Stand for the Soviet Village*, which is based on the two intersecting planes, is more abstract in appearance. Yet the subtle and recognizable contours quickly betray the stand's referential locale: this is a hammer and sickle, the symbol of the new Soviet state. Unlike its abstract predecessors, the Constructivists' spatial constructions, Kulagina's stand is functional, utilizing at once four poster panels, which, in this case, contain statistical information.

12 El Lissitzky: *Self-Portrait,* Pressa, 1928. Photomontage. Gelatin silver print. Private Archive. Cat. 60

great variation in the photographs' sealing and layers of juxtaposition.[53] Furthermore, the frieze's cinematic qualities, reflected in the uninterrupted succession of images, were reminiscent of contemporary documentary newsreels. Given these particular visual and thematic characteristics, Küppers's categorical tone with respect to its authorship must be questioned: "The artist Syenkin [*sic*], who had just arrived from Moscow, was mounting, *according to Lissitzky's design* [my emphasis], the gigantic photo-mural which reflected the history of the Soviet Press."[54] A series of documents attests to the fact that Senkin was far more than a mere executor of Lissitzky's ideas; he no doubt contributed substantially to the general concept of the frieze, based on both his and Klutsis's work in political photomontage, which depended heavily on documentary film practices.[55] The obvious proof of Senkin's greater involvement in the production of the frieze is the Pressa catalogue that was produced after the exhibition and acknowledged his partial authorship. Yet another document, a small photograph of the Pressa frieze that Senkin gave to Kruchenykh and identified as "[his] frieze from the Cologne Exhibition Pressa," suggests an even greater role (Archive, figs. 8–9).[56]

A similarly strong authorial claim to the frieze and to other Pressa designs comes from Klutsis, who in a letter to Valentina Kulagina, his wife and a Pressa designer, gives vent to his adverse reaction to the Pressa exhibition: "There are some illustrations in the catalogue of the Cologne exhibition: a much discussed frieze with an inscription 'von Lissitzky and S. Sen'kin.' Also, there are works by Prusakov, Borisov, Plaksin, Naumov; several photographs of installation views. By the way, the compositional devices are all mine, only they are better in my execution. Scums! As one might expect, neither your nor my works are there" (Archive, fig. 7).[57] Whereas Senkin overtly usurps authorship of the frieze, Klutsis's complaints are more complex and show his insistence upon specific characteristics that he had invented for his propaganda material.[58] Klutsis's letter also reveals that no matter how Productivist theory refuted the importance of autonomous authorship and annihilated the significance of a single art object, even the loyalest supporters of this ideology could not surrender to the anonymity of collective work without some discomfort.

As far as Lissitzky is concerned, Pressa undoubtedly seduced him with its ambitious scale and with the possibility of immediately realizing many ideas, as had been the case with his photomontage cover for Lev Tolstoy's complete works, two million copies of which were promptly printed in 1928 (plate 53). But despite his genuine excitement about the opportunities associated with his position as an official Soviet designer, Lissitzky still doubted whether, in the context of Soviet commissions of the Pressa scale, it was possible to preserve his formal pursuits and to maintain his longing for international status. The signs of this schism, which Yve-Alain Bois discussed in terms of "Lissitzky 2" and "Lissitzky 3," are apparent from two letters Lissitzky addressed to his Soviet and Western colleagues.[59] On August 30, 1928, he reported to Senkin from Cologne: "Here at the exhibition the success is increasing. I finished Lenin's corner. ... A book with selections of reviews in the international press has been published; there is hardly a single example that does not express delight with respect to design. All this is

53 For further discussion of Klutsis's and Senkin's early photomontages, see my *Soviet Photograph, 1924–1937* (New Haven: Yale University Press, 1996), 9–34. Significantly, in their political photomontages, Klutsis and Senkin simultaneously practiced such techniques as multiple exposures, though they limited its application to works of private subject matter.
54 Quoted in Lissitzky-Küppers, *Lissitzky,* 85. For further descriptions by Küppers of Pressa, see 84–85.
55 For example, around 1926 Klutsis made a connection between his photomontage designs and contemporary film by working on a number of covers for the magazine *Kino-Front* (Cine-Front). For his designs he used various documentary film stills.
56 Next to it is the double-exposure image *Varia organizuet pionerov* (Varia Organizes Pioneers), whose 1926 date coincides with Lissitzky's design for a frieze with runners.
57 Klutsis to Valentina Kulagina, letter of June 11, 1928 (Private Archive). Despite Klutsis's conclusion that his and Kulagina's designs were not included in Pressa, two official photographs of Pressa designs bear her signature.
58 For an analysis of Klutsis's design and photomontage techniques, see my *Soviet Photograph,* 9–23.
59 Yve-Alain Bois, "El Lissitzky: Radical Reversibility," *Art in America* 76, no. 4 (April 1988): 165.

good, the political success of the exhibition is beyond a doubt."[60] In a different mood and with a different list of concerns, Lissitzky wrote to the architect J. J. P. Oud: "It was a great success for us, but artistically it remains an unsatisfying achievement, as the haste and lack of time violate the plans and necessary completion of the form, and then it actually ends up being stage scenery."[61]

Among the numerous photos of the Pressa installations, one in particular inspires conclusions about this chapter of Lissitzky's career. Three artists, Lissitzky, Senkin, and Nikolai Simon, appear in a tight lineup, separated only by the loose pages of the Pressa catalogue they hold (fig. 13).[62] Lissitzky, like Senkin, wanted this photograph to be in Kruchenykh's archive, and in his dedication to the poet, he identified the Pressa project as mainly his and referred to the two artists as his helpers—which is not to say that Lissitzky is implying that Pressa was just his project. Rather, this inscription prompts one to think that he identified not so much with the exhibition's numerous details and content, about which he reported to Senkin, but with its large-scale architectural aspects, whose failure he admitted to Oud.[63]

Before Lissitzky returned to Moscow and further surrendered himself to the Soviet Productivist paradigm, in a nostalgic gesture toward internationalism, he accepted an invitation from Schroll-Verlag to design covers for a series of books entitled *Neues Bauen in der Welt* (*New Building in the World*) and to write the first volume, which was on Russia (plates 77–82). He then traveled to Paris, where, with Ehrenburg's camera, he photographed the Eiffel Tower "from nearly every possible viewpoint" (plates 62–67).[64] Both projects placed him in proximity to architecture and revealed his destiny to realize its surrogates. This was once again true upon his return to Moscow when he agreed to restructure the auditorium of the Meyerhold Theater building. I believe it was during his involvement in this project (which was never realized) that Lissitzky came across a set of puppet-mannequins made in 1924 for Meyerhold's production of Mikhail Podgaetskii's *Daesh Evropu* (*Give Us Europe*). The play was based partially on Ehrenburg's novel, so Lissitzky may have paid particular attention to the props because of his recent visit with the writer. One of the puppets, as seen in the remaining photograph of *Give Us Europe,* is strikingly similar to the shape of the puppet-mannequin that Lissitzky used around this time to make a series of photograms (plate 68, figs. 14–15). Providing an additional reference to Ehrenburg, the puppet-mannequins observe through a magnifying glass the photograph of Paris Lissitzky had just taken with the writer's camera.[65] These associations lend Lissitzky's photograms with puppet-mannequins an important place in his career. After all, it was Ehrenburg's *6 povestei o legkikh kontsakh* (*6 Tales with Easy Endings,* 1922; plates 3–5) that inspired Lissitzky to make his first photo collages. It was also through the collaboration with Ehrenburg on the magazine *Veshch* that Lissitzky debuted in the West. Paying homage to Ehrenburg in the puppet-mannequin photograms, Lissitzky acknowledged the end of the epoch that began upon his arrival in Berlin in 1922.

13 Scholz (?), *El Lissitzky, Sergei Senkin, Nikolai Simon at Pressa*, Cologne, 1928. Gelatin silver print. Cat. 197

60 Quoted in Khardzhiev, "Pamiati khudozhnika Lisitskogo," 30.
61 Letter to J. J. P. Oud, December 26, 1928. Quoted in *El Lissitzky: Architect, Painter, Photographer, Typographer, 1890–1941*, 24.
62 This photograph of the three artists emerges metaphorically as an antithesis to the kind of collaboration Lissitzky undertook earlier for *Merz* with Schwitters and for *Die Kunstismen. Les ismes de l'art. The Isms of Art, 1924–1914* with Arp. If the individual styles of participating artists were not hard to detect in these publications, the Soviet model, which envisaged the erasure of the authorial traces, is aptly conveyed by the bodily unity of Lissitzky and his Soviet colleagues.
63 Although Nisbet suggests similarly that Lissitzky was more concerned with the "initial experience" of Pressa—which was dependent, for example, on his architectural design of the exterior of the entrance door—he does not question the methods of execution applied in the frieze and routinely lines it up with Lissitzky's previous photo-based projects, such as the Pelikan designs and the photomontage with runners. See Nisbet, *El Lissitzky*, 38.
64 Quoted in Lissitzky-Küppers, *Lissitzky*, 87.
65 For a scene from *Give Us Europe* where one can see the puppets, see Herbert Marshall, *The Pictorial History of the Russian Theater* (New York: Crown, 1977), 133.

14 Page from *Soviet Photo*, no. 10, 1929.
Larry Zeman and Howard Garfinkel, Productive Arts,
Brooklyn Heights, Ohio. Cat. 133 (Photo: William Short)

15 El Lissitzky: *Untitled*, ca. 1928. Photogram.
29.4 x 23.4 cm. Lost in 1998

66 Khardzhiev, "Lisitskii—konstruktor knigi,"
155.
67 Ibid.
68 Anonymous, "Nadpis' i ee razvitie," a clip-
ping from the magazine *Sovetskii ekran* (Soviet Screen), located in RGALI.
69 Ibid.
70 Lissitzky's distancing from the circle of
photomontage practitioners is also evident in
his not joining the photomontage section of
the October (Oktiabr) group in 1930.
71 Praising Vertov's German, Küppers notes:
"I came to Moscow from Germany to see Lissitzky only in 1927 and hardly knew a word
in Russian. Only the high culture of Vertov
and his knowledge of [German] made it possible to collaborate." S. Lisitskaia-Küppers,
"Skvoz' dal' minuvshikh let," *Dziga Vertov v
vospominaniiakh sovremennikov*, ed. Vertova
Svilova and A. L. Vinogradova (Moscow:
Iskusstvo, 1976), 184.
72 Ibid.
73 Ibid.
74 Ibid., 187

Film, Photo, and a Friendship with Dziga Vertov

There are many references to Lissitzky's interest in film, one of which goes back to the earliest experiments with graphic design. In 1922, he designed and published in Berlin a book entitled *Suprematichesky skaz pro dva kvadrata v 6ti postroikakh* (*Suprematist Story of Two Squares in 6 Constructions*), which Khardzhiev compared to "a cartoon … where all the 'stills' are connected by an undisturbed movement of simple, equivalent figures within a time sequence which is finalized with the triumph of the Red square."[66] Furthermore, Khardziev explained that in this book Lissitzky planned to resolve "the problem with the formal arrangement of the movement … with the aid of a camera. But the film interpretation of *Suprematist Story of Two Squares in 6 Constructions* was never realized."[67]

At exactly the same time in the Soviet Union, the documentary filmmaker Dziga Vertov was working on the typography of his newsreels' subtitles. The author of an article entitled "A Subtitle and Its Development with Kinoki," signed only with an initial, notes that in his *Cine-Pravdas* Vertov began to "'construct' a subtitle in a still, selecting a simplified typeset, emphasizing the key words, and situating [subtitles] in a specific construction. The emphasis was on reading a subtitle as quickly as possible on a screen."[68] The article concluded that Vertov's *Chelovek s kino apparatom* (*The Man with a Movie Camera*, 1929; Archive, figs. 12.1–12.4), which had no subtitles, "had approached the creation of 'absolute kinopis' [absolute cine-writing] that relied on a complete separation from the language of literature."[69] Lissitzky's consideration of cinematic devices to enhance his new typographic language and Vertov's simultaneous use of typography to amplify the reception of his films established the first link between these two figures of the Soviet avant-garde. Furthermore, both Vertov's *kinopis* and Lissitzky's *fotopis* relied on improvisation and the power of an image whose rendering was based on intense preoccupation with formal scrutiny.

The two men met in 1929, the year that Vertov released *The Man with a Movie Camera* and Lissitzky published his essay "Fotopis." That same year Lissitzky also received his next government commission: to design the Soviet pavilion of the Internationale Ausstellung des Deutschen Werkbunds Film und Foto (International Exhibition of Film and Photo). Perhaps owing to the difficult lessons Lissitzky had learned from his collaborative experience with Pressa, he assumed responsibility for the general planning of the exhibition and had Küppers select all the photographs and film stills for enlargement.[70] When Vertov was introduced to Küppers at VOKS (Vsesouznoe Obshchestvo Kulturnoi Sviazi s Zagranitsei, or the All-Union Society of Cultural Relations with Abroad), he immediately invited Lissitzky and her to watch *The Man with a Movie Camera*.[71] In Küppers's words, the film "deeply moved and impressed"[72] them, and things they "simply took for granted … suddenly became clear and comprehensible."[73] Similarly, Lissitzky reported to his Western acquaintances that "in our film industry, works by Dziga Vertov succeed in revolutionizing cinematography. … [In them] only the non-staged material of life itself is used, [shaping] the most polemical example of film production. … He has truly discovered a new path in cinematography—a hundred percent *kinoiazyk* [film language]."[74]

As with Pressa, the planning of and the exhibits for Film and Photo were executed in Moscow. Only the meetings now took place in Lissitzky's own "modest apartment" where "a small collective (consisting of the film directors Sergei Eisenstein, Vertov, and the art critic N. Kaufman) made the final selections of film stills for enlargement."[75] Neither Lissitzky nor Küppers accompanied the exhibition material to Stuttgart; instead they asked that Vertov oversee the project. Vertov, in his first letter from Germany, wrote: "Today, at eleven in the morning, is the opening of the exhibition. ... The film-section will open on the 13 of June. My lecture will not take place now. The Russian [photo] section will be ready only today. ... I am advising that you write to Richter and [Gustav] Stotz ... so that the USSR room (with respect to its design and film program) will remain exactly the way it was defined in advance. ... Tomorrow, I plan to go to Munich and from there to Frankfurt. ... Only from Essen is there firm and clear agreement."[76] Two weeks later Vertov wrote again, comforting Lissitzky on the outcome of the pavilion: "First of all I want to calm you down about the room in Stuttgart. In terms of construction, the room looks better than all the other rooms. It was not completely ready for the opening, due only to the fault of our Russian dawdling. It will function fully on the day of the opening of the film exhibition, which is on the 13th."[77]

After completing his role as the Soviet representative at Film and Photo, Vertov visited Hanover, where the presentation of his lecture "What Is *Kinoglaz* [Cine-Eye]?" was arranged.[78] Küppers, who promoted Vertov's work as passionately as she had Lissitzky's, once again introduced a major Soviet avant-garde practitioner into the cultural milieu of Hanover. From Berlin, Vertov acknowledged his gratitude to Küppers: "Your care of me leaves me much obliged. You have already done a lot for me, and I want to embrace you 100.000 times. ... In Hanover I gave my first two lectures and accompanied them with demonstrations of fragments from my films. ... As soon as I pronounce either of your names, the eyes of any Hanover companion sparkle with a greeting shine."[79] And to Lissitzky, Vertov reported: "I saw your room [*Abstract Cabinet*] in the Hanover museum. I sat there for a long time, looked around, groped."[80]

A letter from Kiev, written shortly after Vertov returned, documents further his collaboration with Lissitzky. "I was told by Shutko while passing through Moscow," Vertov wrote, "that the date for submitting a book about *kinoglaz* is well approaching. He spoke about your participation as the designer of the book, of the photo material, etc. If by now, you and Shutko have discussed this matter, then do not hesitate to let me know which photo materials, stills, negatives, positives, I should order for you."[81] Although there is no evidence that such a book was ever designed and published, a photo collage composed of Vertov's enlargement of an eye (also used by Rodchenko in 1924 in his posters for Vertov's kinoglaz), along with a miniature portrait of Vertov implanted directly into the pupil, has been recently located in the Lissitzky family archive (plate 74). In this interpretation of kinoglaz, Lissitzky emphasized Vertov's autonomous optics as the main force behind patterns of representation in kinoglaz. Thus, Lissitzky's model differed from Vertov's rendering of kinoglaz as seen in *The Man with a Movie Camera*. There the camera lens and the human eye are unified. Vertov's resulting mechanical eye was therefore "a socially constructed artifact" deprived of individualized optics.

16 Umbo (Otto Umbehr): *Dziga Vertov*, Berlin, 1929. RGALI, Moscow. Cat. 226

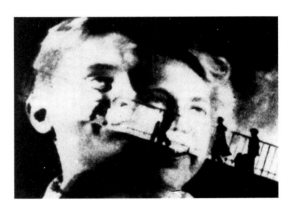

17 Dziga Vertov: Still from the film *Enthusiasm*, 1930–31

75 Ibid., 185. Significantly, photojournalists were excluded from these meetings. The exhibition included works by Aleksandr Rodchenko, Arkady Shaikhet, Max Alpert, Dmitry Debabov, Semen Fridliand, and Boris Ignatovich as well as photographs from Press Clishe, the photo agency established in 1926 as part of TASS. Also included were photomontages by Senkin, Elkin, Klutsis, Telingater, and Varvara Stepanova and film stills by Lev Kuleshov, Mikhail Kaufman, Abram Room, Esphir Shub, Vsevolod Pudovkin, Vertov, Eisenstein, and Roman Karmen. For more on this exhibition, see Ulrich Pohlmann's essay in this volume. As in the case of the All-Union Printing Trades Exhibition, in *Film and Photo* Lissitzky exhibited a mixture of images, including *Portrait of Arp, Self-Portrait* (Constructor), a photogram with a puppet-mannequin, and a photograph of a soldier guarding the Shablovskaia radio tower in Moscow (plate 83).
76 Letter of May 18, 1929, RGALI, f. 2091, op. 2, ed. khr. 294.
77 Letter of June 7, 1929, RGALI, f. 2091, op. 2, ed. khr. 343, ll. 5–8.
78 *Kinoglaz* was the name of a series of newsreels produced by Vertov in 1924. Similar to his other documentary films, *Kinoglaz* was based on spontaneous filming of Soviet reality. For a discussion of Vertov's idea of kinoglaz, see Annette Michelson's introduction in *Kino-Eye: The Writings of Dziga Vertov*, ed. Annette Michelson (Berkeley: University of California Press, 1984), xv–ixi.

18 El Lissitzky: *Sophie Küppers with Two Children* (Kurt and Hans Küppers), ca. 1930. Gelatin silver print. 12.3 x 17.3 cm. Berlinische Galerie, Landesmuseum für Moderne Kunst, Photography and Architecture

In 1930, with the release of his new film *Entuziazm* or *Simfonia Donbassa* (*Enthusiasm* or *Symphony of Donbass*), Vertov once again found, in Lissitzky and Küppers, zealous support for his revolutionary production. Years later, Küppers remembered the "incredible impression" that *Enthusiasm* made upon Lissitzky and her: "With what drama young builders of new industry appealed to us from the screen! … This was an absolutely harmonious construction made from sounds, the noise of cars, blastfurnaces, and mines. We were amazed by the composition and musicality of our friend's new work."[82] In *Enthusiasm,* Vertov adopted the double-faced composition Lissitzky had conceived in 1929 as a poster for the Russian Exhibition in Zurich (plates 75–76). In doing so, Vertov gave Lissitzky an opportunity to see how his compositions worked in a motion picture—an experiment that Lissitzky had hoped to try since his making of the *Suprematist Story of Two Squares in 6 Constructions.*[83]

Although straight photography is rare in Lissitzky's oeuvre, questions remain concerning the connection between Vertov and him in this domain. For the most part, Lissitzky thought about making photographic projects during his illness. Hence he experimented with forms that did not require complicated production—media such as multiple exposures and photograms—work that moved away from the streets and into the dark room. To obtain negatives for his photographic experiments, Lissitzky was sometimes compelled to take photographs, which, to avoid unnecessary physical strain, he usually limited to a single sight (such as the Eiffel Tower) or to an easily available group of models (friends and family). Typical examples of such images are Küppers's profile (Letters, fig. 7), a variation of which appeared in a photomontage of Küppers with her two sons (fig. 18), and photograms with puppets-mannequins that included Lissitzky's photograph of Paris (plates 67–68). Most examples of Lissitzky's straight photography, however, do not reflect any of the popular modernist techniques of the time, particularly taking photographs from above or below the vantage point. Given his association

79 Quoted in Lissitzky-Küppers, "Skvoz' dal' minuvshikh let," 188. During his lecture Vertov projected fragments of his films on a ceiling.
80 Letter of June 7, 1929, RGALI, f. 2091, op. 2, ed. khr. 343, ll. 5–8.
81 Undated letter written in 1929, RGALI, f. 2091, op. 2, ed. khr. 294.
82 Küppers, "Skvoz' dal' minuvshikh let," 191. This was the first full-length sound documentary made in the Soviet Union, despite the minimal technical equipment available. See Vertov, "Zaiavlenie avtora," RGALI, f. 2091, op. 1, ed. khr. 42, ll. 7–8. With *Enthusiasm* Vertov once again was invited on a European tour and visited London and Paris.
83 In 1934 Lissitzky wrote "Iliada Leninizma," in which he acclaimed the representational strategies of Vertov's new film *Three Songs of Lenin* (Archive, figs. 13.1–13.5); "Iliada Leninizma," RGALI, f. 2091, op. 2, ed. khr. 46.

with the Bauhaus, Lissitzky was no doubt familiar with these new photographic devices but avoided using them because of the daring physical activity involved. Instead, as his photographs and existing portraits of him with a camera illustrate, he was determined to take pictures using a technique that Rodchenko negatively termed "belly-button level" (Letters, fig. 6).[84] In light of what has been said, a set of family photographs (those of Küppers's children and of Küppers herself) is difficult to recognize as Lissitzky's precisely because, in them, the position that the photographer takes is atypical for him (figs. 20–21).

A small photograph taken by Vertov's wife, Elizaveta Svilova (fig. 19), may settle questions as to the authorship of these images.[85] In Svilova's snapshot, Vertov is photographed in profile and in a playful position, looking up toward Küppers's son, who sits high on a fire escape, joyful over his unreachability. The boy wears a *tubeteika,* a traditional Asian cap, an image that is similar to another portrait of Küppers's sons: a photomontage of the two boys' heads in profile (Letters, fig. 14). Here, in accordance with Lissitzky's photographic methods, Küppers's sons, caught inside in a motionless and staged position, appear serious and entirely removed from the joy and mobility of outdoor games. Variations in both the location and details of Svilova's photograph are repeated in a series of images whose authorship I question. Some of the photographs show Küppers's sons posing on the same fire escape for an invisible photographer (Letters, fig. 15); others record them standing on the ground beside the same building, looking upward with a grimace at the photographer (figs. 20–21). It is particularly difficult to imagine Lissitzky in this last scenario—that is, standing on a fire escape—when one looks at the photomontage of Lissitzky's multiple portraits that Josef Albers took at the Bauhaus in 1928. In one of the portraits, Lissitzky is caught by Albers sitting on a chair with a camera on his lap, obviously exhausted from having taken some pictures (fig. 5).[86]

The same gap exists between Lissitzky's predominantly belly-button portraits of Küppers (as they appear in his photomontages; fig. 18) and the portrait of her now in the collection of Berlinische Gallery, where Küppers's gaze is distinctly upward. To attribute this particular portrait of Küppers to Vertov is especially

19 Elizaveta Svilova: *Dziga Vertov and Sophie Küppers's Son,* ca. 1930–31. Priska Pasquer, Photographic Art Consulting, Cologne. Cat. 229

20 El Lissitzky: *Kurt and Hans Küppers,* 1930. Gelatin silver print. Private Archive. Cat. 89

21 El Lissitzky; *Kurt and Hans Küppers.* 1930. Gelatin silver print. 23.8 x 15.2 cm. Private Archive

84 It would be engaging to undertake a comparative analysis of Lissitzky's and Rodchenko's transition from abstract painting to photo collage around 1922. Both artists grounded their first experiments with photographic elements within the framework of formal innovations of their paintings. Similarly, in the photographic imagery that immediately followed their first photo collages they resisted the spatial flexibility of Constructivism and relied on the preciseness of a frontal vantage point. Whereas by 1927 Rodchenko returned to the practice of photography with multiple viewpoints, Lissitzky continued to insist on the observational simplicity of his photographic compositions. It is also important to note that Rodchenko left for his first visit to the West during the same year that Lissitzky returned from his stay abroad.
85 According to Küppers, Svilova also often photographed their newborn son Jen, whose nickname was "Bubka." Küppers notes that she and Lissitzky "received an entire album with pictures of the little one as a present." A collage of Jen's double portrait glued on a cardboard may very well be one of the pages from Svilova's album (Letters, this vol., fig. 13; Küppers, "Skvoz' dal' minuvshikh let," 191). Svilova also took photographs of Lissitzky before he died on December 30, 1941.
86 Given that during the same trip Lissitzky borrowed Ehrenburg's camera to photograph Paris, it is likely that in Albers's photomontage, Lissitzky once again uses someone else's camera.

tempting when one reads the notes she wrote in 1930, shortly before she and Lissitzky left to design the Soviet pavilions at the Internationale Hygiene-Ausstellung (International Hygiene Exhibition) in Dresden and the Internationale Pelz-Fachausstellung (International Fur Trade Exhibition) in Leipzig (plates 84–86, 88).[87] "In connection with the work on these two exhibitions," Küppers writes, "Lissitzky and I had to again go abroad for a long time, and as a result, part from Vertov. Then shortly before the departure, he made several of my portraits, which I still have. … In the winter of 1930/31 [after their return] he visited us often. It is hard to forget his attention and love toward our kids."[88]

In conclusion, one might choose to agree with Khardzhiev, who wrote that "Lissitzky and Vertov followed each other's achievements with pleasure."[89] One might add that they adopted certain tools from each other's work. If that is true, the series of photographs in question represents Lissitzky's homage to Vertov's film techniques. If we instead attribute these photographs to Vertov, we might gain more than we lose. Within Lissitzky's overall photographic production, the questioned images look rather misplaced and random; if by Vertov, however, they would stand as noteworthy examples of his photography, making them a significant addition to the known frame enlargements he left behind.

Aching Propaganda: Photography, Illness, and Collaboration

After the enormous success of the two Soviet pavilions designed for the International Hygiene Exhibition and International Fur Trade Exhibition, Lissitzky and Küppers returned to a hot summer in Moscow. Immediately after, Küppers and her children left for a remote village near Riazan, where Lissitzky addressed the following letter: "I was in the Ogonek-Pravda office and must now see whether I can rescue anything of my design. The whole program has been changed. … So in fact a new design has to be made, but the foundations have already been started on. Maybe I will have to write to the newspaper—'Please do not accuse me of the death of my design.'"[90] The apocalyptic terms that Lissitzky used to describe the

87 Küppers also stresses that Vertov made photo portraits of young student-artists from the "Institute of Peoples of the North" for use in Lissitzky's design of the International Fur Trade Exhibition. See Küppers, "Skvoz' dal' minuvshikh let," 190.
88 Ibid.
89 Khardzhiev, "El Lisitskii—konstruktor knigi," 161.

changing policies in the Soviet design industry serves as a metaphor for this last phase of his career, which began with the opening of the decade and ended with his death in 1941.

I shall not present here a structural or iconographic analysis of Lissitzky's late photographic work as it was used in magazine and book designs. That has been done before.[91] Instead, my intent is to illuminate the interdependence between Lissitzky's progressive illness and the working strategies he devised in response to it. As we shall see, throughout the 1930s Lissitzky vacillated, out of necessity, between moments of exhilarating work and periods of serious recuperation. Moreover, although Lissitzky's commitment to Soviet propaganda consumed much of his time and energy, the government commissions he received, and the various privileges associated with them, in fact prolonged his life.

In spite of Lissitzky's ominous outlook at the beginning of the 1930s, by 1932 things were looking brighter, in both his work and his health. He was now strong enough to travel to Sverdlovsk, whose Recreational Park (plate 97) he was commissioned to design, and to visit the newly launched Dnieper Dam (Dneproges). The second trip related to Lissitzky's first assignment for IZOGIZ (the State Publishing House for Art): to design an issue of *SSSR na stroike* (*USSR in Construction*) commemorating the construction of Dnieper Dam (plate 98). Lissitzky's new contract with this organization, responsible for most of the state-subsidized publications, secured his livelihood and his access to medical treatments for the rest of the decade. The photographer Max Alpert, who took a photograph of Lissitzky during their trip to Dneproges, records him in the state of rare physical resilience essential for photojournalists who traveled long distances and subjected themselves to uncomfortable living conditions (Letters, fig. 6). Alpert's photograph is misleading, however, if we are to believe that it certifies Lissitzky's responsibility for taking the numerous photographs needed to document the giant industrial sight. As the credits in the resulting issue of *USSR in Construction* testify, Lissitzky went to Dnieper Dam only to tell Alpert *what* to photograph.

Thus, as before, Lissitzky's involvement with straight photography was brief and left no significant imprint on his subsequent projects. His earlier career as a book designer, however, revived by his contract with IZOGIZ, took on a new phase. Lissitzky himself described it as a conscious move away from a "constructive" to a *monternaia* (montaged) book. "We are approaching," he wrote in 1932, "the book constructed like a film: plot, development, highpoint, denoument [sic]."[92] Küppers attributed Lissitzky's reevaluation of his book format and the way he presented documentary photographic material in *USSR in Construction* to his appropriation of Vertov's strategies of free-running images in his early newsreels. Küppers also summed up Lissitzky's new activities as the logical continuation of his career as an exhibition designer, primarily because, as she claimed, he employed "the same 'collective' system for working."[93] To illustrate her point, Küppers outlined in detail the way each issue of *USSR in Construction* was composed: "Writers, scholars, artists, and photographers met together in the editorial office. Each number treated just one basic theme, which was determined by the chief editor in conjunction with the writer who was responsible for the 'scenario.' Lissitzky, after intense consultations with the writers of the text, transformed this 'scenario' into

90 Quoted in Lissitzky-Küppers, *Lissitzky*, 95.
91 See Victor Margolin, *The Struggle for Utopia: Rodchenko, Lissitzky, Moholy-Nagy, 1917–1946* (Chicago: University of Chicago Press, 1997), 162–213; and my *Soviet Photograph*, 127–74.
92 El Lissitzky, "Do Not Separate Form from Content!" 62. In this translation the word *monternaia* is translated as "assembled" and therefore misses the reference to film.
93 Lissitzky-Küppers, *Lissitzky*, p. 97.

23 Anonymous: *El Lissitzky in Bed*, 1928.
Gelatin silver print. Private Archive. Cat. 264

24 Anonymous: Max Alpert and Georgy Petrusov at
the offices of *USSR in Construction*, ca. 1934.
Howard Schickler Fine Art, New York. Cat. 264

a visual exposition. On the rough layout he sketched the outline of the photos that were taken by the photographers, taught them the rudiments of composition, and gave them the most precise instructions for obtaining the required material—with a view of the appropriate interpretation of the theme."[94] It was precisely this well-organized preparatory framework that would later allow Lissitzky to continue with his designs "even when his illness confined [him] to his bed."[95]

Predictably, the two trips that Lissitzky took around the Soviet Union were too ambitious and ultimately caused his already frail health to deteriorate severely. As a result, for his next IZOGIZ project—the design of the album *Raboche-krestianskaia krasnaia armia (Workers'-Peasants' Red Army*; plate 104)—he was unable to travel to Moscow from his home in Skhodnia and settled instead in the capital's Military Hotel. Although Lissitzky was provided with many archival photographs and sources for this volume (fig. 26), he also managed to sketch compositions that were later staged at the Moscow Mezhrabpom (Organization of Proletarian Solidarity; fig. 25). In spite of special accommodations, however, Lissitzky was further drained by this project. As a reward for the "exceptional work" he had done, he received a *putevka* (a government-subsidized pass) to an excellent military sanitarium in the Crimean town of Gurzuf. Apart from the substantial amount of money he received for *Workers'-Peasants' Red Army* and several issues of *USSR in Construction*—which enabled him, even while he was ill, to adequately support his family of four—the privileges granted him were priceless. Following a rapid recuperation in Gurzuf, Lissitzky was ready to travel with Küppers along the Volga River to plan the upcoming issues of the new magazine *Na stroike MTS i sovkhozov (At the Construction of MTS and of Collective Farms;* plates 107–108, fig. 27). During the course of this trip he met the photographer Mikhail Prekhner in Stalingrad, the future author of Lissitzky's famous portraits (Letters, fig. 1; Chronology, fig. 5). Immediately recognizing Prekhner as "one of the most gifted young photographers"of the time, Lissitzky made sure to include him in his group of photojournalists for the first issue of *At the Construction of MTS and of Collective Farms.*

Although artists often had to adjust to the special circumstances of Lissitzky's health, his pattern of collaboration with other Soviet photojournalists, as described earlier by Küppers, was not out of the ordinary; often it was practiced by other

designers of *USSR in Construction,* including Rodchenko and Stepanova. What is unique about the structure of Lissitzky's late design productions, however, was his increasing dependence on Küppers. This fact, though rarely discussed, deserves attention, because Küppers was not a professional designer or photographer.[96]

Their working relationship began only two years after their marriage, when Lissitzky, distraught by the complexities of collaboration during Pressa asked Küppers to assist him in the collection of visuals for Film and Photo. Küppers's involvement in this project was perfectly appropriate: she was educated as an art historian, and because of her experience as an art dealer, she was familiar with archival work and knew how to deal with art in practical terms. Furthermore, she was able to approach material from a Western standpoint, which ultimately contributed to a wider reception of Lissitzky's work within the West. Only after her full participation in the design of the two Soviet pavilions for the hygiene and fur exhibitions was she officially recognized as Lissitzky's assistant. On July 19, 1930, he informed Küppers of the following news : "I was in VOKS. They send you their warmest regards. They have no reports and no catalogues from Dresden [of the Hygiene Exhibition] or Leipzig [of the Fur Trade Exhibition]. So, I gave each of them a copy and showed them photographs of your section. They are very pleased and continue to repeat that if it hadn't been for you they would not have risked sending these things. As things stand, they regard you as an assistant."[97] Thus, the very mention of a "separate section" by Küppers testifies to an involvement that was initially archival and gradually evolved into actual design, including the production of photomontages.

It was not until Lissitzky became sick again in 1934 that Küppers resumed her responsibilities as assistant. It was Lissitzky who initially arranged and negotiated the commissions, but it was Küppers who made their production possible. Well aware of this, he later paid homage to her: "It is necessary, especially in my autobiography, to emphasize that in all my work, in the *USSR in Construction* in particular, my most active and devoted helper was my wife Sophia Khristianovna Lisitskaia Kuppers."[98] In 1934, along with Lissitzky, Küppers was acknowledged for the first time as the designer of several issues of *USSR in Construction* and of the book *Sovetskie subtropiki* (*Soviet Subtropics*; plate 101). The extent of her par-

25 Anonymous: Georgy Zelma photographing a scene staged by El Lissitzky for an issue of *USSR in Construction* devoted to the fifteenth anniversary of the Red Army. International Workers Aid Film Studio, ca. 1932. Howard Schickler Fine Art, New York. Cat. 252

26 Georgy Zelma: El Lissitzky working on the album *Workers'-Peasants' Red Army*, 1934. Private Collection. Cat. 247

96 Lissitzky-Küppers, *Lissitzky,* 97. Prekhner's portraits of Lissitzky have been misdated in several publications. Because he wears a suit and tie in these portraits, I believe Prekhner took them after they returned from a trip on the Volga River.
97 Lissitzky-Küppers, *Lissitzky,* 95.
98 El Lisitskii, *Avtobiografiia,* July 1941, RGALI, f. 2361, op. 1, ed. khr. 58, ll. 22 −23.

ticipation is not clear in either of these publications, since there is no apparent distinction between their respective contributions. Also in 1934, during Lissitzky's stay at the military sanitarium, Küppers was listed as the sole author of all the photomontages in issue 5 of *At the Construction of MTS and of Collective Farms*. Her compositional renderings varied from the simple insertion of small photo stills into large spreads of fields to ambitious but awkwardly designed pages with multiple scenarios (figs. 28.1–28.3).

Despite his many health problems, in 1935 Lissitzky once again gathered enough strength to continue his work, producing an issue of *USSR in Construction* as well as the detailed seven-volume publication *Industria sotsializma* (*Industry of Socialism*; plate 109). This picture survey of the industrial progress achieved during two Five Year Plans brought Lissitzky yet another handsome financial reward and an opportunity to stay at a sanitarium in the Georgian mountain village of Abastumani. Before leaving for his three-month cure, Lissitzky prepared an initial layout for his next major design project: a large album of lithographs called *Pishchevaia industria* (*Food Industry*, 1936; plate 110). In his letters from Abastumani, Lissitzky regularly instructed Küppers on how to proceed with the album's design; her role as author in this project was therefore operative rather than creative. This concept of the new Soviet author, formulated in the contemporary writings of Tretiakov, repudiated the traditional approach to the making of art as a synthesis between creativity and professionalism. As a result, this operative ideology gave birth to an army of amateur photographers and designers who were ready to work for regional newspapers, magazines, and workers' clubs. Lissitzky's debt to Tretiakov's radical authorial ideas is evident in a 1932 letter to Tschichold, in which he contrasts the concept of artistic creation with the expeditious production of commissioned work.[99]

It was Küppers who negotiated final approval from high-ranking officials for *Food Industry*. She also frequently visited the editorial office of IZOGIZ, where she had to deal with the three editors who, according to her, "vied with each other in their inspirations and in the production of new photographic material."[100] This coincided with Lissitzky's conviction that "the little people with whom one is forced to prepare work" presented more of an obstacle in the production of propaganda publications than the high-ranking officials who sanctioned them.[101] Combining these organizational functions with the design of the album, Küppers nevertheless believed that she was simply "carrying on" Lissitzky's "most precise details about the [required] work."[102] As the last of Lissitzky's letter from Abastumani testified, however, he viewed Küppers's role in the production of *Food Industry* differently. "You seem to be generally satisfied with the work," he observes; "you have done it from the beginning completely by yourself."[103]

Submitted at the end of 1935 as a project codesigned by Lissitzky and Küppers, the album was produced in just two weeks. Significantly, unlike Lissitzky's previously designed books and albums, *Food Industry* was not for sale and was printed in the limited edition of fifteen hundred copies. The final version consisted of fifty-eight lithographs of drawings, photomontages, and single-frame photographs, each with a descriptive title, displayed in a case 20 by 16 inches made of gray satin. A booklet containing a speech by the commissar of food industry, Anas-

99 See Lissitzky's letter of September 29, 1932, Letters, this vol., 203–4.
100 Lissitzky-Küppers, *Lissitzky*, 98.
101 See Lissitzky's letter of July 16, 1935, Letters, this vol., 212.
102 Lissitzky-Küppers, *Lissitzky*, 98.
103 See Lissitzky's letter of August 29, 1935, Letters, this vol., 221.

tas Mikoian, provided only three days before the album went to the printer, was also included. Entitled "Questions of the Food Industry in Connection with the Stakhanov Movement," Mikoian's text encouraged Soviet workers to do superhuman labor and to maintain high levels of productivity. The lithographs—straight photographic images and photomontages alike—were signed by photographers and included such well-known names as Vladimir Gruntal, Anatoly Skurikhin, and Semen Fridliand. Küppers signed only one image: that of a statuesque sunflower towering over a bed of sunflower heads set in the foreground to indicate their readiness to be processed into a popular Soviet oil.[104] Although this is the only photomontage that bears her signature, it is likely, particularly if we are to rely on Lissitzky's remark "until you have to do montage," that Küppers was responsible for most of the album's composed photographic imagery.[105] Yet in the end, she chose to sign the lithographs with the names of the better-known photojournalists who provided the photographs.

Lissitzky's letters reveal that he advised Küppers not so much on the album's photographic aspects as on the cover, case, and color choices for the paper. Lissitzky also prevented Küppers from making dangerous iconographic "slips" in political themes, cautioning her on critical points: "When you glue on the star," he wrote, "you must place within it the cut-out of Stalin."[106] After all, as a foreigner Küppers could easily overlook the rigid regulations and codes of political correctness in the Soviet Union. As far as photographic imagery is concerned, however, only one photomontage in the album had explicit political significance: it depicted Mikoian during the presentation of the speech mentioned earlier. Separated from the audience that he is addressing, Mikoian is surrounded by a wave of male and female portraits that are all identified by name on the bottom of the lithograph and described as "the best people of the food industry." The prototype for this compositional format, where a body of people appear in close physical proximity, was first introduced in 1931 by Klutsis in his photomontage *SSSR— Udarnaia brigada mirovogo proletariata* (*USSR—World Shock Brigade*). But unlike Klutsis's well-structured and coordinated parade of Soviet workers and politicians, "the best people of the food industry" is an awkward mass of heads that conflict in

27 El Lissitzky: Cover for the magazine
At the Construction of MTS and of Sovkhozy, no. 1, 1934.
Lithography. Private Collection

28.1–28.3 Sophie Küppers: Cover and two pages from the magazine *At the Construction of MTS and of Sovkhozy*, no. 5, 1934. Lithography. 36.4 x 26.2 cm.
Private Collection

104 Curiously, Peter Nisbet's reading of Küppers's lithograph as "a monumental daisy emerging from behind pomegranates" reflects his attempt to endow this image with a nonutilitarian dimension, thus romanticizing it in a way that would come across as decadent for the Soviet mentality. The question that comes to mind is why Küppers would depict a flower that is of no use for the Soviet food industry. It was precisely because of its usefulness that the sunflower became a frequent image in Soviet agricultural representations. See Peter Nisbet, *El Lissitzky, 1890–1941*, 199.
105 See Lissitzky's letter of June 16, 1935, Letters, this vol., 206.
106 Ibid., July 9, 1935, 209.

size, direction, and facial expression. Presented in such odd form, this particular group of Soviet "overachievers" ends up distorting Soviet reality rather than portraying it. At the time of the portfolio's design, such unintended "surrealization" in political photomontage became commonplace, primarily because of the requirement to illustrate a variety of narratives with diverse imagery. The contradictory corrections of editors contributed further to the compositional disunity of many photomontages, resulting in the exclusion of this kind of technique from Soviet representation. This ungainly attempt at conveying a political message was replaced by socialist realist painting, which offered a far more convincing way of concealing the scars of censorship.

Apart from the explicit political iconography of the best people of the food industry, the portfolio represented various aspects of food productivity rather than food consumption, in opposition to the Western formula of advertising. Furthermore, all the lithographs were packed into a case and distributed primarily to libraries thereby excluding the sort of display necessary for a commodity.[107] Consequently the producer-consumer model, constructed by this album, did not depend on whether the consumer discovered a product through representation and went out to buy it; rather, the Soviet model of consumerism, which can be identified here as the "Stalinist psychedelic commodity," depended on the euphoric effects of representation itself.[108] *Food Industry* later became an object of sacral rather than secular significance and was appropriately deposited into the vaults of libraries and archives. In this capacity, the album provided the third and final model (prior to the return of painting) of the Soviet—or Stalinist—object. Although the portfolio was not promoted on the visual level, the contents, when viewed, say, in a library, did not estrange the viewer (as did the Constructivist abstract objects). Similarly, as mentioned earlier, the social object, with its emphasis on function and its powerful mechanisms of display, could not constrast more strongly with *Food Industry*'s neglect of the subject's "im/pulse to see" and the object's complete lack of utility.

While recognizing the difference between the social object and the Stalinist object, we must also remember that both were related to productive and receptive standards of collective optics. In the case of Lissitzky, the intrusion of this visual paradigm occurred when he agreed to unite with other Soviet artists for the Pressa designs. This intervention disturbed the foundation of mainstream modernism in his abstract work. Lissitzky's two diverse opinions about the outcome of Pressa signified his recognition that his customary visual mechanisms were threatened. He evaluated the installation in the Soviet pavilion negatively when discussing it with the Western architect Oud, complaining to him that the installation was not satisfactory with regard to a purified modernist (read Western) optical scaling. Yet when he communicated with his Soviet colleague Senkin, Lissitzky judged the very same project in positive terms, finding satisfaction in the visual power that Pressa gained from the collective vision of a synthesized rather than fragmented reality. After Pressa, Lissitzky resisted, if unintentionally, the intrusion of the Soviet optical paradigm into his art, which explains why he asked Küppers to collaborate with him on the design of three more pavilions at international exhibitions. Küppers's foreign identity secured his relative Otherness with respect to the

107 Since perestroika, some of these publications have been removed from reading rooms in libraries and placed among the rare books. It is important to note that in general these sorts of publications were available to the masses.
108 This phrase is from Victor Tupitsyn, "Civitas Solis: Ghetto as Paradise," *Parallax*, University of Leeds, 1996, 139. Tupitsyn calls the postabstract (affirmative) avant-garde "Socialist modernism," thereby distinguishing it from Socialist realism on the basis that the latter was unable to create a style of its own. See also his "Romancing the Negative: Boris Mikhaylov's New Photographs," in *Boris Michailov: Les Misérables* (Hanover: Sprengel Museum, 1998), n. p.

Soviet optical machine, and yet it simultaneously established the context for collective work that undercut his subjectivism. Later, Lissitzky's work for IZOGIZ forced him back into a community of collaborators, which increased the power of collective vision every time Lissitzky became physically debilitated. Lissitzky's physical absence from the design process of *Food Industry* contributed to the kind of representation in which collective optics was briefly interrupted. It was not Lissitzky, however, but Küppers who escaped from the arena of the Soviet visual apparatus.

Earlier I mentioned that, in Küppers's mind, *Food Industry* seemed to be aligned with a Western model of commodity advertising—an approach that allowed her to feel at ease with the project. Similarly, unaware of the official intention to promote the album from functioning on a visual level, she made the photographic images visually effective. Feeding into these two false assumptions, Küppers resisted entangled narratives and spatial illusionism, the two main properties of late Soviet photographic representation. In doing so, she liberated both the object, which was lost within a crowd of details, and the subject, who was obscured by a politically conditioned arsenal of characters. The resulting pictures of cigarettes, automobiles, perfume, spaghetti, clams, and caviar—most rendered through virtually extinct modernist devices of spatial compression and fragmentation—were designed for a wall rather than a case.[109]

Realizing her transgression of the late Soviet visual canon, Küppers began to obstruct the sense of collective consciousness on which Soviet representations were based. Much later, in the 1960s, she recorded her introduction to Soviet communal reality, through her first cooking experience: "In the kitchen, which overlooked a nearby church," remembers Küppers, "the meals were prepared on paraffin cookers. Two friendly old women, who lived in a little room close by, helped me at the beginning, because it was very difficult for me. I did the cooking on my electric ring, with one pan, some Jena glass dishes and some cooking utensils, a procedure which seemed quite inconceivable to the neighbors."[110] The scene described brings to mind one image from the album: the lithograph of a woman pleasantly cooking alone in a kitchen. Perhaps this is Küppers, removed from the communal reality she described. Whether or not this is a self-portrait, here she constructed a picture imbued with Western logic, namely, that collective participation in production was to be followed by individual consumption of commodities.

By the time Küppers began to design the album, she fully qualified for the status of a pioneering Soviet woman who was equal to men in the workplace but still burdened by domestic responsibilities carried out in inefficient space. Küppers's iconographic choices in *Food Industry* reveal (and simultaneously compensate for) her fantasies about and desire for lost (Western) and unattainable (Soviet) spaces. Lissitzky detected this schism in Küppers as early as 1932, when he wrote to Tschichold that regardless of Küppers's apparent endurance of Soviet life, "the engine" would still have to be "oiled" and that he hoped to send Küppers "to Munich during the winter for a cure."[111] He therefore recognized that his wife would be able to retain a Soviet female identity only if, in the words of Walter Benjamin, her "optical unconscious" was at least occasionally revivified by the

109 The visual validity of the *Food Industry* album was at once recognized by Ute Eskildsen, director of the Folkwang Museum's department of photography, who during the installation of my exhibition *Glaube, Hoffnung, Anpassung: Sowjetische Bilder, 1928–1945* suggested that we frame and hang these lithographs on the wall rather than put them in the vitrines.
110 Lissitzky-Küppers, *Lissitzky*, 82.
111 See Lissitzky's letter of September 29, 1932, Letters, this vol., 204.

29.1 Design for *USSR in Construction*, nos. 9–12, 1937. Priska Pasquer, Photographic Art Consulting, Cologne. Cat. 112

29.2 Design for *USSR in Construction*, nos. 9–12, 1937. Statens Konstmuseer, Moderna Museet, Stockholm. Cat. 113

112 Elena Semenova, "From My Reminiscences," 24.
113 After Lissitzky died, Küppers worked as a designer of various exhibitions, including the Exhibition of American Film in the House of Architects and a large exhibition dedicated to Charlie Chaplin in the House of Cinematography. She was later exiled with her son Jen to Novosibirsk, where she died on December 10, 1978.
114 Lissitzky got together with some dadaists in 1922 at the Düsseldorf Congress of Progressive Artists and then again at the Dada-Constructivist meeting at Weimar. The reference to Dada is particularly evident from Lissitzky's representation of Tatlin, the dadaists' hero since the 1920 Dada Fair in Berlin, in his maquette for Ilia Ehrenburg's *6 Tales with Easy Endings*. Combining the Constructivist *Proun* space with photo collage was Lissitzky's attempt to synthesize the two visual principles of these, at the time, radical movements.
115 Lissitzky-Küppers, *Lissitzky,* 54.

Western order of things. No longer able to return to the West, however, throughout the 1930s Küppers could "cure" herself only through representation, something she attempted to do in the *Food Industry* album. More than ever, Lissitzky, in desperate need of a medical cure, continued to strain himself with magazine, book, and architectural designs until "he was no longer able to move around physically."[112] With the coming of World War II in 1941, the possibility of a cure was irreversibly halted for both Lissitzky and Küppers. Lissitzky was deprived of medical attention because his high-ranking protectors, now absorbed by the events of the war, could no longer help him. Similarly, as a German, Küppers qualified for enemy status; with Lissitzky dying in her arms, she suffered from extreme cultural and personal displacement. For the moment, her children, both German and Russian, were her only link to an unrecoverable past, but they were also her sole incentive to face an unknown future.[113]

One question will always linger among Lissitzky scholars: What kind of artist would he have been had he not gotten sick in 1923? To claim that his sudden impairment led him to embrace figuration and photography would be inaccurate, because his first experiments in photographic media, as exemplified by the photocollage illustrations for Ehrenburg's *6 Tales with Easy Endings,* date from 1922 and were inspired by his acquaintance with the Dadaists.[114] Moreover, these photocollages exhibit Lissitzky's conscious break with abstraction by means of intruding upon the *Proun* space with a photographic image. Similarly, to assume that his sickness introduced him to commissioned work that clashed with his creative course would be equally misleading. Lissitzky had already been involved in work for the Soviet government in 1919–20, when he designed such Suprematist posters as *Stanki depo fabrik zavodov zhdut vas* (*The Factory and Plant Workbenches Await You*) and *Beat the Whites with the Red Wedge*. Was Lissitzky therefore implying that he preferred socialist commissions to capitalist ones when he commented, with respect to the Pelikan designs, that he "loath[ed] the entire business," calling it the "face of capitalism"?[115] I would say most likely not, because in 1935, he recalled that very experience of working for a capitalist firm with nostalgic pleasure, juxtaposing it with the frustrating moments associated with *Food Industry*. Why, then, did he express all these contradictory signals of pleasure and despair in relation to

various periods and commissions? Was it the artist's perpetual dissatisfaction with the fact that he could never concentrate solely on architecture as he had hoped to upon his return to Moscow? Or was it anguish over the clash between his desire to construct a sense of conceptual totality in his oeuvre within troubled personal and political circumstances? Regardless of the answers, by continually shifting styles, media, and sociopolitical contexts, Lissitzky, like other major Soviet avant-garde artists, deprived his future scholars of the stability required for the study of a modernist artist. Worse yet, in 1941, as if anticipating the historian's desire to sort his work into "major" and "minor," Lissitzky equalized his incomparable experiments, violating even established media classifications. Recognizing the radicalness of his gesture, Lissitzky, five months before his death, wrote: "The word design does not convey the full creative substance of our work. I *dare* to say that the work on the 'essense' of certain magazine issues [of *USSR in Construction*] and others was no less intense than in a painting" (emphasis added).[116]

29.3 Design for *USSR in Construction,* nos. 9–12, 1937. Priska Pasquer, Photographic Art Consulting, Cologne. Cat. 114

29.4 Design for *USSR in Construction,* nos. 9–12, 1937. Priska Pasquer, Photographic Art Consulting, Cologne. Cat. 115

116 El Lisitskii, *Avtobiografiia,* July 1941, RGALI, f. 2361, op. 1, ed. khr. 58, ll. 22–23.

Ulrich Pohlmann

El Lissitzky's Exhibition Designs:
The Influence of His Work in Germany, Italy, and the United States, 1923–1943

Space is there for man, not man for space.
—El Lissitzky, 1923

The concept of an "event culture" has increasingly permeated modern-day life, particularly in art museums and galleries of the Western world. Spectacularly mounted exhibitions that often boast the latest in electronic media encourage visitors to become actively involved with art and thus turn their visit into an unforgettable event. The precursors of this development include exhibition scenarios from the 1920s. These, too, were intended to mobilize the public through the use of neon lighting, film and, above all, photography. The stand and exhibition designs by the Soviet artist El Lissitzky hold a special place within this tradition—the artist himself has designated them as his most important artistic works. Two facts may have been decisive here: first, Lissitzky saw in these works the possibility of actively influencing the restructuring of the young Soviet state; second, these exhibitions offered him the unique opportunity of lending concrete form to his ideas in his capacity as managing "engineer" in a collective. The most famous of Lissitzky's installations were carried out in Germany and are extremely well documented, like the Internationale Presse-Ausstellung Pressa in Cologne in 1928 and the Internationale Ausstellung des Deutschen Werkbunds Film und Foto (International Exhibition of Film and Photo) in Stuttgart in 1929.[1] It is not my task to document El Lissitzky's designs. Instead I shall focus on how Lissitzky's design influenced exhibitions of a more political-propagandistic nature, such as those that took place in National Socialist Germany and fascist Italy between 1932 and 1937. In doing so I shall make particular reference to photography and photomontage.

The Soviet Pavilion at the Pressa in Cologne, 1928

Before El Lissitzky was commissioned by Anatoly Lunacharsky to assume the artistic direction of the Soviet pavilion at the Pressa in Cologne, he had already completed important installations in Germany—for example, his "Proun Room" at the Grosse Kunstaustellung (Great Art Exhibition) in Berlin in 1923; his "Raum für konstruktivistische Kunst" ("Room for Constructivist Art") within the Internationale Kunstausstellung in Dresden in 1926; and his *Kabinett des Abstrakten (Abstract Cabinet)* in the Provinzialmuseum in Hanover in 1927. In these structures, Lissitzky developed the essential features of his exhibition architecture: the active involvement of the visitors owing to movable wall elements and the possibility of experiencing the room as an optically dynamic form. Yet whereas the activation of perception in the abstract rooms in Dresden and Hanover served more to substantiate an individual artistic concept, work on the Russian pavilion in Cologne, carried out by a collective of thirty-seven artists, presented Lissitzky with totally new, concrete tasks.[2] The objective was to present advances in the press sector of the socialist state in twenty so-called demonstration rooms. Also included was the presentation of such themes as the industrialization and electrification of the country; the living conditions of the proletariat; trades unions; agriculture; and social life within the new political system. Seen by more than five million visitors, the exhibition constituted a highly effective showcase on the Soviet Union for the West, so that even conservative political personalities like Konrad Adenauer, lord mayor of Cologne, reacted quite open-mindedly toward the socialist state after visiting the Pressa. Despite philosophical, political, and religious differences, the Pressa exhibition fulfilled a need for international understanding among nations.[3]

The head commissar, A. B. Khalatov, had drawn attention to the novel design of the Soviet pavilion in the accompanying catalogue: "In our section, we present

1 Cf. Ute Eskildsen and Jan-Christopher Horak, *Film und Foto der Zwanziger Jahre* (Stuttgart, 1929); Inka Graeve, "Internationale Ausstellung des Deutschen Werkbunds Film und Foto," in *Stationen der Moderne: Die bedeutenden Kunstausstellungen des 20. Jahrhunderts in Deutschland* (Berlin, 1988), 237–73.
2 For the names of the artists involved in the design, cf. Sophie Lissitzky-Küppers, *El Lissitzky: Maler, Architekt, Typograf, Fotograf* (Dresden, 1967), 81n65. The members of the working committee behind the Soviet pavilion are listed in *Amtlicher Ausstellungskatalog PRESSA—Internationale Presse-Ausstellung* (Cologne, 1928), 302–7.
3 Cf. *PRESSA Kulturschau am Rhein*, ed. Internationale Presse-Ausstellung (Cologne, 1928).

1 El Lissitzky and Sergei Senkin: Detail of the photofrieze at the Soviet pavilion at Pressa. Cologne, 1928

our material not in the form of passive diagrams and drawings, but as a fusion of artistically and dynamically structured objects, constructions, models, etc. This kind of presentation enables a large degree of vividness and is best suited to revealing the dynamic essence of the phenomena of the year."[4] He clearly rejected what Georg Simmel had aptly described as a "paralysis of the power of perception," which the visitor experienced in the face of the random juxtaposition of heterogeneous exhibition items.[5]

Igor Riazantsev noted the most significant technical innovations of the Soviet pavilion: the "process of structuring the room in zones to form a surround for 'focal point' exhibits; the unusual shapes of the decorative constructions; the creation of self-moving objects; the extensive use of photomontage; the utilisation of light and film as design components."[6] It was at the Pressa that photography and photomontage experienced a breakthrough as design elements, though they represented but one element of the multimedia interplay of kinetic objects, statistics, models, neon advertisements, and illustrations.

However, the photofrieze designed by Lissitzky and Sergei Senkin, and presented under the motto "The education of the masses is the main task of the Pressa in the transitional period from capitalism to communism" established exhibition history. This photofrieze, 3.8 meters high, 23.5 meters long, and installed at a height of about 3 meters, appeared in the section entitled "Federal Republics" (fig. 1). In his decision to use friezelike photo panoramas, Lissitzky was employing a technique that had already been tried and tested at world and industrial exhibitions since 1900. For example, at an exhibition on cities held in Dresden in 1903, the Neue Photographische Gesellschaft (New Photographic Society) of Berlin had erected a photo panorama of the Gulf of Naples that measured 12 meters long and 1.5 meters high.[7] Similarly, at the Internationale Photographische Ausstellung (International Photography Exhibition) in Dresden in 1909, four large-format photographic panoramas of mountains were displayed in the Hall of Honor. But whereas these presentations were still competing with the spatial illusionism of nineteenth-century panorama painting, Lissitzky produced something totally new by foregoing a unified central perspective in favor of the "optical rhythm of the montage" (Dziga Vertov). Red cloth triangles subdivided the photofrieze into zones of enlarged press

4 A. B. Khalatov, quoted in *Frühe Kölner Kunstausstellungen*, ed. Wulf Herzogenrath (Cologne, 1981), 92.
5 Georg Simmel, "Berliner Gewerbe-Ausstellung," in *Die Zeit*, no. 95, Vienna, July 25, 1896, 59–60.
6 Igor W. Rjasanzev, "El Lissitzky und die 'Pressa' in Köln 1928," in *El Lissitzky: Maler, Architekt, Typograf, Fotograf*, Staatliche Galerie Moritzburg (Halle, 1982), 80–81.
7 Cf. *Photographische Chronik* 87 (1903): 549–51. Cf. Wolfgang Kemp, *Foto-Essays zur Geschichte und Theorie der Fotografie* (Munich, 1978), 38.

photographs illustrating the conditions that prevailed in industry, agriculture, the army, and sports.

One striking feature of Lissitzky's design is the "filmic" mise-en-scène of the pictorial material.[8] There can be little doubt that the continual change in format and the use of individual portraits, group photos, and mass shots reflect the designers' dialectical understanding of the image. One of the best-known and most publicized extracts from this photofrieze, taken from its center, depicts the theme of press photography in the Soviet state. Alongside the charismatic figure of Lenin we see a press photographer documenting the event not from an isolated distance but within the space and the moment, and inseparably bound up with social reality. Photography, as a medium of enlightenment, is obviously at the service of socialism. This obvious trust in the argumentative power of the photograph, shown without text and thus speaking for itself, was something completely new in exhibition design and constituted an important turning point that would influence subsequent Soviet exhibitions.[9] *In nuce,* the photofrieze proclaimed the principle behind such later exhibitions as the Family of Man, organized by Edward Steichen in 1955, in which photographs became symbols of a universal language and were hung without captions.

Margarita Tupitsyn has pointed out that before the Pressa, Lissitzky had no practical experience in the production of agitprop photomontages.[10] This abrupt transition from abstract designs for fair stands to concrete political iconography suggests that Gustav Klutsis and Senkin, who were far more experienced in the art of photomontage, strongly influenced Lissitzky's design of the photofrieze and that in particular Klutsis's involvement in the conception of the Pressa photofrieze was more decisive than has been acknowledged.[11] Curiously enough, despite the considerable impact that the Pressa photofrieze had on leading creative designers in large firms, Lissitzky was not satisfied with the outward *form* of the pavilion as it was finally realized, apart from its political content.[12]

The accordion-fold brochure on the Soviet pavilion, which Lissitzky designed after the exhibition opening to accompany the catalogue, may help explain the transposition of his artistic ideas. Consisting of five photomontages, the original designs of which are preserved in the Museum Ludwig in Cologne, the brochure contains views of the interior and exterior of the Soviet pavilion and the most important installations and exhibition items. More so than the heterogeneous arrangement of the exhibition objects, this brochure gives the impression of a homogeneous design aesthetic. The miniature reproduction of individual items makes the concrete political message, such as the increase in productivity in socialism or the alphabetization of the masses, recede into the background allowing the formal aspect to become more immediate. This is further emphasized by the strict orthogonal arrangement of the pictorial sections; these seldom overlap and are subordinate to a screen.

Lissitzky's design was clearly distinguishable from the sober, objective arrangements of other Pressa exhibitions, in which the medium of photography played other roles. A conventional section of photographs, gathered under the heading "Photography and Reproduction," for example, included a historical collection of photos by Erich Stenger, a group exhibition by the Society of German Photographers, and a presentation of so-called illustration photography, a synonym for press photography in its various realms, from sports events to political reportage in the illustrated daily or weekly press.[13]

8 Cf. Kai-Uwe Hemken, *El Lissitzky: Revolution und Avantgarde* (Cologne, 1990), 145.
9 Margarita Tupitsyn, *The Soviet Photograph, 1924–1937* (New Haven: Yale University Press, 1996), 56–57.
10 Ibid., 59. Cf. Benjamin H. D. Buchloh, "From Faktura to Factography," *October* 30 (1984): 83–119.
11 Tupitsyn, *Soviet Photograph,* 60.
12 "The big companies who had carried out the advertising constructions on the exhibition grounds sent their directors to Lissitzky to learn about propaganda from him. But the kind of agitation being carried on at the Soviet pavilion was quite different than that, for example, on the big tower of the Hag coffee company, where even a cup of coffee free of charge failed to convince many people" (Lissitzky-Küppers, *El Lissitzky,* 82 n 2.
13 Cf. *Amtlicher Ausstellungskatalog PRESSA–Internationale Presse-Ausstellung,* 203–5. *Das Atelier des Photographen,* vol. 35, 1928, 126–28.

The Film and Photography Exhibition in Stuttgart, 1929

El Lissitzky's design for the Soviet section of the 1929 Film and Photography Exhibition in Stuttgart, organized by the Deutscher Werkbund and better known as FiFo, constituted the most unusual and daring example of exhibition architecture of the entire show. As to its genesis, existing documents are contradictory. According to the catalogue, Lissitzky was commissioned by VOKS (the All-Russian Society for Foreign Cultural Relations) and responsible for the selection and presentation of the exhibits, whereas Stuttgart companies were in charge of carrying out the construction work.[14] On the other hand, Lissitzky's wife, Sophie Küppers, who is not mentioned in the catalogue, reports that her husband designed only the exhibition system, while she herself undertook the selection of photographs and films.[15] Because few photographs of the Stuttgart installation have survived, the content and presentation of the Soviet section remain vague. It obviously had no spectacular design element equivalent to the Pressa photofrieze, which was on show in Stuttgart in draft form and as a catalogue brochure. Nor did photomontage play an important role, although FiFo included numerous photomontages by John Heartfield, Willi Baumeister, Herbert Bayer, Max Burchartz, George Grosz, and Hannah Höch, demonstrating its application not just in product publicity but in political agitation.[16]

If one is to credit contemporary critiques, then a preference for documentary photography and photo reportage obviously marked the selection of Soviet photographs and films, which included works by thirty photojournalists, cameramen, and film directors—among them Max Alpert, Dmitry Debadov, Boris Ignatovich, Klutsis, Lissitzky, Nikolai Petrov, Aleksandr Rodchenko, Arkady Shaikhet, Senkin, Varvara Stepanova, Sergei Eisenstein, Mikhail Kaufman, Roman Karmen, Vsevolod Pudovkin, Esfir Shub, Dziga Vertov, and Abram Room.[17] Having replaced painting, photo reportage had been given the task of authentically documenting the restructuring of society, as the catalogue contribution by Vitaly Zhemchuzhny points out: "This turbulent reality could not be captured within the framework of traditional 'painterly' compositions. The change in theme demanded a change in the formal technical photographic methods, a search for specific, more suitable methods that sprang from the unique character of the photographic material. New and unexpected forms of foreshortening, unusual perspectives, daring combinations of light and shade

2–3 Anonymous: Installation view of the Soviet section at Film and Photo Exhibition, photo and film sections. Stuttgart, 1929. Cat. 198–99

14 Cf. *Internationale Ausstellung des Deutschen Werkbunds Film und Foto* (Stuttgart, 1929; rpt. 1975), 73.
15 Cf. Lissitzky-Küppers, *El Lissitzky*, 85.
16 Cf. Adolf Reitz, "Die Fotomontage in der Ausstellung Film und Foto," *Stuttgarter Neues Tagblatt*, July 2, 1929.
17 For a list of the artists who participated, see *Internationale Ausstellung des Deutschen Werkbunds Film und Foto*, 73–74.

4 Anonymous: Installation view of the Soviet section at Film and Photo Exhibition, photo section. Berlin, 1930

were availed of in order to reproduce the excerpts from social reality as sharply and precisely as possible."[18]

The second characteristic of Lissitzky's design was the symbiotic presentation of film and photography, which, from the point of view of content, was in keeping with Osip Brik's observation in 1928 that "photography was the basis of cinematography" and that filmmakers should orient themselves around the success and advances in contemporary photography.[19] At FiFo, the Russian section was the only one to succeed in presenting the close links between film and photography. Enlargements of stills from films by Vertov and Eisenstein were mounted on transparent lath constructions of varying colors and hovered freely, and the walls were covered with orthogonal arrangements of film sequences and individual takes, presumably reportage photographs (figs. 2–3). The presence of several daylight film projectors indicate that extracts from the latest Soviet films were shown. Confident of inherent capability of photographs to communicate, the photographers apparently chose to do without explanatory captions.

It is more than likely that Lissitzky's lucid architecture was inspired by the L- and T-systems designed by the Austrian architect Friedrich Kiesler for the Internationale Ausstellung neuer Theatertechnik (the International Exhibition of New Theatre Technology) in Vienna in 1924, in which Lissitzky was also involved. For the purposes of creating a space continuum, Kiesler's "elementary architecture," indebted to the ideas of Constructivism, set out to eliminate any "separation between floor, walls and ceiling."[20] In Lissitzky's case, this principle, which created an inspiring photographic and film production owing to the simultaneous perception of the two media, became a symbol of the mobility and dynamism of the young socialist state. As a contemporary critic points out: "What you have here is the power of agitation, propaganda tools; the shrewd selection drums into the visitor's head that even art has only one goal, and that is, to be at the service of politics. But photography has the task of capturing and documenting the era of social restructuring in its works. … That this kind of photography is deeply rooted in real life ought to be as laudably acknowledged as the pleasing fact that the Soviets have no intention of falling victim to the inevitably tiring surface divisions so familiar to us from Europe's nonfigura-

18 W. Zhemchuzhni, "Russland und Fotografie," in Internationale Ausstellung des Deutschen Werkbunds Film und Foto, 15.
19 Osip Brik, editorial in the magazine Sovetskoe Kino (Soviet Cinema), nos. 4–5 (1926): 23, quoted by Tupitsyn, Soviet Photograph, 37.
20 Frederick Kiesler, quoted by Cynthia Goodman, "The Art of Revolutionary Display Techniques," in Lisa Phillips, Frederick Kiesler (New York: Whitney Museum of American Art, 1989), 57.

tive photography, to whose representative, László Moholy-Nagy, a whole room is devoted."[21]

In spite of this polemic on experiments with light in the field of nonfigurative photography, the factographic documentary aspect of the Soviet exhibition was not all that far removed from the official credo behind the event formulated by Moholy-Nagy in the entrance hall of FiFo. He, too, referred to the "great social responsibility of the photographer who, with the existing elementary photographic means, carries out a task which could not be achieved with any other means. His work must be an unadulterated document of contemporary reality. Photography's frame of reference ought not rest on a photographic aesthetic, but instead on the human and social intensity of what is optically grasped. For a productive person this intensity is the one and only valid criterion."[22]

Nevertheless, there was a world of difference between photos from the realms of advertising, journalism, and book design and politically commissioned photos intended to represent in a positive light the socialist states of the USSR. In his essay "Beautiful Photographs, Cheap Photographs," written for *Die Weltbühne,* the Hungarian art theoretician and writer Ernst Kallai criticized many of the photographs exhibited at FiFo as extravagant, formal tinkering and as "optical feuilleton" without any social or political relevance, suited at best for illustrating "snobby" society magazines like *Vogue* and *Dame*.[23]

Consequently, the innovative impact of FiFo on contemporary photography was vehemently debated in Germany. The experimental techniques in particular, such as the photogram and photomontage, irritated traditional amateur and commercial photographers.[24] Yet the reaction of the media to Lissitzky's exhibition works was surprisingly restrained. In one of the most popular publications on the photography of the Neue Sachlichkeit (New Objectivity), *Es kommt der neue Fotograf* (Here Comes the New Photographer), edited by Werner Graeff and published by Hermann Reckendorff in Berlin in 1929, the only reproduction is of Lissitzky's "Proun Room" at the Great Art Exhibition of 1923 in Berlin.[25] A photography volume entitled *Foto-Auge,* edited in 1929 by Franz Roh and Jan Tschichold, in collaboration with Gustav Stotz, and published after the exhibition closed, presented seventy-six motifs from the FiFo, including three photographs by Lissitzky, though none of his photomontages, with the exception of his *Self-Portrait* (Constructor), done in 1924 (plate 14).[26]

As a result of its resounding success with the public, the FiFo exhibition went on tour to Zurich, Berlin, Danzig, Vienna, Agram, Munich, Tokyo, and Osaka. The size, content, and presentation of the Soviet section varied, as an installation view of the "Russia" stand in Berlin in 1930 clearly demonstrates, with its extensive series of pictures by Rodchenko, Lissitzky, and Arkady Shaikhet (fig. 4). The presentation in Vienna was restricted to sixty exhibits by twenty-two photographers, typographers, and filmmakers, among them Alpert, Debadov, Eisenstein, Fridliand, Ignatovich, Karmen, Kaufman, Klutsis, Kuleshov, Lissitzky, Novitsky, Pudovkin, Rodchenko, Zaitsev, Saveliev, Shaikhet, Shub, Stepanova, Sternberg, and Vertov. Lissitzky had the largest number of works in the show: posters, book covers, ten photographs, and the catalogue and photofrieze from the Pressa.[27]

Although he was the supervisor and designer of the touring exhibition, Lissitzky apparently had no official commission, so that details of organization were in the hands of local event managers. In Munich, for example, the exhibition was shown under the heading "Das Lichtbild" (The Photograph) from June to September 1930; committee members included Wolfgang von Wersin, director of the Neue Samm-

21 Rudolf Junk, in *Photographische Korrespondenz* 65 (1929): 230. Similar statements were made by W. Warstat, "Der internationale Stand der bildmässigen Photographie," in *Deutscher Kamera Almanach 1931,* 1930, 37–38.

22 László Moholy-Nagy, quoted by A. Schwoerer, "Film und Foto," *Photo-Woche* 19 (1928–29): 1040.

23 Ernst Kallai, "Schöne Photos, billige Photos," *Die Weltbühne* 25, no. 46 (1929): 736–38, rpt. in Ernst Kallai, *Vision und Formgesetz: Aufsätze über Kunst und Künstler, 1921–1933* (Leipzig, 1986), 141–44.

24 Cf. E. Haceel, "Bemerkungen zu Film und Foto in Stuttgart," in *Photographische Chronik* (1929), 214–15. Similarly negative statements are recorded in *Die Camera* (1929), 332–34, and *Photofreund,* no. 24 (1929): 480–82.

25 The chapter "Fotomontagen" in this book is illustrated with works by Werner Graeff, Willi Baumeister, Alice Nerlinger, Umbo, and Herbert Bayer.

26 The photographs are El Lissitzky's *Constructor,* "komposition" (no. 6), and the poster "Russische Ausstellung, Kunstgewerbemuseum Zürich" (1929). It is not known whether works by Lissitzky were included in the 1931 Berlin exhibition of photomontage. Cf. *Der Photograph,* no. 38 (1931): 150–51.

27 Cf. *Internationale Ausstellung Film und Foto: Wanderausstellung des Deutschen Werkbundes* (Vienna, 1930; rpt. 1975), 12.

5 El Lissitzky: View of the entry hall of the Soviet pavilion at the International Hygiene Exhibition. Dresden, 1930

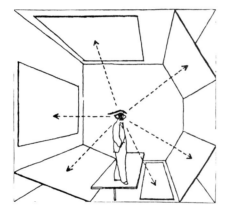

6 Herbert Bayer: Exhibition sketch, ca. 1936

28 G. Boltianskii, in the catalogue *Internationale Ausstellung Das Lichtbild* (Munich, 1930), 35.
29 For a detailed description of the exhibitions in Leipzig and Dresden, cf. Hemken, *Revolution und Avantgarde*, 151–60.
30 Lissitzky used the same arrangement for the cover of the catalogue *Sowjet-Pavilion auf der Internationalen Hygiene-Ausstellung Dresden 1930*.
31 Cf. Nicola Hille, "Macht der Bilder—Bilder der Macht. Beispiele politischer Fotomontage der 30er Jahre," *Fotogeschichte* 17, no. 66 (1997): 23–31.

lung im Bayerischen Nationalmuseum; Paul Renner, typographer and head of the Master School for Germany's Book Printers; the art historian Franz Roh; and the conservative commercial photographer Eduard Wasow of Munich. As a complement to the FiFo show, some of whose exhibits had been damaged in previous presentations, the Munich committee mounted a separate, four-part exhibition comprising scientific photography, photo reportage, advertising photography, and abstract art photography, with participants from England, France, the United States, Scandinavia, and the Soviet Union.

The section on photo reportage contained a large collection entitled "Russian Reportage Photographs," which VOKS had placed at the disposal of the touring exhibition and which consisted mainly of documentary works. Alongside the known professional photographers, amateurs were gradually gaining importance. Georgy Boltiansky, a photography critic, noted: "From the large collection of Russian photographs, which comprises many thousands of pictures, we ourselves have selected these examples. Something of the hardy and unfettered vitality that is to be felt in Russian films can also be felt in Russian photography. What characterizes Soviet reportage photography as one of the leading forms of photography? Freshness, originality and novelty of viewpoint, dynamism, daring, sharpness and clarity in light and shade, emphasis on detail, and a clarity of composition that destroys the aesthetics of painting and brings it closer to that of film-making. What contribution does Soviet reportage photography make? Pictures of the new life, of work in factories, of restructured working methods in production in the city and in agriculture in the country, of cultural and national life. From reportage photography, its teachers, its mistakes and its achievements, the worker-photographer circles in the Soviet Union can also learn. The army of worker-photographers in the Soviet Union, mustered at the personal initiative of the proletariat in independent circles in towns and villages, has almost reached a total of 100,000 people."[28]

Because El Lissitzky's works received no mention in press reports of the Munich exhibition, the extent of his participation is uncertain.

The International Fur Trade Exhibition in Leipzig and the International Hygiene Exhibition in Dresden, 1930

Lissitzky's designs for the Internationale Hygiene-Ausstellung (International Hygiene Exhibition) in Dresden and the Internationale Pelz-Fachausstellung (International Fur Trade Exhibition) in Leipzig, both mounted in 1930, hark back to the ensemble for the Soviet Pressa pavilion, which consisted of three-dimensional objects, picture panels, models, and photomontages. These two events offered the Soviet Union an opportunity to present its achievements in the fur trade and the developments in its health system to a large public in the West. Technically, the Soviet section at the International Hygiene Exhibition was the more interesting and multifaceted of the two.[29] At the Dresden exhibition, visitors to the Soviet section were greeted by a large-format photomontage of a worker under the heading "Gesundung der Werktätigen" (Recovery of the Workers); Lissitzky had cleverly superimposed a photograph by Arkady Shaikhet onto the worker's torso (fig. 5, plate 84). In a vertical direction ran a friezelike strip of portraits of Soviet professional groups and citizens.[30] Innovations included the use of a large photomontage at the entrance to an exhibition and the inclusion of the ceiling, which was completely papered with large-format posters, as exhibition space. This was the first time that Lissitzky had applied the principle of mobilizing the observer to the whole room area, as demonstrated in a sketch done by Herbert Bayer in 1936 (fig. 6).

Mostra della Rivoluzione Fascista in Rome, 1932

Although the formal, Constructivist style of many of the objects on show in Cologne and Dresden was not always easily understood by the visitors, Lissitzky's exhibition installations were enthusiastically received by designers and advertising experts. The presentation forms and pictorial techniques developed and used by Lissitzky, Senkin, and Klutsis were particularly evident in the politically oriented exhibitions of such totalitarian countries as Germany and Italy. The "left-wing" techniques of photomontage and large-format photographs were frequently used as propagandistic wall decoration championing the cult of the Führer.[31] This resulted in a contradictory mixture of modernist aesthetic form and reactionary political content.

These techniques again appeared at the Mostra della Rivoluzione Fascista (Exhibition of the Fascist Revolution) at the Palazzo dell' Esposizione in Rome in 1932, which Mussolini commissioned in celebration of the ten-year jubilee of the March on Rome. This exhibition was the first conceptual propaganda show devoted to historicizing a political movement and party.[32] The high artistic level of the exhibition resulted from the collaboration of some thirty architects, painters, and sculptors, including such prominent avant-garde artists as Giuseppe Terragni, representing *architettura razionale;* Enrico Prampolini, a member of the Secondo Futurismo; and Mario Sironi and Lucio Fontana, members of the traditionalist Novecento group.[33] The primary aim of the show, the concept and content of which can be touched on only briefly here, was to prejudice the visitor in favor of the fascist party. To achieve this, the organizers modeled their presentations after Lissitzky's designs for Cologne, Leipzig, and Dresden, without mentioning this influence in the catalogue; his signature is sometimes evident even in the minor details of this show. Endeavoring to imbue the stands and rooms with an optical dynamism, as Lissitzky had done, the Italian artists used all the wall and ceiling space and combined in montagelike fashion such diverse materials as wood, glass, steel, and marble, which, when merged with large-format photomontages, newspapers, posters, and other documentary materials formed a futurist-Constructivist environment. The deliberate pathos and showy monumentalism of Italian fascism were embodied in the use of "precious" materials such as marble.

Unlike Lissitzky's designs, whose documentary information was aimed at enlightenment, the Roman exhibition was obviously a symbolic mise-en-scène. These differences become apparent when one examines the entrance area, the Sala O, designed by Giuseppe Terragni (fig. 7). At the center of this spectacular scenario, under the heading "How Mussolini's fiery words entice the Italian people with the force of turbines and convert them to fascism," is a huge photomontage of a great mass of people being "ground" by three enormous turbine wheels ascending diagonally. A greatly enlarged text written by Mussolini in 1922, in which he set the date for the March on Rome and issued the command "Adunate" (Gather), represents the driving force behind this huge gathering of people who, by means of the turbines, are forced into empty molds shaped in the form of raised hands—the symbol of affirmative participation—an iconographic borrowing possibly from Gustav Klutsis's famous poster *Let Us Fulfill the Plan of the Great Projects* (*Vypolnim plan velikhikh rabot,* 1930). Other design elements reminiscent of Pressa[34] are found in the "Sacrario dei martiri," by Adalberto Libera and Antonio Valente (fig. 8); out of its center rose a "blood-red" stand with a tall metal cross and the inscription "Per la patria immortale" bathed in bluish-red light, while the neon word *presente* flashed endlessly on the domed walls. The formal similarities with the Soviet star on the Pressa pavilion,

7 Giuseppe Terragni: "Sala O" at the exhibition Mostra della Rivoluzione Fascista. Rome, 1932

8 Adalberto Libera and Antonio Valente: "Sacrario dei martiri" at the exhibition Mostra della Rivoluzione Fascista. Rome, 1932

32 Cf. Tupitsyn, *Soviet Photograph,* 29, on Rodchenko's photomontages "History of the VKP (b)," which were published by the Communist Academy in collaboration with the Museum of the Revolution in 1925–26.
33 For details on the exhibition, cf. catalogue *Nationale Faschistische Partei: Ausstellung der Faschistischen Revolution—Erste Zehnjahresfeier des Marsches auf Rom* (Rome, 1933). For a survey of Giuseppe Terragni's works, cf. Stefan Germer and Achim Preiss, *Giuseppe Terragni, 1904–43: Moderne und Faschismus in Italien* (Munich, 1991).
34 For example, Marcello Nizzoli and Dante Dini, in designing the figure "Movimento dei Combattenti" in Hall G, adapted the "Die Presse und die Sowjetfrau" created by Mikhail Plaksin for the Pressa 1928. Both designs consisted of photographs, word and image collages, and press reports.

9 Herbert Bayer: Room 5 of the German section at the Exposition Internationale des Arts Décoratifs. Paris, 1930. Bauhaus Archive, Berlin

surrounded by neon bands and illuminated in red, are as apparent as the differences in content. Whereas the Soviet star symbolized international communism and the Soviet state, the fascist Hall of Honor became a sacred votive room where fascist ideology and Catholicism melded into a cryptic rite.

In Italy, the exhibition techniques developed for the Mostra della Rivoluzione Fascista were later taken up principally by the architect Erberto Carboni, whose work was highly regarded by Walter Gropius and Herbert Bayer. Carboni collaborated on the Mostra Internazionale della Stampa Cattolica in Rome (1936), the Milan Triennial (1936), the Exposition Universelle in Paris (1937), and the Mostra d'Oltremare di Napoli (Overseas Exhibition) in Naples (1940), all of which repeatedly used large photomontages.[35]

National Socialist Exhibitions in Berlin, 1933–1937

Whereas Lissitzky's exhibition installations were inspired by the utopia of a better, socialist society, his innovations were modified in Germany in the 1930s so as to function as a technical model for a form of "visual communication" in which photography became a universally understood pictorial language. The painter, commercial artist, and photographer Herbert Bayer is usually associated with this model. An advertising designer, Bayer managed the renowned international advertising agency "studio dorlands" and exerted a decisive influence on the design of posters and exhibitions in Germany and the United States in the 1930s and 1940s.[36] Through his designs for the Deutsche Werkbund pavilion at the Exposition Internationale des Arts Décoratifs (Decorative Arts Exhibition) in Paris in 1930 (fig. 9) and the Deutsche Bau-Ausstellung (German Architecture Exhibition) in Berlin in 1931, Bayer, inspired by Lissitzky's model for the Soviet pavilion at Pressa, developed the principles of modern communications design. Bayer, who knew Lissitzky's work firsthand, used large-format photographs to create a room ensemble in Paris that abandoned the rigid arrangement of exhibits on walls in favor of large-format photographs mounted at an angle from ceiling to floor. The architect Walter Gropius, with whom Bayer had worked on several exhibitions up until 1934, introduced another novel design element in Berlin: a free-standing ramp from which the visitor had an almost bird's-eye view of the complete exhibition ensemble, which was made up of large-format photographs, statistics, graphs, and accompanying texts. In the 1930s and 1940s, the ramp became a permanent feature of exhibition architecture in both Germany and the United States.

Like Lissitzky, Bayer carefully planned how to achieve "extended vision" well in advance of exhibitions, based on sketches and models of the stands and rooms. This method entailed the use of a kind of guideline with precise viewing instructions for the visitors, who were escorted by an optical system of signals, complete with directional arrows. One assumes that Bayer also adopted the use of kinetic objects from Lissitzky's Pressa installation, for example, when he mounted large-format photographs on slats kept in constant motion by electric motors, thereby creating moving supports that offered continually varying images.

Bayer understood exhibition design primarily as an ideology-free form of communication, as did his friend the theoretician Alexander Dorner. Yet what began as harmless product advertising for industry and the crafts was to assume a clear political meaning and, as of 1933, function in the service of the National Socialists (NS) regime. The highly effective advertising techniques developed for product publicity could also be adapted to the political aims of the National Socialists and were to

35 Cf. Erberto Carboni, *Exhibitions and Displays*, with an introduction by Herbert Bayer (Milan, 1957).
36 For more on Herbert Bayer, cf. Rolf Sachsse, "Von Österreich aus: Herbert Bayer," *Camera Austria* 46 (1994): 3–11; Arthur A. Cohen, *Herbert Bayer* (Cambridge, Mass., 1984); and the catalogue *Herbert Bayer: Das künstlerische Werk, 1918–1938* (Berlin: Bauhaus-Archiv, 1982).

10–11 Anonymous: Hall of Honor and entrance hall at the exhibition The Camera. Berlin,1933

influence the design of their costly exhibitions. Both at home and abroad, these exhibitions took on a considerable propagandistic importance as they attempted to present National Socialist ideology bathed in an aura of modernity. Although official Third Reich publications defamed the experiments of the New Vision school as "cultural Bolshevism," "degenerate," or "Jew-ridden," experimental design elements such as large-format photographs and photomontages were repeatedly used in exhibitions to advance ideological rhetoric.

The first successful National Socialist propaganda event of this kind was the exhibition Die Kamera (The Camera). Organized in October 1933 by the Deutscher Werkbund to succeed the legendary FiFo, it strove to convert German photographers, as well as the general public, to the aims of the new regime.[37] Under Joseph Goebbels's motto "The experience of the individual has become the experience of the people, thanks solely to the camera," associations of amateur and commercial photographers and the photographic industry exhibited their achievements, accompanied by special didactic shows on such themes as the history of photography and scientific photography. A striking citation of 1920s avant-garde aesthetics at that exhibition, for which Bayer designed the catalogue, was the Hall of Honor and the entrance hall (figs. 10–11). The Hall of Honor was dominated by a large photomontage of a *Sturmabteilung* (SA) column dedicated as a theatrical monument to the "Martyrs of the Movement" and reminiscent of the "Sacrario dei martiri" at the 1932 exhibition in Rome. On show in the entrance hall were sixteen huge enlargements of press photographs of Nationalsozialistische Deutsche Arbeiterpartei (NSDAP) mass marches and meetings taken by Heinrich Hoffmann (Hitler's personal photographer) and aimed at illustrating and historically immortalizing the "History of the National Socialist Movement." Unlike Lissitzky's multipart photofrieze in Cologne, however, the National Socialist designers focused on a central-perspective illusionism that integrated the observer into the omnipresent fascist mass rituals, allowing him or her to become that "ornament of the mass" in which social antagonisms were apparently canceled out.[38]

At the extravagant exhibitions Deutsches Volk—Deutsche Arbeit (German People—German Work), Wunder des Lebens (Miracle of Life), Deutschland (Germany), and Gebt mir vier Jahre Zeit! (Give Me Four Years' Time!), staged in praise of the NS state at the fairgrounds in Berlin between 1934 and 1937, large-format photographs and photomontages were employed extensively. The 1934 Deutsches Volk—Deutsche Arbeit was one of the first comprehensive presentations of National Socialist policy. The focal points were large photographs of Hitler and historical photos of the NSDAP mounted under the title Das Reich der Deutschen (The Realm of the

37 I refer here to my essay "Nicht beziehungslose Kunst, sondern politische Waffe: Fotoausstellungen als Mittel der Ästhetisierung von Politik und Ökonomie im Nationalsozialismus," *Fotogeschichte* 8, no. 28 (1988): 17–31.

38 There is little doubt that the use of large-format photographs was also inspired by the American "photomurals" exhibited at the Musuem of Modern Art in 1932 and commonly used during the New Deal. Cf. *Murals by American Painters and Photographers* (New York: Museum of Modern Art, 1932). These photomurals were also discussed in the German press: cf. E. Trieb, "Monumentalphotos als Wandschmuck," *Der Photograph*, no. 36 (1933): 142–43.

12 Anonymous: Photomontage before the Hall of Honour at the Deutschland exhibition. Berlin, 1936

13 Herbert Bayer: Double page from the prospectus for the catalogue of the Deutschland exhibition. Berlin, 1936

Germans) in the Hall of Honor. In addition to this, photographs of negroid and Jewish children were juxtaposed with statistics and portraits of German men and women; in one large photograph a blond giant of a man—a "protector of the German race"—was accompanied by the following comment: "The occupiers of the Rhineland retreated … leaving 600 bastards. In Berlin, 10 genetically healthy families have 17 children on average—10 genetically sick families, by contrast, have 35 children. … Here the cheerful faces of young unadulterated German manhood speak a silent but so much more compelling language. The Race Laws aim to maintain the health and power of our people."[39] Here the mass destruction of "worthless" life through euthanasia and concentration camps seemed to be a logical, if unspoken, consequence of National Socialist policy. Similar messages were communicated by the exhibition Das Wunder des Lebens in Dresden in 1935, a "comprehensive show on National Socialist genetic theory, the fostering of the race and the promotion of health," which on the surface continued the tradition of the hygiene exhibitions, while at the same time propagandistically preparing the way for the so-called Nuremberg Laws, or *Blutschutzgesetz* (Race Protection Law), passed in September 1935.

The Deutschland exhibition, mounted on the occasion of the 1936 Olympic Games in Berlin, was a costly spectacle aimed at vividly impressing upon the world the economic and cultural advances Germany had made under the NS regime. Under the motto "Volk ohne Raum" (People without Space), the entrance to the Hall of Honor was dominated by a photomontage of Hitler designed to justify the aggressive expansionist policy of the National Socialists (fig. 12). Formally speaking, the monumental photomontage schematically reflects the hierarchical structure of the NS state and the cult of the Führer; the latter looms larger than life from the center of a pyramid made up of an ornamental mass of people, surrounded by his faithful followers, representatives of the party, the military, and the Reich labor service.

The artistic form of the photomontage also played an important role in the brochure for the exhibition catalogue, which was designed by Bayer. This brochure, publicized in the magazine *Gebrauchsgraphik* in 1936, contained twenty-eight montages made up of graphic art, engravings, and photographs.[40] The latter originated from various photographic agencies and from Fritz Henle, Martin Hürlimann, Albert Renger-Patzsch, Erich and Hans Retzlaff, and Bayer. From the point of view of content, the brochure presented Germany as a fruitful and peaceful idyll, a state that was thriving under National Socialism. Bayer also shifted the dynamic central point of the German Reich and the Olympic events, to the foreground. The brochure contained views of cultivated landscapes, a rural population conscious of its traditions, idyllic small-town life, and examples of important architectural styles, from the redbrick Gothic of northern Germany to Karl Schinkel's classicist structures. Portraits of Bach, Beethoven, Goethe, Schiller, Kant, and Gutenberg symbolized a Germany of musicians, poets, and thinkers—a national image that contrasted sharply with the reality of National Socialist cultural policy, which resulted in the wholesale exodus of modern artists. What at a fleeting glance looked like a harmless advertising brochure put out by a tourist agency took on a more concrete political character in the photomontage of a large crowd at a mass rally of National Socialists (fig. 13). Copied into the integral ornament of the mass, which Bayer had produced by cleverly repeating the motif, were not only the swastika, the NS symbol per se, but also the heads of a farmer, a worker, and a soldier, who as representatives of the people were attentive listeners and willing followers of Hitler. The message ran: "The Führer speaks! Millions hear him. The working population, the farming com-

39 *Amtlicher Katalog und Führer Das Wunder des Lebens* (Berlin, 1935), n.p.
40 *Gebrauchsgraphik* 13, no. 4 (1936).

munity, the military in their regained freedom, are the pillars of National Socialist Germany."

Bayer's photomontage on the cult of the Führer and totalitarian dominance is one of the rare examples of applied experimental techniques in German photography between 1933 and 1945. Eberhard Hölscher, editor of the journal *Gebrauchsgraphik*, claimed that Bayer's work stimulated in the observer "the inactive associative powers of his subconscious" and persuaded "even the indifferent and reluctant observer to pay heed and collaborate, intellectually and actively."[41] One characteristic of the photomontages used for the NS exhibitions is that dialectical relations no longer existed between individual, heterogeneous, pictorial fragments, having been replaced by affirmative pictorial statements. The theatrical representations served the sole aim of heroizing or monumentalizing the supposed advances made by the political system. This applies particularly to Give Me Four Years' Time! mounted in Berlin in 1937, surely the most complex exhibition ever planned by the National Socialist regime, in which photography, large-format photo panoramas and photomontages were put to use for propaganda purposes for the last time. In the entrance hall to this megalomaniacal mise-en-scène were nine "Bilderbücher der Geschichte" (Picture Books of History), each with six large-format photographs measuring six meters wide and nine meters high and illustrating the most important stages in National Socialist policy, which moved to the "powerful tones of symphonic music and manly poetic words" (fig. 14). With the help of precisely controlled lighting, the room was transformed architecturally into a sacred, immaterial, emotional space that drew the visitor into the collective experience of National Socialist myths. The other exhibition halls radiated a similar theatrical pathos. Against the backdrop of huge photomontages, whose production had been possible only since the invention of modern techniques for enlargement in 1933, there were life-size models of the Reichsautobahn, machines, and Wehrmacht arsenals, harbingers of war and fetishes of technology still celebrated by NS propaganda as "indisputable evidence of our unshakeable peace policy."[42] Other large photomontages in the exhibition had as their theme the cultic mystification of the Führer, as illustrated by an enormous twenty-meter-high portrait of Hitler surrounded by farmers, industrial workers, and smoking factory chimneys ("Der Führer ruft das ganze deutsche Volk"—The Führer calls upon all the people), measuring all of forty by eighteen meters (fig. 15). Despite the involvement of Egon Eiermann, an important German architect, in the design of the exhibition halls, the photomontages are rather crude and are the work of anonymous technicians. As in the huge monuments created by the politically conformist NS sculptors Josef Thorak and Arno Breker, in these huge photomontages, too, the political "movement" fossilized into a pathetic formula with a noticeably aggressive tenor.

14 Taubert-Neumann: Entry hall at the exhibition Give Me Four Years' Time! with "Picture Books of History." Berlin, 1937

15 Anonymous: Hall II of the exhibition Give Me Four Years' Time! Berlin, 1937

Road to Victory, 1942

Interestingly enough, the year 1937 marks a return to painting as a design instrument in state exhibitions and a turning away from photography and photomontage in favor of "synthetic compositions" in the style of socialist realism transitions evidenced not only in the USSR but in Germany as well.[43] For the interior of the German pavilion at the 1937 Exposition Universelle in Paris, the architect Albert Speer chose expansive tapestries and mosaics characterized by a "quiet reserve" rather than photographs.[44]

In the United States, by contrast, photomontage and large-format photographs enjoyed a renaissance thanks to Bayer, who had emigrated to New York in 1938. Bayer

41 Eberhard Hölscher, "Herbert Bayer," *Gebrauchsgraphik* 13, no. 4 (1936): 18–19.
42 Quoted in Pohlmann, "Nicht beziehungslose Kunst," 27.
43 Cf. Tupitsyn, *Soviet Photograph,* 134.
44 *Der Photograph* 47 (1937): 318–19.

16 Herbert Bayer: Detail of the exhibition Road to Victory at the Museum of Modern Art, New York, 1942. Bauhaus Archive, Berlin

45 Richard Paul Lohse, *Neue Ausstellungsgestaltung* (German, English, French) (Erenbach-Zürich, 1953), 230.
46 Alexander Dorner, *The Way Beyond Art: The Work of Herbert Bayer* (New York, 1947), 209–10. See also "Road to Victory, 1942: A Procession of Photographs of the Nation at War," *Bulletin of the Museum of Modern Art* 9, nos. 5–6 (June 1942): 2–21.
47 Dorner, *Way Beyond Art*, 209–10.
48 Cf. *Bulletin of the Museum of Modern Art* 11, no. 1 (August 1943): 2–21. There is a picture of the installation in the *Bulletin of the Museum of Modern Art* 11, no. 2 (October–November 1943): 16.

succeeded in pursuing his career in America without a break and advanced to become a much sought after designer, mounting such successful exhibitions as Bauhaus 1919 –28 (1939), Road to Victory (1942) and Airways to Peace (1943) at the Museum of Modern Art in New York. At first Bayer reverted to the political propaganda exhibition of the 1930s; Road to Victory: A Procession of Photographs of the Nation at War consisted exclusively of photographs. This exhibition, curated by Edward Steichen, with a text by Carl Sandburg, was commissioned by the United States government after the country entered World War II. It was "part of the propaganda campaign which the American government carried out to mobilize the public, persuade them of the necessity of the war effort by the USA, and spur the individual to participate."[45] Out of ten thousand black-and-white photographs, Steichen selected 150 motifs taken almost exclusively from state archives and American press agencies. The formats ranged from images as small as 30 by 40 centimeters up to enlarged "photomurals" 2.5 by 12 meters. The photographers had been obliged to subordinate themselves to the overall context of the exhibition and were therefore not named in the captions.

For this exhibition, Bayer developed a plan with eleven stations, a form reminiscent of the NS exhibitions. In keeping with his method of "extended vision," the photographs were placed at varying angles on the floor and in front of the walls (fig. 16) so that, in the words of Dorner, the exhibition seemed like one "gigantic photomontage rising up in the spectator's mind as he walked along."[46] Basically, the narrative sequence of the photographs conformed to the dramaturgy of Bayer's Deutschland brochure of 1936. First the visitor was led into a timeless continuum, only then to be confronted with the political message. The interplay of texts and photographs represented war as a proof of the worth of the younger generation. Political connections, causes, and consequences, such as the battle against German and Italian fascism, were not touched on in the exhibition; instead the war was characterized as a cyclical change in generations, as a fateful, natural reaction that required the commitment of each American citizen. Dorner wrote about the enormous public response to the show, which traveled to San Francisco, Cleveland, Detroit, Chicago, and London: "The pictures and the ideas and activities they [the photographs] represented interpenetrated in the minds of the visitors, interacting and creating associations and spontaneous reactions. The visitor was led from one such reaction to another and finally to the climactic reaction, to intense sympathy with the life of the USA and an ardent wish to help it and share its aims. One entirely forgot that one was in an exhibition. The photographs avoided all idealistic symbolism, with its static, freezing effect. … The arrangement of the photographs was an active cooperation with the physiological and psychological activities of the visitor."[47]

The most spectacular installation at the exhibition, Airways to Peace, also designed by Bayer and mounted at the Museum of Modern Art in August 1943, was a photomural of war photographs more than thirty meters long, under the motto "War over the World." This mural was integrated into the life-size silhouette of the Liberator bomber that had been graphically transcribed onto the wall.[48] What had initially seemed paradoxical, even inconceivable, for ideological reasons, had become a political reality: the type of design idiom Lissitzky had created for Soviet exhibitions had eventually been adopted by leading designers in the National Socialist and fascist states of Germany and Italy, respectively. Finally, under the influence of Bayer, Lissitzky's revolutionary mode of designing exhibitions became acceptable for the capitalist West and the American public.

Plates

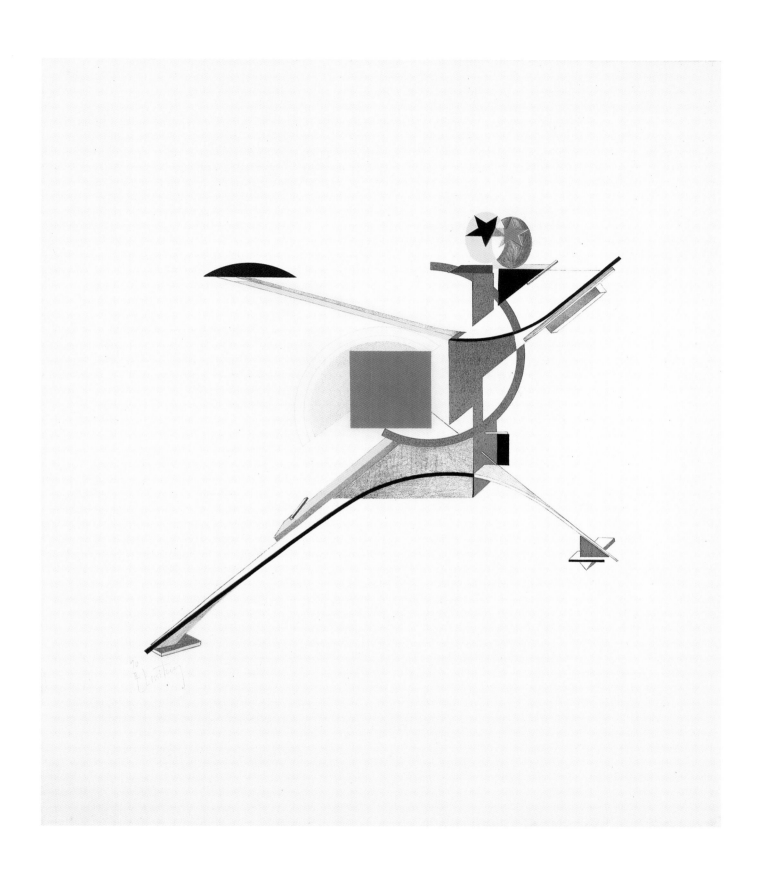

1 *The New.* Plate 10 from Figurine Portfolio for *Victory over the Sun.* 1920–23.
Lithography. Sprengel Museum Hannover. Cat. 125

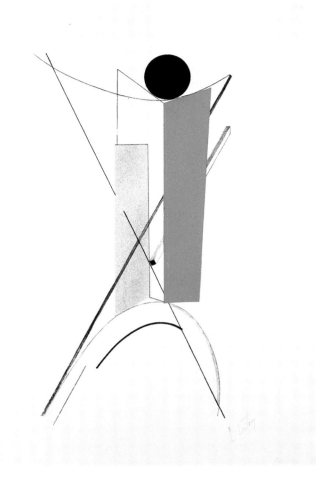

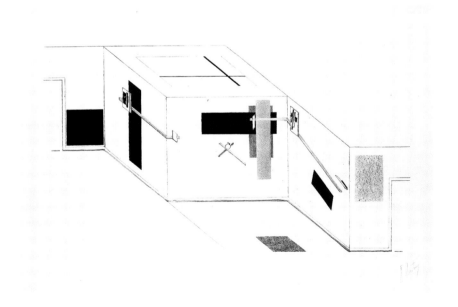

2.1 – 2.2 Kestner Portfolio. *Proun* (1919 – 23).
Plates 3 and 6. 1923. Lithography.
Sprengel Museum Hannover. Cat. 122

3 Maquette for an illustration for *6 Tales with Easy Endings*. 1921–22.
Photo collage, ink, pencil on cardboard. Private Collection. Cat. 1

4 Maquette for an illustration for *6 Tales with Easy Endings*. 1921–22.
Photo collage, pencil, gouache, ink on cardboard. State Tretiakov Gallery, Moscow. Cat. 2

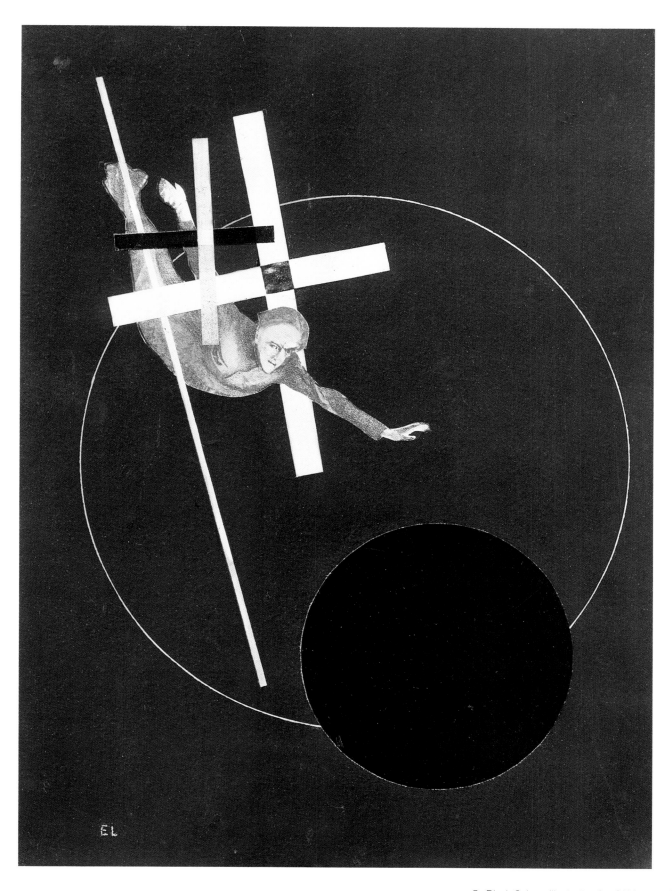

5 *Black Sphere*. Illustration for *6 Tales with Easy Endings*.
1921–22. Gelatin silver print. Private Archive. Cat. 3

6 *Proun B 111* (Self-Portrait). 1922. Photo collage. Private Collection.
Courtesy Galerie Gmurzynska, Cologne. Cat. 4

7 *In the Studio*. Ca. 1923. Gelatin silver print. Metropolitan Museum
of Art, Ford Motor Company Collection, New York. Cat. 10

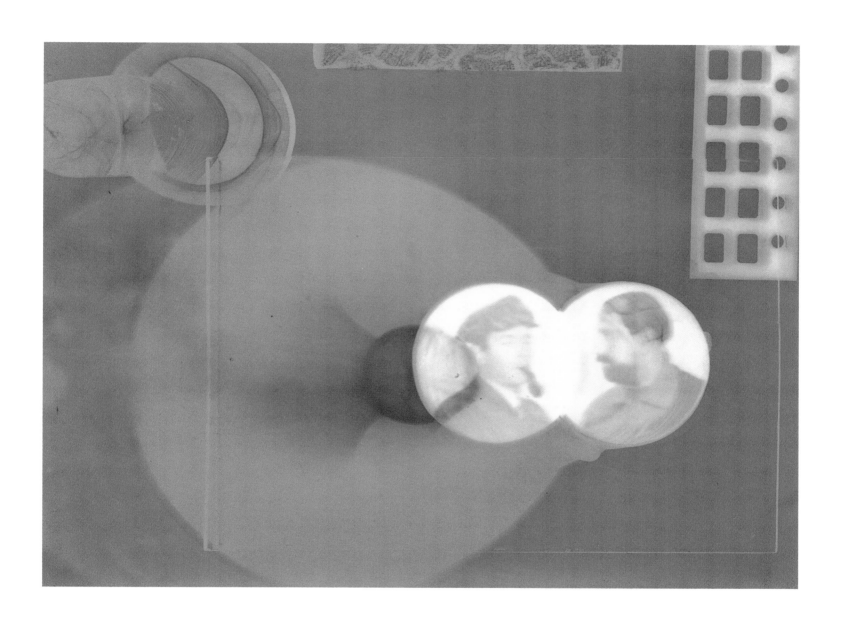

8 *Untitled* (Lissitzky and Huszar). 1923. Photogram.
The Art Institute of Chicago. Mary L. and Leigh B. Block Collection. Cat. 7

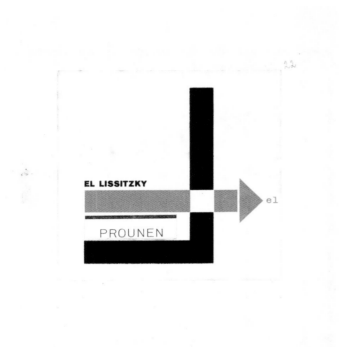

9.1–9.2 Maquette for the book *Prounen.* Ca. 1924. Gelatin silver prints, lithographs, and collage on paper. Russian State Archive for Literature and Art, Moscow. Cat. 14

10 *Untitled* (Hand with a Compass). 1924. Gelatin silver print. Sprengel Museum Hannover. Permanent loan. Collection of Ann and Jürgen Wilde. Cat. 30

11 *Self-Portrait*. 1924. Gelatin silver print.
Barry Friedman Ltd., New York. Cat. 31

12 *Self-Portrait*. 1924. Modern print from original glass negative.
Sprengel Museum Hannover. Permanent loan.
Niedersächsische Sparkassenstiftung. Cat. 32

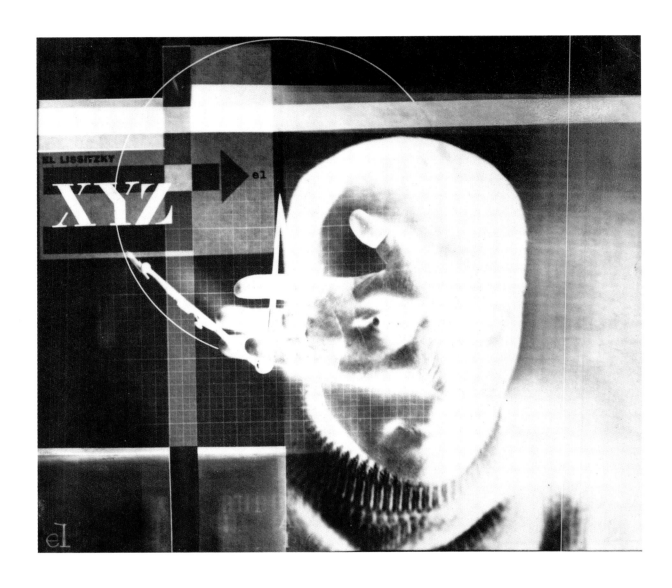

13 *Self-Portrait* (Constructor). 1924. Gelatin silver print (negative).
Galerie Berinson, Berlin. Cat. 33

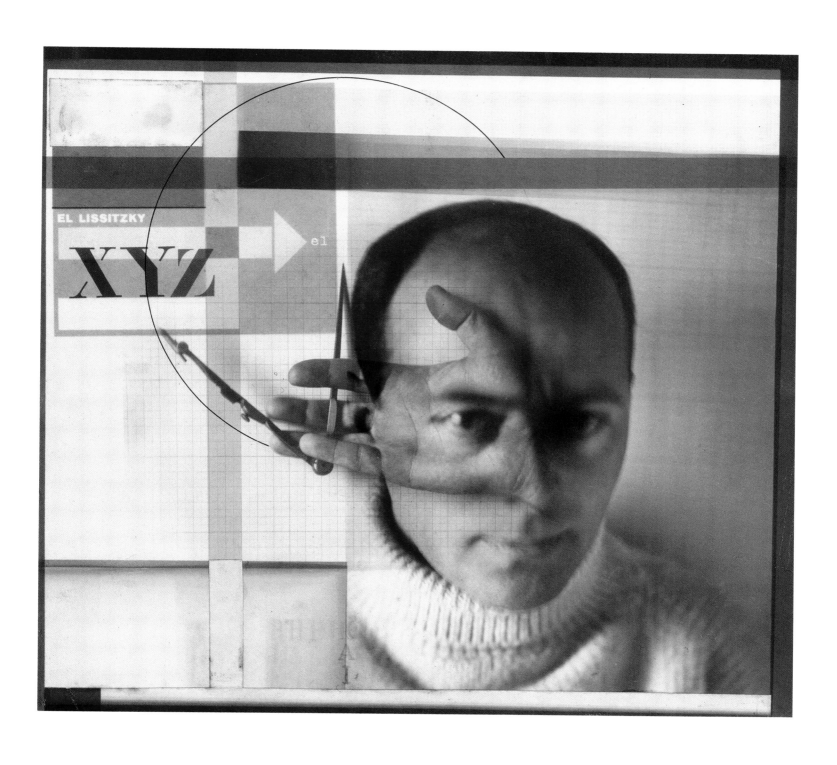

14 *Self-Portrait* (Constructor). 1924. Gelatin silver print, collage.
State Tretiakov Gallery, Moscow. Cat. 34

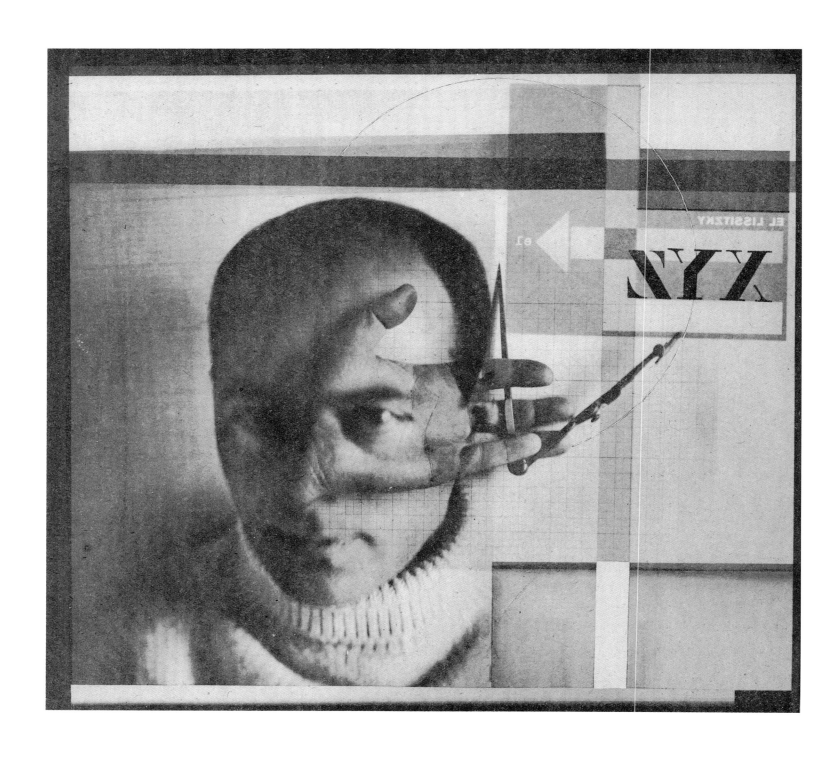

15 *Self-Portrait* (Constructor). Ca. 1924. Halftone photo lithograph.
Private Archive. Cat. 127

16 *Self Portrait.* 1924. Gelatin silver print. Collection of
Gilman Paper Company, New York. Cat. 35

17 *Untitled.* Ca. 1924. Gelatin silver print with text.
Collection of Thomas Walther, New York. Cat. 9

18 *Kurt Schwitters*. Ca. 1924. Modern print from original glass negative.
Sprengel Museum Hannover. Permanent loan.
Niedersächsische Sparkassenstiftung. Cat. 27

19 *Kurt Schwitters*. Ca. 1924. Modern print from original glass negative.
Sprengel Museum Hannover. Permanent loan.
Niedersächsische Sparkassenstiftung. Cat. 28

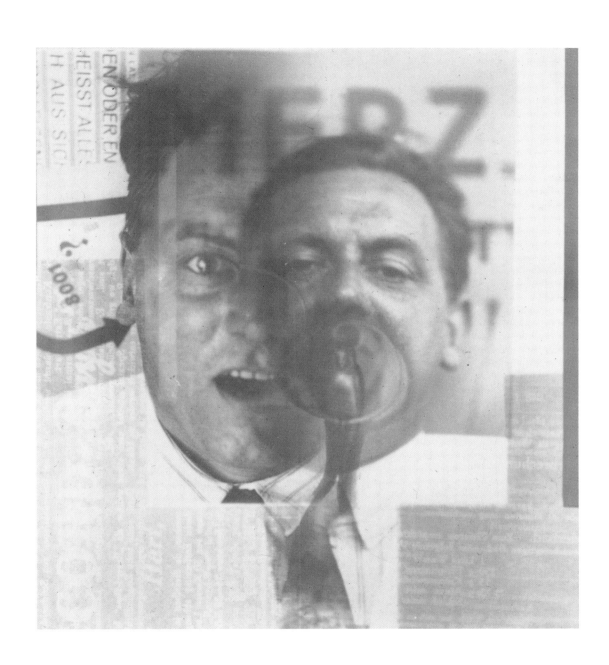

20 *Kurt Schwitters*. Ca. 1924. Gelatin silver print.
Collection of Thomas Walther, New York. Cat. 29

21 Cover for the book *Notes of a Poet*. IZOGIZ, Moscow. 1928.
Letterpress. Galerie Schlégl—Nicole Schlégl, Zurich. Cat. 135

22 *Hans Arp*. 1924. Gelatin silver print with text.
Russian State Archive for Literature and Art, Moscow. Cat. 12

23 *Hans Arp.* 1924. Gelatin silver print.
Galerie Berinson, Berlin. Cat. 13

24 *Pelikan Ink.* 1924. Photogram.
Galerie Berinson, Berlin. Cat. 15

25 *Pelikan Ink*. 1924. Photogram.
Collection of Manfred Heiting, Amsterdam. Cat. 16

26 *Pelikan Ink.* 1924. Photogram.
Russian State Archive for Literature and Art, Moscow. Cat. 17

27 *Pelikan Ink, Typewriter Ribbon, Carbon Paper.* 1924. Gelatin silver print.
Russian State Archive for Literature and Art, Moscow. Cat. 18

28 *Pelikan Carbon Paper.* 1924. Photogram.
Russian State Archive for Literature and Art, Moscow. Cat. 19

29 *Pelikan Carbon Paper.* 1924. Photogram.
Russian State Archive for Literature and Art, Moscow. Cat. 20

30 *Pelikan Carbon Paper.* 1924. Photogram.
Russian State Archive for Literature and Art, Moscow. Cat. 21

31 *Pelikan Carbon Paper.* 1924. Photogram.
Russian State Archive for Literature and Art, Moscow. Cat. 22

32 Design for Pelikan (advertisment for typewriter carbon paper). 1924.
Gelatin silver print. Russian State Archive for Literature and Art, Moscow. Cat. 23

33 Pelikan carbon paper. 1924. Photogram.
Russian State Archive for Literature and Art, Moscow. Cat. 24

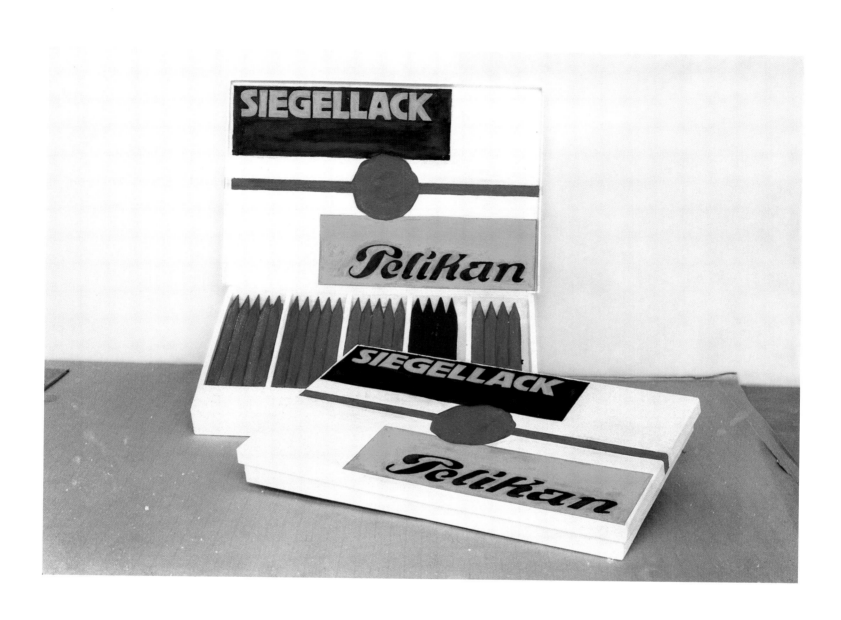

34 *Pelikan Sealing Wax.* 1924. Gelatin silver print, gouache.
Russian State Archive for Literature and Art, Moscow. Cat. 24

35 *Pelikan Drawing Ink*. 1924. Lithography.
Museum für Kunst und Gewerbe, Hamburg. Cat. 128

МОСКВА
1927

АРХИТЕКТУРА

АРХИТЕКТУРА

ВХУТЕМАС
АРХ

36 Cover for *VKhUTEMAS Architecture*. VKhUTEMAS, Moscow. 1927. Letterpress.
Collection of Larry Zeman and Howard Garfinkel, Productive Arts, Brooklyn Heights, Ohio. Cat. 130

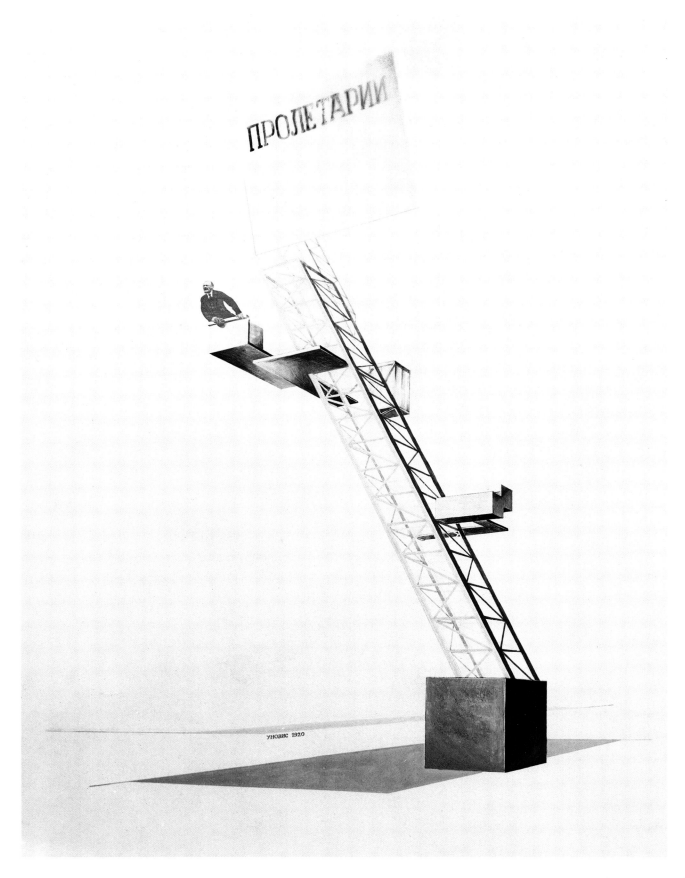

37 *Lenin Tribune* (with Ilia Chashnik). 1920–24.
Gelatin silver print. Private Archive. Cat. 6

38 *Untitled* (Superimposed Portrait). 1926–30. Photomontage.
Gelatin silver print. Museum of Modern Art, New York,
Gift of Shirley C. Burden and David H. McAlpin by exchange. Cat. 44

39 *Record* (Runner). 1926. Photomontage. Gelatin silver print.
Collection of Thomas Walther, New York. Cat. 41

40 *Runner in the City.* 1926. Photo collage.
Metropolitan Museum of Art, New York, Ford Motor Company Collection,
Gift of Ford Motor Company and John C. Waddell. Cat. 42

41 *Record* (Runner). 1926. Photo collage.
Galerie Berinson, Berlin. Cat. 43

105

42 *Footballer.* 1926. Gelatin silver print.
Alexander Kaplen, New York. Cat. 45

43 *Untitled* (Pliers and Wire). Ca. 1927. Photogram.
Galerie Berinson, Berlin. Cat. 39

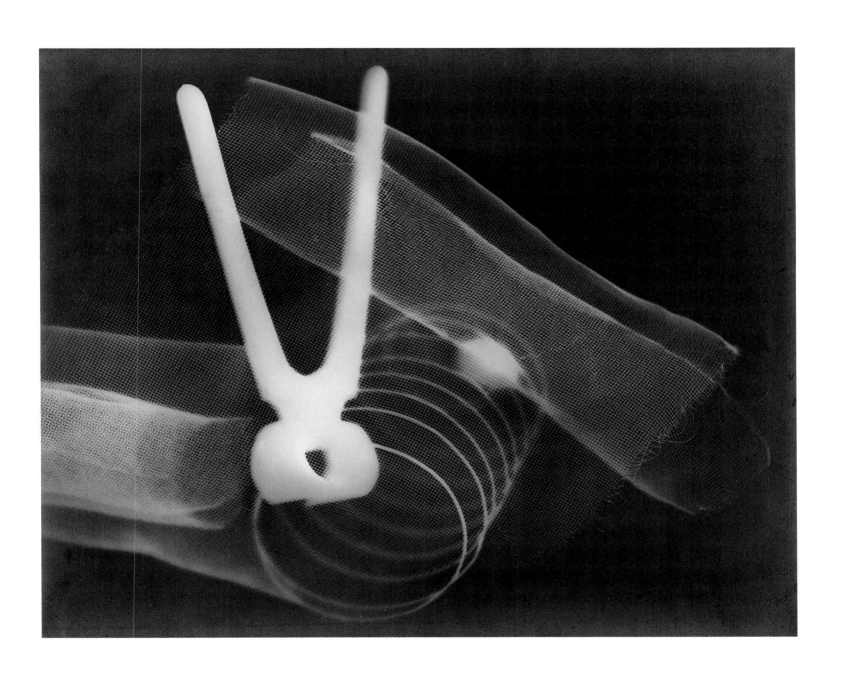

44 *Untitled* (Pliers and Wire). Ca. 1927. Photogram.
Galerie Berinson, Berlin. Cat. 40

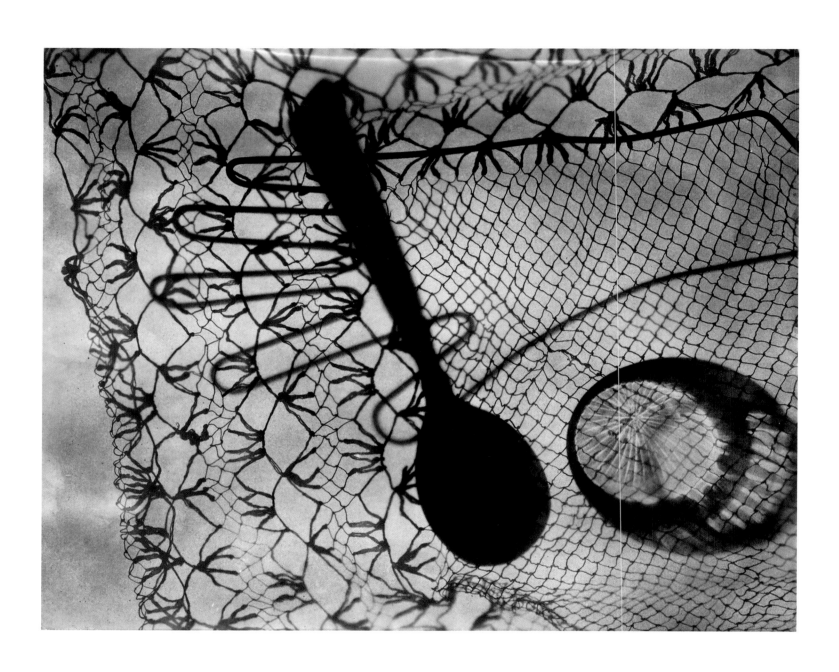

45 *Untitled* (Composition with Spoon). Ca. 1923–27.
Photogram. Collection of WAVE PBK, Cologne. Cat. 11

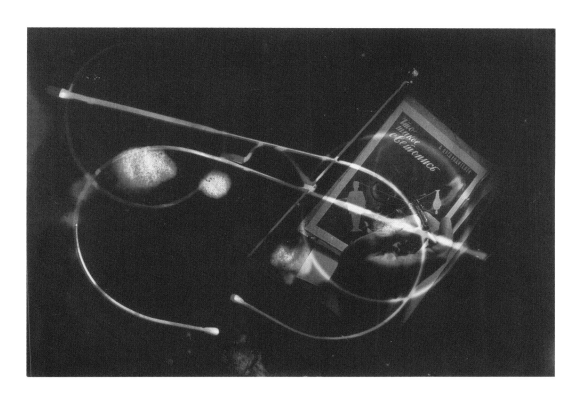

46 *Untitled* (What Is Svetopis?). Ca. 1928.
Attributed to El Lissitzky. Believed to be
Grigory Miller. Photogram. Collection of
Gilman Paper Company, New York. Cat. 59

46.1 Grigory Miller. Cover for the book
What Is Svetopis? by A. Predvoditelev.
Letterpress. Private Collection. Cat. 187

111

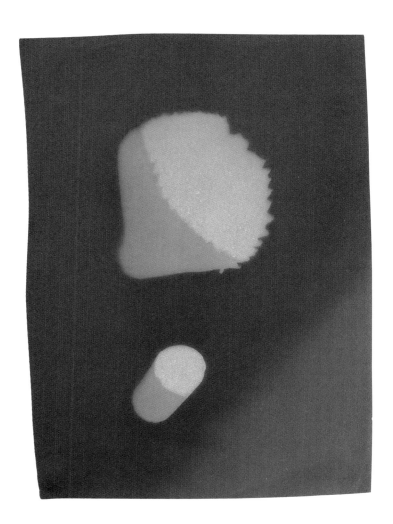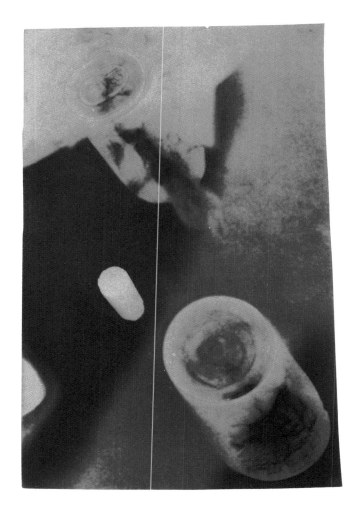

47.1 – 47.2 *Untitled.* Ca. 1927. Cyanotype. Russian State
Archive for Literature and Art, Moscow. Cats. 48, 49

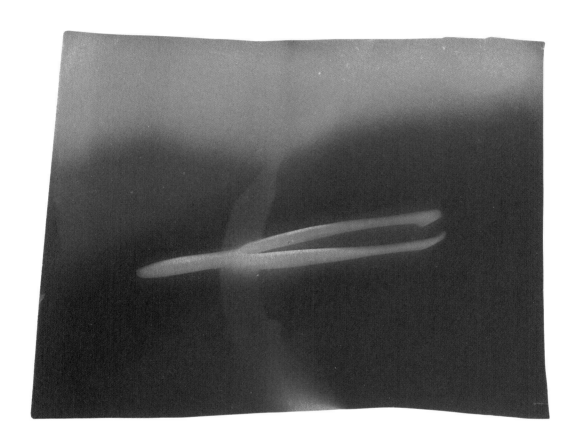

47.3 *Untitled.* Ca. 1927. Cyanotype. Russian State
Archive for Literature and Art, Moscow. Cat. 50

48 *Untitled.* N.d. Gouache on paper.
Russian State Archive for Literature and Art, Moscow. Cat. 53

49 *For the Voice*, a poem by Vladimir Mayakovski. 1923. Gelatin silver print.
Russian State Archive for Literature and Art, Moscow. Cat. 8

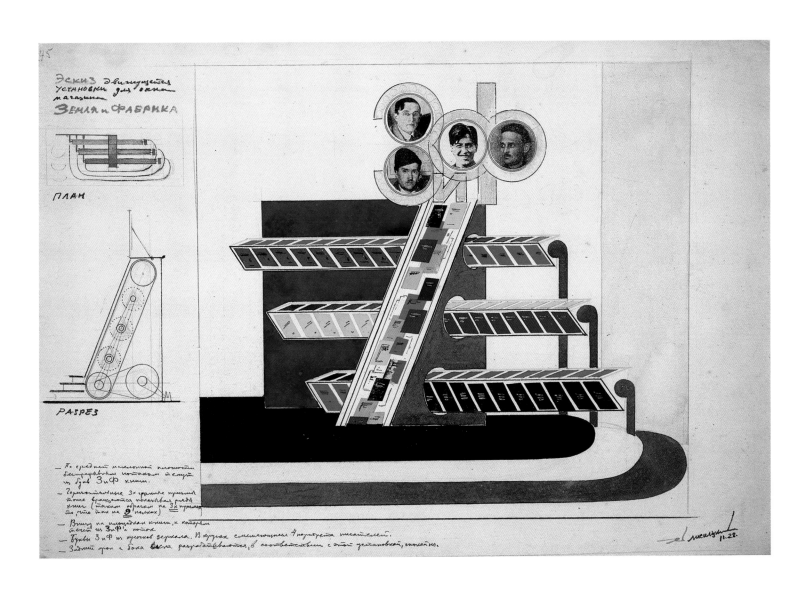

50 Design for a window mobile for a bookstore of the Land and Factory Publishing House. 1928.
Photo collage, gouache, ink, pencil on cardboard. State Tretiakov Gallery, Moscow. Cat. 56

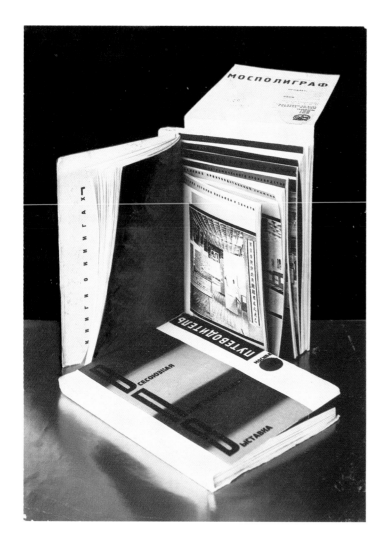

51 Guide for the All-Union Printing Trades Exhibition, with Solomon Telingater. 1927. Gelatin silver print, retouched. Private Archive. Cat. 46

52 Guide for the All-Union Printing Trades Exhibition, with Solomon Telingater. 1927. Gelatin silver print. Private Archive. Cat. 47

ПОЛНОЕ
СОБРАНИЕ
ХУДОЖЕСТВЕННЫХ
ПРОИЗВЕДЕНИЙ
ЛЬВА
НИКОЛАЕВИЧА
ТОЛСТОГО

ТОМ 1
ВЫПУСК 2
ГОСУДАРСТВЕННОЕ 1928
ИЗДАТЕЛЬСТВО

53 Maquette for the cover of the complete edition of Lev Tolstoy's novels. 1928.
Photo collage. Russian State Archive for Literature and Art, Moscow. Cat. 57

54 Cover design for the brochure of the Soviet pavilion at Pressa, Cologne. 1928.
Gouache on paper, collage. Russian State Archive for Literature and Art, Moscow. Cat. 54

55 Catalogue for the Soviet pavilion at Pressa, Cologne. 1928. Gelatin silver print,
photo collage, ink. Art Gallery of New South Wales, Australia. Cat. 55

56 Foldout from the catalogue for the Soviet pavilion at Pressa,
Cologne. 1928. Letterpress. Collection of David King, London. Cat. 134

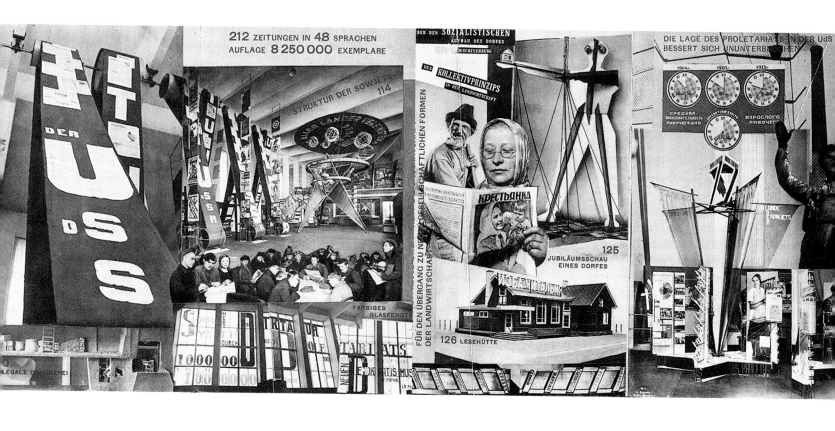

56 Foldout from the catalogue for the Soviet pavilion at Pressa,
Cologne. 1928. Letterpress. Collection of David King, London. Cat. 134

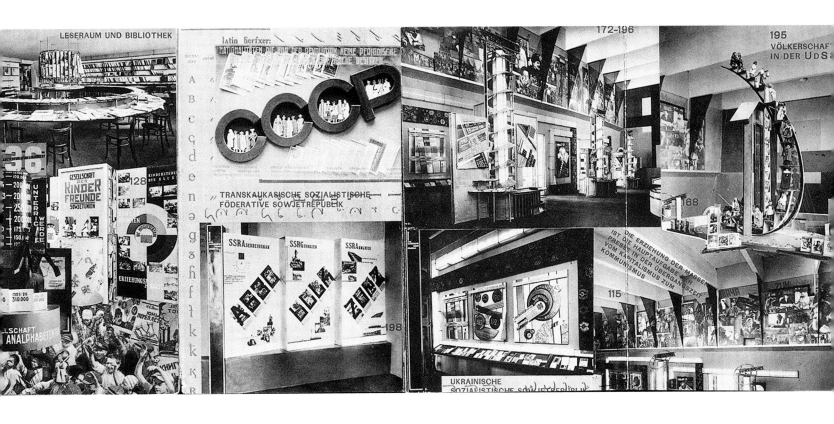

56 Foldout from the catalogue for the Soviet pavilion at Pressa,
Cologne. 1928. Letterpress. Collection of David King, London. Cat. 134

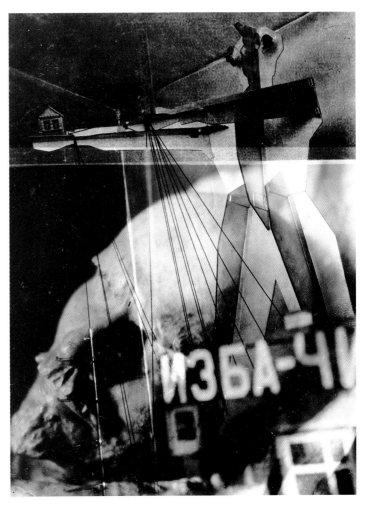

57 Installation view of *Anniversary Show of a Village*, designed for Pressa and preinstalled in GUM (State Universal Store), Moscow. 1928. Gelatin silver print. Russian State Archive for Literature and Art, Moscow. Cat. 52

58 *Untitled.* Detail from the Soviet pavilion of Pressa, Cologne. 1928. Gelatin silver print. Private Archive. Cat. 51

125

59 Flagpole for the Soviet pavilion at Pressa, Cologne. 1928. Gouache, ink, photo collage on paper. State Tretiakov Gallery, Moscow. Cat. 58

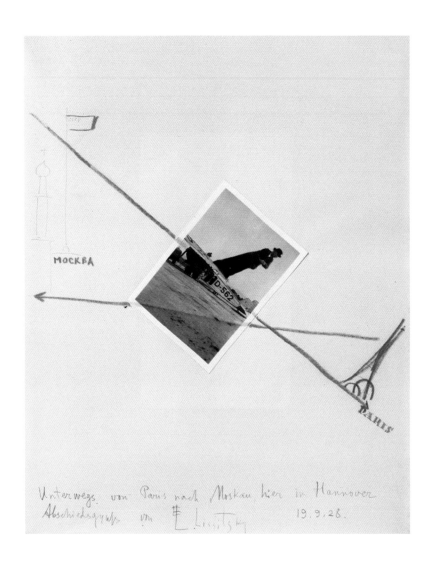

60 *Untitled.* Page from the Bode family guest book, Hannover. 1928. Photo collage,
graphite pencil. Sprengel Museum Hannover. Private collection on permanent loan. Cat. 61

61 *Der Wolkenbügel (Cloud Stirrup)*. 1924–25. Photomontage, retouched.
Russian State Archive for Literature and Art, Moscow. Cat. 36

62 *Eiffel Tower.* 1928. Gelatin silver print.
Galerie Gmurzynska, Cologne. Cat. 62

63 *Eiffel Tower.* 1928. Gelatin silver print.
Private Archive. Cat. 63

64 *Eiffel Tower.* 1928. Gelatin silver print.
Galerie Gmurzynska, Cologne. Cat. 64

65 *Eiffel Tower.* 1928. Gelatin silver print.
Galerie Gmurzynska, Cologne. Cat. 65

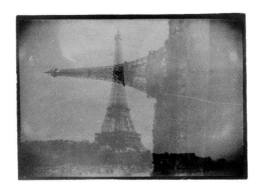

66.1– 66.5 *Eiffel Tower.* 1928. Contact gelatin
silver print. Private Archive. Cat. 66–70

67 *Eiffel Tower.* 1928. Gelatin silver print.
Private Archive. Cat. 71

68 *Untitled*. Ca. 1928. Photogram. Russian State
Archive for Literature and Art, Moscow. Cat. 77

ИЛЬЯ ЭРЕНБУРГ
Портрет работы
Эль Лисицкого

5

69 Cover and illustrations for the book *My Paris*. IZOGIZ. Moscow. 1933. Letterpress.
Larry Zeman and Howard Garfinkel, Productive Arts, Brooklyn Heights, Ohio. Cat. 150

70–71 Design for cover and illustrations for *My Paris*. Ca. 1933. Gelatin silver print.
Russian State Archive for Literature and Art, Moscow. Cats. 103, 104

72 Cover for the magazine *Artists' Brigade*, no. 4. 1931. Letterpress. Larry Zeman and Howard Garfinkel, Productive Arts, Brooklyn Heights, Ohio. Cat. 145 (Photo: William Short)

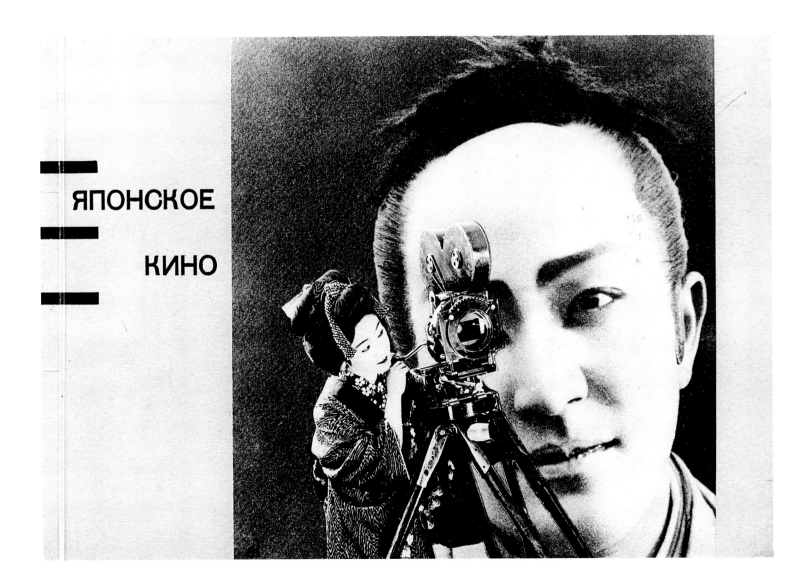

ЯПОНСКОЕ

КИНО

73 Cover for the catalogue of the Japanese Cinema Exhibition. Gosznak, Moscow. 1929.
Letterpress. Stedelijk Van Abbemuseum, Eindhoven. Cat. 136

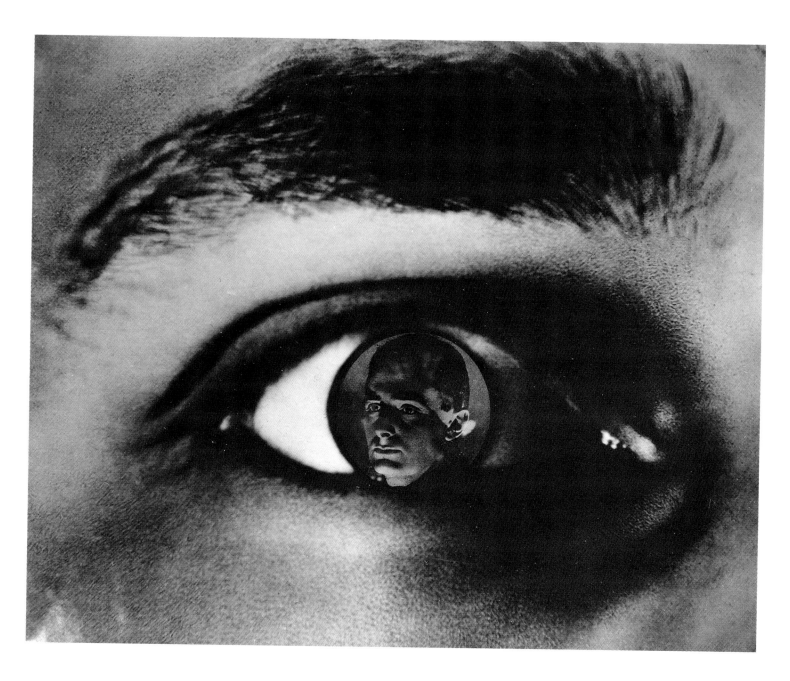

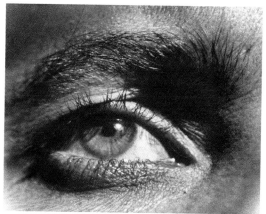

74 Maquette for "Kinoglaz," an unpublished book by Dziga Vertov. 1929. Photomontage, retouched. Collection of Manfred Heiting, Amsterdam. Cat. 80

74.1 Still from *Man with a Movie Camera*. 1929. Gelatin silver print. Collection of Manfred Heiting, Amsterdam. Cat. 211

75 Poster design for the Russian Exhibition in the
Kunstgewerbemuseum, Zurich. 1929. Gelatin silver print.
Staatliche Galerie Moritzburg Halle, Landeskunstmuseum
Sachsen-Anhalt, Photography Collection. Cat. 79

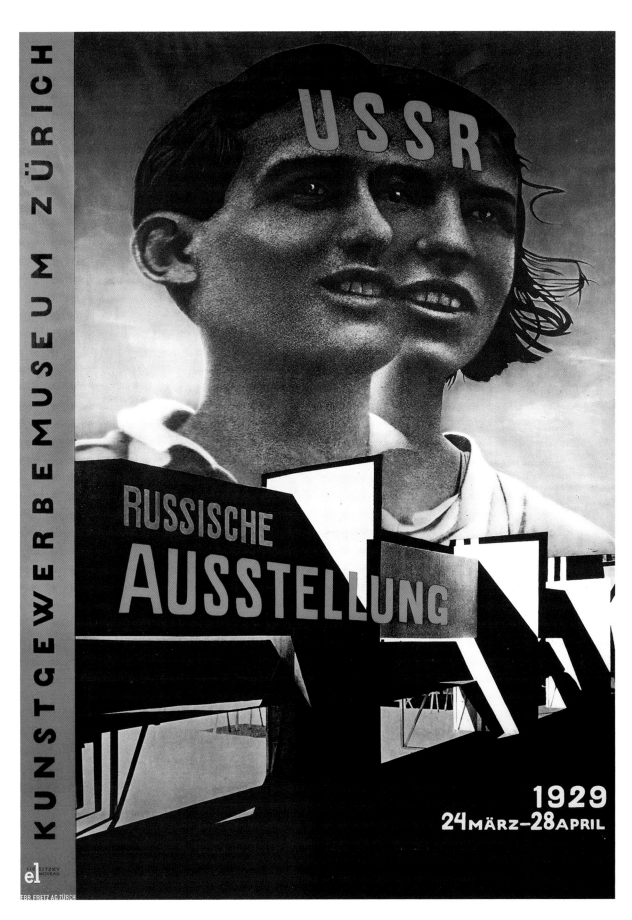

76 Poster for the Russian Exhibition at the Kunstgewerbemuseum, Zürich. 1929.
Lithography. Schule für Gestaltung, Plakatsammlung, Basel. Cat. 138

77 Cover design for *Frankreich: Neues Bauen in der Welt*, vol. 3, by Roger Ginzburger. 1929–30.
Photomontage. Gelatin silver print. Barry Friedman Ltd. New York. Cat. 83

78 Cover design for *Amerika: Neues Bauen in der Welt*, vol. 2, by Richard J. Neutra. 1929–30.
Photomontage. Gelatin silver print. Collection of Thomas Walther, New York. Cat. 82

79 Cover design for *Russland: Neues Bauen in der Welt,* vol. 1, by El Lissitzky. 1929–30.
Photomontage. Gelatin silver print. Collection of Thomas Walther, New York. Cat. 81

79.1 Boris Ignatovich. *Untitled.* 1929. Gelatin silver print
(printed in the 1960s). Private Collection. Cat. 188

80 Cover for *Russland: Neues Bauen in der Welt*, vol. 1, by El Lissitzky. 1930.
Letterpress. Collection of Ann and Jürgen Wilde. Cat. 139

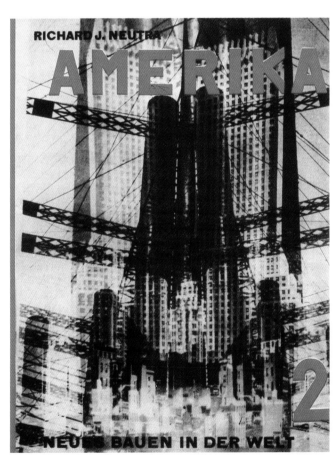

81 Cover for *Amerika: Neues Bauen in der Welt*, vol. 2, by Richard
J. Neutra. 1930. Letterpress. IVAM. Instituto Valenciano de Arte Moderno.
Generalitat Valencia. Cat. 140

82 Cover for *Frankreich: Neues Bauen in der Welt*, vol. 3, by Roger Ginzburger.
1930. Letterpress. Collection of Ann and Jürgen Wilde. Cat. 141

83 Soldier near the Shabolovskaia radio tower. 1929. Gelatin silver print.
Russian State Archive for Literature and Art, Moscow. Cat. 78

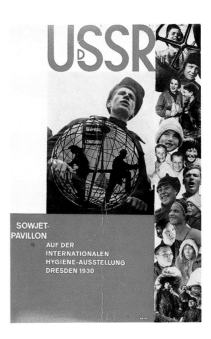

84 *Untitled.* Detail from the Soviet pavilion of the International
Hygiene Exhibition, Dresden. 1930. Photomontage. Gelatin silver print.
Collection of Robert Shapazian, Los Angeles. Cat. 84

85 Cover for the catalogue of the Soviet pavilion at the International
Hygiene Exhibition, Dresden. 1930. Letterpress.
Bibliothek des Deutschen Hygiene-Museums, Dresden. Cat. 142

86 *Untitled*. Detail from the Soviet pavilion of the International Hygiene Exhibition, Dresden. 1930. Photomontage. Gelatin silver print. Private Archive. Cat. 85

87 *Untitled.* Page from Alexander Dorner's guest book. Hanover. 1930.
Photo collage with text. Sprengel Museum Hannover. Cat. 87

el

89 *Untitled* (Lenin). 1930. Photomontage.
Gelatin silver print. Private Archive. Cat. 92

90 *Untitled*. N.d. Photomontage. Russian State
Archive for Literature and Art, Moscow. Cat. 99

91 Design for *USSR in Construction*. 1930. Photomontage.
Gelatin silver print. Russian State Archive for Literature and Art,
Moscow. Cat. 96

91.1 Dmitry Debabov, *Smokestacks*. 1929. Gelatin silver print.
Howard Schickler Fine Art, New York. Cat. 251

92 Design for *USSR in Construction*. 1930. Photomontage. Gelatin silver print.
Russian State Archive for Literature and Art, Moscow. Cat. 97

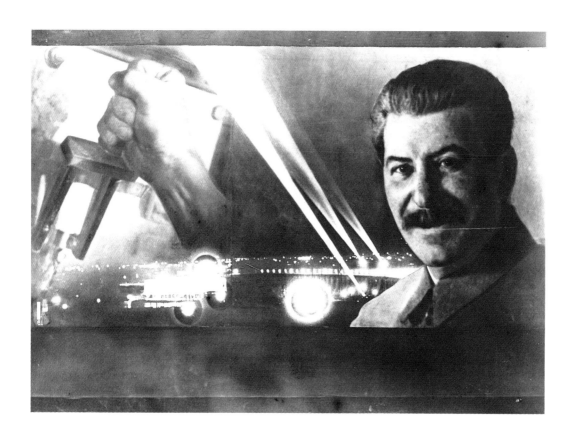

93 Design of a double page for *USSR in Construction*, no. 10.
1932. Photomontage. Gelatin silver print. Priska Pasquer,
Photographic Art Consulting, Cologne. Cat. 100

94 Design for *USSR in Construction*, no. 10. 1932.
Photomontage. Gelatin silver print. Howard Schickler Fine Art,
New York. Cat. 101

95 Cover design for *USSR in Construction*, no. 10. 1936.
Photomontage. Gelatin silver print with text. Russian State
Archive for Literature and Art, Moscow. Cat. 106

96 Design for *USSR in Construction*, no. 10. 1934.
Photomontage. Gelatin silver print. Russian State Archive
for Literature and Art, Moscow. Cat. 107

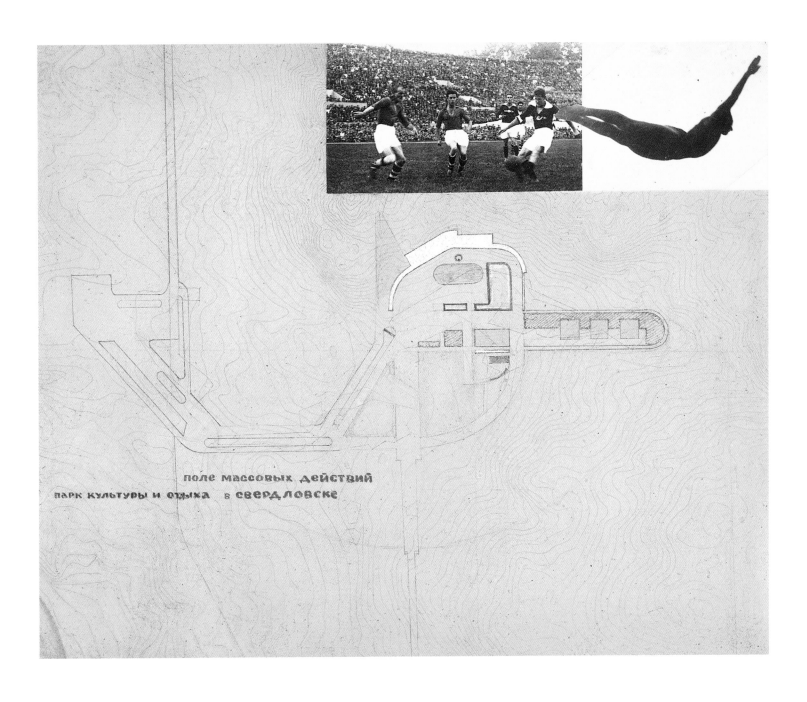

поле массовых действий
парк культуры и отдыха в свердловске

97 Architectural design for the field for mass activities in Recreational Park in
Sverdlovsk. 1932. Photo collage, pencil on cardboard. Private Archive. Cat. 102

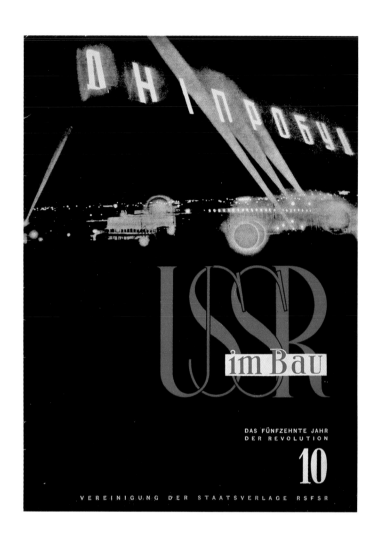

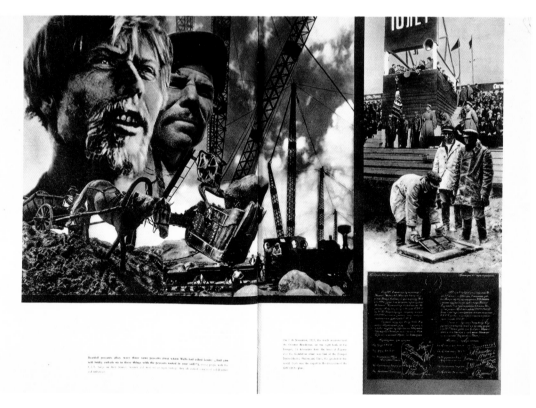

98 *USSR in Construction*, no. 10. 1932. Devoted to the construction of Dnieper Dam. Lithography and gravure.
Larry Zeman and Howard Garfinkel, Productive Arts, Brooklyn Heights, Ohio. Cat. 146 (Photo: William Short)

99 *USSR in Construction*, no. 2. 1933. Devoted to the fifteenth anniversary of the Red Army. Lithography and gravure.
Larry Zeman and Howard Garfinkel, Productive Arts, Brooklyn Heights, Ohio. Cat. 147 (Photo: William Short)

100 USSR Building Socialism. IZOGIZ. Moscow. 1933. Lithography. Larry Zeman and Howard Garfinkel,
Productive Arts, Brooklyn Heights, Ohio. Cat. 149 (Photo: William Short)

101 *Soviet Subtropics*, with Sophie Küppers. Newspaper and Magazine Union, Moscow, 1934. Letterpress and lithography. Larry Zeman and Howard Garfinkel, Productive Arts, Brooklyn Heights, Ohio. Cat. 155 (Photo: William Short)

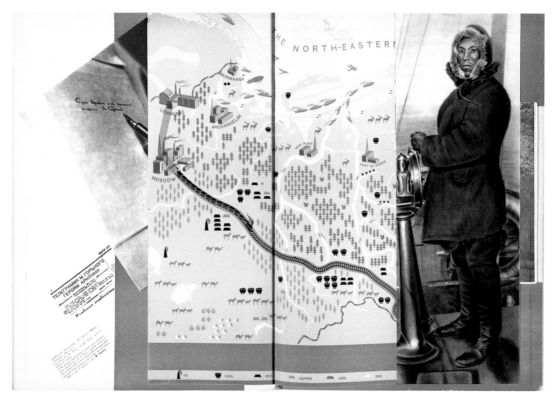

102 *USSR in Construction*, no. 9. 1933. Devoted to the Soviet Arctic. Lithography and gravure.
Larry Zeman and Howard Garfinkel, Productive Arts, Brooklyn Heights, Ohio. Cat. 102 (Photo: William Short)

103 *USSR in Construction,* with Sophie Küppers, no. 2. 1934. Devoted to the four bolshevik victories. Lithography and gravure. Larry Zeman and Howard Garfinkel, Productive Arts, Brooklyn Heights, Ohio. Cat. 151 (Photo: William Short)

104 Workers'-Peasants' Red Army. IZOGIZ, Moscow. 1934. Lithography. Larry Zeman and Howard Garfinkel, Productive Arts, Brooklyn Heights, Ohio. Cat. 152 (Photo: William Short)

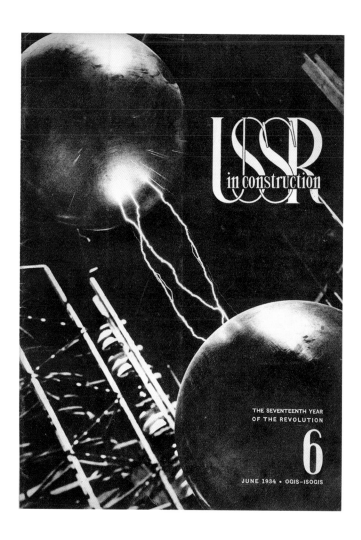

105 *USSR in Construction*, with Sophie Küppers, no. 6. 1934. Devoted to Soviet science. Lithography and gravure.
Larry Zeman and Howard Garfinkel, Productive Arts, Brooklyn Heights, Ohio. Cat. 153 (Photo: William Short)

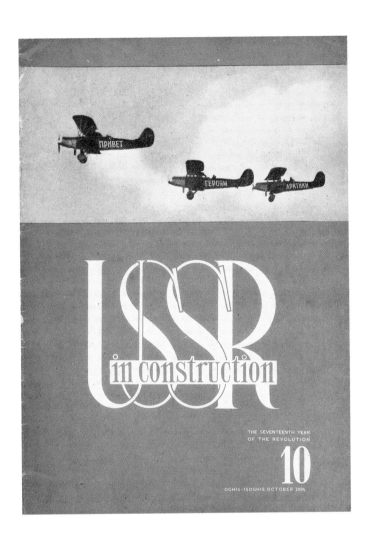

106 *USSR in Construction*, with Sophie Küppers, no. 10. 1934. Devoted to the epic of the Cheluskin exploration. Lithography and gravure. Larry Zeman and Howard Garfinkel, Productive Arts, Brooklyn Heights, Ohio. Cat. 154 (Photo: William Short)

107 *At the Construction of MTS and Sovkhozy,* no. 4. 1934.
Lithography and gravure. Larry Zeman and Howard Garfinkel, Productive Arts,
Brooklyn Heights, Ohio. Cat. 156 (Photo: William Short)

108 *At the Construction of MTS and Sovkhozy,* no. 2. 1935. Lithography and
gravure. Larry Zeman and Howard Garfinkel, Productive Arts, Brooklyn Heights,
Ohio. Cat. 157 (Photo: William Short)

109 *Industry of Socialism.* Stroim, Moscow, 1935.
Larry Zeman and Howard Garfinkel, Productive Arts,
Brooklyn Heights, Ohio. Cat. 158 (Photo: William Short)

110 *Food Industry*, with Sophie Küppers. 1936. Lithography.
Museum Folkwang, Essen. Cat. 162 (Photo: William Short)

Бекон — отличная тара. Банк «склада сахарных»   Фото А. Хлебников

Советский шоколад на международном промышленном на земле   Фото В. Осколков

Советский аппарат в руке; были сотня советских и русские «флаконы сильный тип»   Фото А. Калинина

Советская тара на будет более лет для нашего хлеба   Фото — Мальш

Советская консервная тара обеспечивает продукт от повреждений   Фото В. Осколков

110 *Food Industry,* with Sophie Küppers. 1936. Lithography.
Museum Folkwang, Essen. Cat. 162 (Photo: William Short)

Думни лица питпрй инустрия

111 *USSR in Construction*, with Sophie Küppers, no. 1. 1937. Devoted to the Workers'-Peasants' Red Navy. Lithography and gravure. Larry Zeman and Howard Garfinkel, Productive Arts, Brooklyn Heights, Ohio. Cat. 163 (Photo: William Short)

112 *USSR in Construction*, nos. 4–5. 1936. Devoted to the fifteenth anniversary of Soviet Georgia. Lithography and gravure. Larry Zeman and Howard Garfinkel, Productive Arts, Brooklyn Heights, Ohio. Cat. 160 (Photo: William Short)

113 *USSR in Construction*, with Sophie Küppers, no. 3. 1937. Devoted to the people of the Ordzhonikidze Territory (Northern Caucasus). Lithography and gravure. Larry Zeman and Howard Garfinkel, Productive Arts, Brooklyn Heights, Ohio. Cat. 164

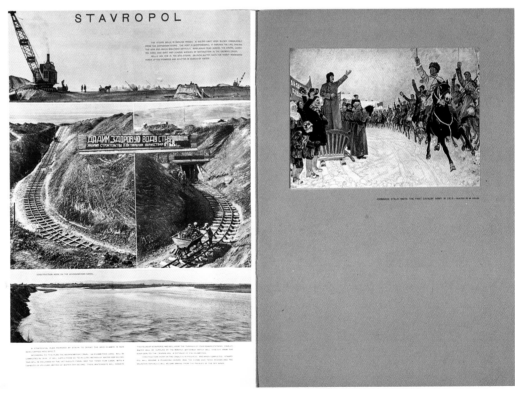

114 Design of a title page for *USSR in Construction*, nos. 9 – 12. 1937.
Photomontage. Gelatin silver print, hand-colored. Private Archive. Cat. 108

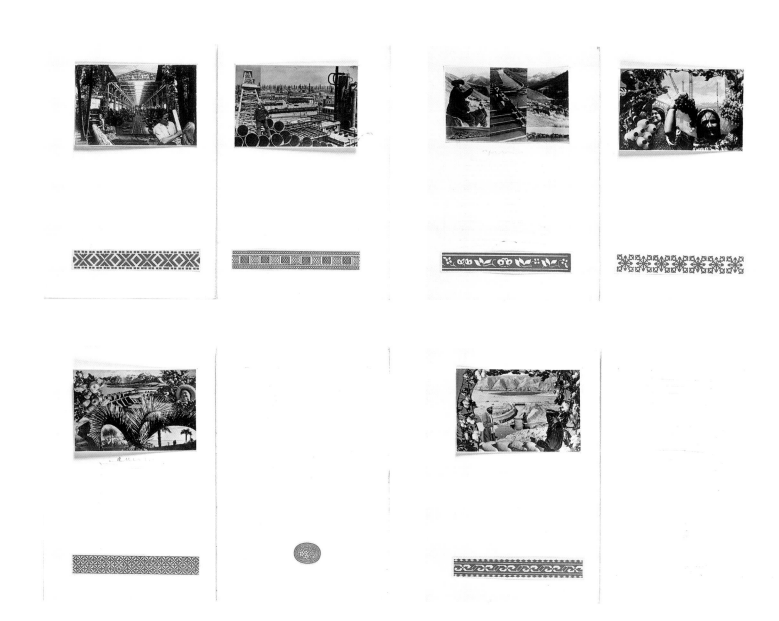

115 Maquette for *USSR in Construction*, nos. 9–12. 1937.
Gelatin silver prints, collage on paper. Private Archive. Cat. 109

116 Design for *USSR in Construction*, nos. 9–12. 1937. Photomontage.
Gelatin silver print. Priska Pasquer, Photographic Art Consulting, Cologne. Cat. 110

117 Design for *USSR in Construction*, nos. 9 – 12. 1937. Photomontage.
Gelatin silver print. Museum Folkwang, Essen. Cat. 111 (Photo: William Short)

118 *USSR in Construction*, with Sophie Küppers, nos. 9–12. 1937.
Devoted to Stalin's Constitution. Lithography and gravure. Larry Zeman
and Howard Garfinkel, Productive Arts, Brooklyn Heights, Ohio. Cat. 165

XX

YEARS
OF THE GREAT
OCTOBER
SOCIALIST
REVOLUTION

USSR in CONSTRUCTION № 9-10-11-12 1937

UKRAINIAN SOVIET SOCIALIST REPUBLIC

	1913	1936
Gross output of large-scale industry (milli./m.) at 1926-27 [note]	2.100	14.600
Teachers (№)	—	1.414.200
Retail trade turnover [milli. rm.]	1.300'	16.400
Elementary and secondary school pupils [thousands]	1.700''	5.200
Students in higher technical school students	26.700	113.600

"WE BOLSHEVIKS WOULD NOT H... SES WE HAVE NOW IF WE HAD NOT... FOR THE PARTY THE CONFIDENC... NON-PARTY WORKERS AND PEASANTS...

THE SUCCES-... ABLE TO WIN MILLIONS OF ... J. STALIN

Article 126

In conformity with the interests of the toilers and in order to develop the organisational initiative and political activity of the masses of the people, citizens of the USSR are ensured the right to unite in public organisations—trade unions, co-operative associations, youth organisations, sport and defence organisations, cultural, technical and scientific societies; and the most active and politically conscious citizens in the ranks of the working class and other strata of the toilers unite in the Communist Party of the Soviet Union (Bolsheviks), which is the vanguard of the toilers in their struggle to strengthen and develop the socialist system and which represents the leading core of all organisations of the toilers, both public and state.

183

119 *All Power to the Soviets.* 1937. Photo collage. Museum Folkwang, Essen. Cat. 120

120 *USSR in Construction*, with Sophie Küppers, nos. 5–6. 1938. Devoted to Far Eastern Territory. Lithography and gravure. Larry Zeman and Howard Garfinkel, Productive Arts, Brooklyn Heights, Ohio. Cat. 166 (Photo: William Short)

121 *USSR in Construction*, with Sophie Küppers, no. 6. 1939. Devoted to the Korobov family. Lithography and gravure. Larry Zeman and Howard Garfinkel, Productive Arts, Brooklyn Heights, Ohio. Cat. 167 (Photo: William Short)

122 *USSR in Construction*, with Sophie Küppers, no. 11. 1940. Devoted to the construction of the warfleet. Lithography and gravure. Larry Zeman and Howard Garfinkel, Productive Arts, Brooklyn Heights, Ohio. Cat. 172 (Photo: William Short)

123 *USSR in Construction,* with Sophie Küppers, no. 11. 1940. Devoted to the Grand Fergana Canal, dedicated to Stalin. Lithography and gravure. Larry Zeman and Howard Garfinkel, Productive Arts, Brooklyn Heights, Ohio. Cat. 169 (Photo: William Short)

124 *USSR in Construction*, nos. 2–3. 1940. Devoted to the Western Ukraine
and Western Belorussia. Lithography and gravure. Larry Zeman and Howard Garfinkel,
Productive Arts, Brooklyn Heights, Ohio. Cat. 170 (Photo: William Short)

125 *USSR in Construction*, with Sophie Küppers, no. 10. 1940. Devoted to Bessarabia
and Northern Bukovina. Lithography and gravure. Larry Zeman and Howard Garfinkel,
Productive Arts, Brooklyn Heights, Ohio. Cat. 171 (Photo: William Short)

126 *Produce More Tanks*, with Nikolai Troshin. 1942. Lithography. Staatliche Galerie Moritzburg, Halle, Landeskunstmuseum Sachsen-Anhalt, Photography Collection. Cat. 174

Archive

Photos from Lissitzky's private archive and
works by artists with whom he collaborated

1.1 Man Ray: Fifth rayogram from the
album *Champs délicieux*. 1922. Copy Print.
Private Archive. Cat. 175

1.2 Man Ray: Sixth rayogram from the
album *Champs délicieux*. 1922. Copy Print.
Private Archive. Cat. 176

1.3 Man Ray: Seventh rayogram from the
album *Champs délicieux*. 1922. Copy Print.
Private Archive. Cat. 177

1.4 Man Ray: Ninth rayogram from the
album *Champs délicieux*. 1922. Copy Print.
Private Archive. Cat. 178

1.5 Man Ray: Twelfth rayogram from the
album *Champs délicieux*. 1922. Copy Print.
Private Archive. Cat. 179

1.1

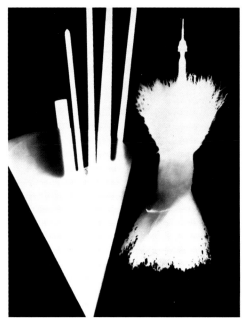

1.2

1.3

1.4

1.5

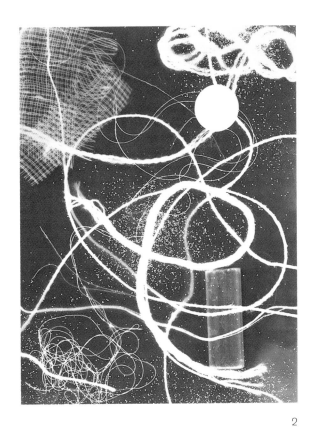

2

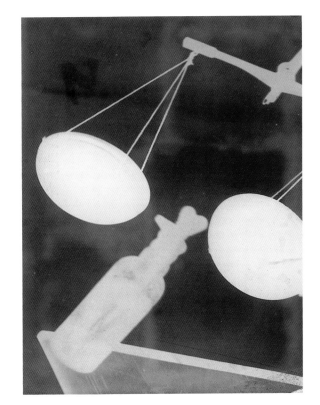

3

4

5

2 Attributed to Georgy Zimin: *Untitled.* Ca. 1927. Photogram.
Russian State Archive for Literature and Art, Moscow. Cat. 180

3 Georgy Zimin: *Untitled.* Ca. 1927. Photogram. Russian State
Archive for Literature and Art, Moscow. Cat. 181

4 Sergei Senkin: *Through Fabric.* 1927. Cyanotype. Russian
State Archive for Literature and Art, Moscow. Cat. 185

5 Attributed to Sergei Senkin: *Untitled.* Ca. 1927. Cyanotype.
Russian State Archive for Literature and Art, Moscow. Cat. 186

6

7

8

9

6 Gustav Klutsis and Sergei Senkin: Dust jacket for *In Memory of Fallen Leaders*. 1927. Lithography. Howard Schickler Fine Art, New York. Cat. 183

7 Gustav Klutsis: View of Valentina Kulagina's Stand for the Soviet Village, designed for Pressa, Moscow. 1928. Gelatin silver print. Priska Pasquer, Photographic Art Consulting, Cologne. Cat. 196

8 Sergei Senkin. *Varia Organizes Pioneers* (left). 1926. *My Frieze from the Cologne Exhibition* (right). 1928. Gelatin silver prints mounted on paper. Russian State Archive for Literature and Art, Moscow. Cat. 193

9 Sergei Senkin: *Untitled* (left). 1927. *Self-Portrait* (right). 1928. Gelatin silver prints mounted on paper. Russian State Archive for Literature and Art, Moscow. Cat. 194

10 Dsiga Wertow [?]: Entwurf einer Anzeige für den Film *Ein Sechstel der Welt*, 1926
Russisches Staatsarchiv für Literatur und Kunst, Moskau

11.1 Dsiga Wertow [?]: Plakat für den Film *Der Mann mit der Filmkamera*, 1929
Russisches Staatsarchiv für Literatur und Kunst, Moskau

11.2 Dsiga Wertow [?]: Anzeige für den Film *Enthusiasmus*, 1930–31
Russisches Staatsarchiv für Literatur und Kunst, Moskau

10

11.1

11.2

195

12.1

12.2

12.3

12.4

13.1

12.1 Dziga Vertov: Still from *Man with a Movie Camera*. 1929.
Collection of Thomas Walther, New York. Cat. 203

12.2–12.4 Dziga Vertov: Still from *Man with a Movie Camera*. 1929. Gelatin
silver print. Russian State Archive for Literature and Art, Moscow. Cat. 204–206

13.1 Dziga Vertov: Still from *Three Songs of Lenin*. 1933–34. Gelatin silver print.
Russian State Archive for Literature and Art, Moscow. Cat. 213

13.2

13.3

13.4

13.2–13.5 Dziga Vertov: Still from *Three Songs of Lenin*. 1933–34. Gelatin silver print. Russian State Archive for Literature and Art, Moscow. Cat. 214–217

13.6 Anonymous: Red Army soldiers march to a movie theater to view *Three Songs of Lenin*. 1934. Gelatin silver print. Russian State Archive for Literature and Art, Moscow. Cat. 224

13.5

13.6

15

14   16

17   18

14 Ivan Shagin: *Nina Kamneva, Who Set a World Record in a Delayed Parachute Jump.* 1930s. Gelatin silver print. Private Archive. Cat. 269

15 Georgy Petrusov: *Socialist Treaty for Competition.* 1934. Gelatin silver print. Collection fredo's. Cat. 262

16 Georgy Petrusov: *Untitled.* 1934. Gelatin silver print. Private Archive. Cat. 263

17 Ivan Shagin: *Untitled.* 1930s. Gelatin silver print. Private Archive. Cat. 270

18 Georgy Petrusov: *Untitled* (the Korobov family). Ca. 1939. Gelatin silver print. Private Archive. Cat. 267

19

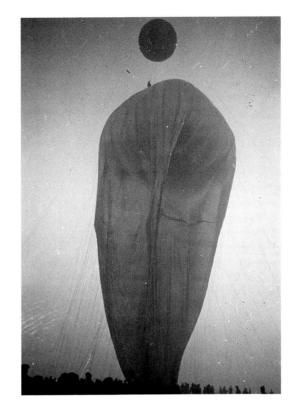

20

21

19 Anonymous: *Roof of the World, German-Russian Joint Pamir Expedition.* 1933.
Gelatin silver print. Sveriges Television, International Historical Press Photo
Collection, Stockholm. Cat. 256

20 (?)Kislov: *The Soviet Stratospheric Balloon "USSR" Breaks the Record.* 1933.
Gelatin silver print. Sveriges Television. International Historical Press Photo
Collection, Stockholm. Cat. 257

21 Eduard Tisse: *9500 Kilometers on Soviet Roads* (The Moscow – Kara-kum –
Moscow Automobile Run). 1933. Gelatin silver print. Sveriges Television,
International Historical Press Photo Collection, Stockholm. Cat. 260

22 Solomon Telingater: Stationery for *USSR in Construction.* 1932

22

Written in awkward German (partially preserved here), this collection of letters, published in English for the first time, relates to El Lissitzky's career as a designer of official propaganda magazines, books, and photo albums.[1] The first two letters were written to the German designer Jan Tschichold: one shortly after Lissitzky's last trip to Germany in 1930, another in 1932 when Lissitzky took on a new position as the designer of *USSR in Construction*. The rest of the correspondence is with Sophie Küppers, Lissitzky's wife of eight years, who moved to Moscow in 1927 from her native Germany. Written during Lissitzky's three-month stay in the Georgian health resort of Abastumani, the letters provide a narrative that is repeatedly structured around three themes: his illness, his and Küppers's relationship and personal life, and the circumstances of Lissitzky's work with mass media in general and on the photo album *Food Industry* in particular. The resulting entanglement of private and public affairs as they developed in the prewar period under Stalin explains why Lissitzky and his colleagues continued to serve the state regardless of the increasing pressure it placed upon their working techniques and artistic principles. Without question, the letters attest to Lissitzky's idealization and sincere endorsement of a Soviet utopia even at the time of its U-turn, but they also exhibit the destructive force of human dependence upon the mechanisms of survival. In Lissitzky's case, his tuberculosis and his wife and three children forced him to rely on influential people whose power was the equivalent of medical insurance and could guarantee him a monthly income. In the process of securing these necessities, Lissitzky demonstrated his skillful ability to negotiate on projects with, and obtain "rewards" from, high-ranking apparatchiks, as well as his admirable willingness to give up his privileges for the sake of his loyalty to Küppers. Because the propaganda publications paid generously, many artists regarded them as a highly competitive source of income rather than simply as a mechanism of coercion or as an opportunity to display one's loyalty to a ruthless regime. This economically based fact is rarely mentioned, because it places Soviet image makers surprisingly close (perhaps, too close) to their Western counterparts. Ironically, one reason why artists such as Lissitzky, Aleksandr Rodchenko, and Gustav Klutsis were sought after to produce much of the propaganda material was their unbeatable reputation in mass-media design, established during the first Five Year Plan.

Lissitzky's growing dependence on Küppers as his codesigner is evident from their correspondence. Because her voice is absent, we can only reconstruct some of her thinking (which is exceptionally stalwart) from other published sources or from Lissitzky's reactions. What is apparent from all the existing references is that by the mid-1930s Küppers had entered the Soviet mass-media establishment as both a designer and negotiator. She therefore fulfilled, not without Lissitzky's assistance, the dream of many Western intellectuals who wanted to participate in postrevolutionary activities in the Soviet Union. (Walter Benjamin's failed attempt to publish his writings in the Soviet press comes to mind.)

Equally important, these letters demonstrate that no matter how much the design principles of the 1920s were degraded in the late examples of Soviet propaganda material, they should not be viewed as precursors of socialist realist methodology. Instead, they are concluding examples of agitational objects, as they had been envisioned since the Constructivists refuted painting in the early 1920s. Lissitzky's concern with the external features of the *Food Industry* album—that is, with its mate-

El Lissitzky's Letters

with an Introduction and Annotations by Margarita Tupitsyn

1 Mikhail Prekhner: *El Lissitzky*. 1934. Gelatin silver print. RGALI, Moscow. Cat. 250

2 El Lissitzky: *Sophie Küppers in the House of Le Corbusier.* Paris. 1928. Gelatin silver print. Private Archive. Cat. 76

3 Max Alpert: *El Lissitzky, Sophie Küppers and Unidentified Person.* Skhodnia. Ca. 1932. Gelatin silver print. RGALI, Moscow. Cat. 246

rials rather than its content—reminds us of the connection between the early and late phases of the Constructivist-Productivist ideology of a cultural object.

Finally, the content of Lissitzky's letters, together with his career as outlined in this volume, opens up new angles for evaluating the history of the Soviet avant-garde. No matter how ruptured that history is on the level of formal search, it is connected by the avant-gardists' continuous attempts to bridge art, politics, and life. Along this path, the avant-garde practitioners were perpetually changing course, not only because of shifting political events but also because of the resistance of artists to accept a single mode of artistic production and distribution. With that aim, the Soviet avant-garde disjointed itself not only from socialist realism, which defended static artistic strategies and depended on the status quo, but, more important, from subsequent artistic manifestations of this century.

These letters are published with a kind permission of the Getty Research Institute for the History of Art and the Humanities.

1 Many of El Lissitzky's letters from this collection were first published in German in Sophie Lissitzky-Küppers and Jen Lissitzky, eds., *El Lissitzky, Proun und Wolkenbügel: Schriften, Briefe, Dokumente* (Dresden: VEB Verlag der Kunst, 1977), 118–76. The letters written from Abastumani were extensively edited not only in an attempt to improve Lissitzky's German but, more important, to suppress their content to some degree. Specifically, Küppers omitted various passages that criticized Soviet institutions or individuals as well as discussions and comments that were especially personal. Küppers's editing is clearly based on her understanding of what Soviet censors considered dissident opinions and frivolous comments in the late 1970s.

Moscow, Kropotkinski Lane 5a, k.4
August 22, 1930

Dear Tschichold,[2]

I received your letter with printed matter in Hanover before my departure, and now your letter with the advertising *phototek* prospectus.[3]

I can hardly be angry with you when you advertise a book of mine without my knowledge. I imagine the matter as follows: I don't want to take upon myself a book about photography and typo-photography *in the USSR;* that is something my wife can do much better and more calmly for this series, and I ask that you or Roh come to an understanding with her directly. After all, she has collected all the materials for the exhibitions in Essen and Stuttgart and is in contact with all of our people. I am prepared to do a small book about my own work, and if you wish to publish it, I'm certain that it will be very good. However, I want to have enough time to do it. I would put the material together in a particularly vivid way. I am also prepared to procure the typography image sequence myself. I have only been here a short time and have a great deal to put in order after a break of 4 months, but I think that I will have some time later for this matter.

Please convey my greetings to your wife; I forwarded her letter to my wife, who is in the country about 300 kilometers from Moscow.

I wish you all success,

Your El Lissitzky

P.S. Give my regards to Herr Roh.

2 Jan Tschichold (1902–74) was a German designer and typographer during the 1920s and the author of *Die Neue Typografie* (*1928*).
3 Refers to the book *Foto-Auge* (*Photo-Eye*), which Tschichold edited in 1929 with the German art historian Franz Roh (1890–1965). Lissitzky's *Self-Portrait* (Constructor) was chosen for the cover.

Skhodnia, October Line, October Street 10
September 29, 1932

Dear tschichold

One must be sick and in bed in order to get any time for private matters. It has been so long since I have been able to write to you. In the meantime, a whole series of messages has arrived from you, and they have made us very happy. Your new short pieces are very nice. In general, your books will have the same importance for our movement as the books Larisch and Jonston had before and you will add your individuality to it too. What prospects do you have for the new edition of the major work on new typography? What is happening with photomontage?

4 Franz Roh and Jan Tschichold: Invitation for *Foto-Auge*. 1929. RGALI, Moscow, f. 2361, op. 1, ed. khr. 3, ll. 3–5.

5 Page from *Izofront: Class Struggle on the Front of Visual Arts*. Publication of October Association. Moscow: IZOGIZ, 1931.
Larry Zeman and Howard Garfinkel, Productive Arts, Brooklyn Heights, Ohio. Cat. 144 (Photo: William Short)

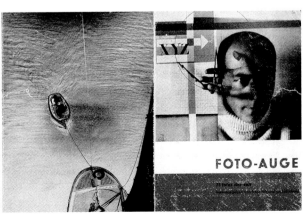

Yes, I can only now thank you after considerable delay for the wonderful compositions that you created from my work, for the magnificent layout, special printings, journals, and the entire cornucopia package. The quality of German book printing gives one pleasure, and we will be proud when we have reached this level.

What am I creating? I don't know whether I am creating anything, but like everyone else here, I am so swamped with work that when I am finished with one thing (and everything must be finished "express") I am blinded to what has been created. We fought against "art," upon whose altar we spit—and now we have it. We don't need any new art monasteries and art forest, but even in the storm in which we are flying one would like to be able to concentrate more, and if not 9 whole months then at least 7 for the execution of the creations.

I thought to take a rest from architecture and busy myself with something easier, quieter that could be done at home as a sort of respite. Then an order came from the government for a large photo book, "15 Years of October," to celebrate the Union.[4] And with that began a hounding and rushing that you lazy Europeans have no idea of. So, I thought that as a revenge for the "soul" I would take over the issue of the journal "USSR in Construction" that is dedicated to the opening of Dneprostroi.[5] We'll see what will become of that. And the result—about 400 montages in about 8 months. If anything of it should turn out to be of value, I will gladly send it to you. And that is only part of the many things that one is given to do every day.

We have been living for a year in the country near Moscow. We are all together here, all 3 boys with us. The big ones have gotten big, and the little one will also become big quickly, in socialist tempo. So, we know for whom we made the revolution and for whom we continue to expend our energies. Our Kurti[6] has already been elected standard bearer of his Pioneer division, and on 7 November he will carry it along with all of Moscow in Red Square. Hansi[7] also spent the summer in camp with the Pioneers and is strong and healthy again. Our Mutti is also creating interesting things: photofrescoes. At the same time she wants to be a shining housewife and model mother; to do all of that here, one must have superhuman powers. She certainly is very strong, but the engine must be oiled, and I hope I can send her to Munich during the winter for a cure.

Let us hear from you

I send you greetings singly and all together

Your *El Lissitzky*

6 Max Alpert: *El Lissitzky at the Dnieper Dam.* 1932. Gelatin silver print. Private Archive. Cat. 245

4 This was published as *SSSR stroit sotsialism* (*The USSR Is Building Socialism*; Moscow: IZOGIZ, 1933); twenty-five thousand copies were printed.
5 Refers to the monthly magazine *SSSR na stroike*, published between 1930 and 1941. It was distributed both locally and abroad and appeared in German, English, French, and Russian editions and later in Spanish. The first issue of *SSSR na stroike* (no. 10, 1932), designed by Lissitzky, was dedicated to the launching of the Dnieper Dam and hydroelectric station. Beginning in 1934, Lissitzky designed *SSSR na stroike* primarily in collaboration with Küppers.
6 Kurt was Küppers's son from a previous marriage.
7 Hans was Küppers's son from a previous marriage. Other names Lissitzky uses for him are "Hanni" and "Hani."

Tiflis
June 6, 1935

The dearest Mama,[8]
You know that my love and respect for you is, in accordance with the cosmic law of gravity, "directly proportional to the square of the distance," i.e., if the distance is   1 kilometer, my love is 2°
Thus when 2   "   "   "   4°
          " 3   "   "   "   18°
          " 4   "   "   "   256°
          " 5   "   "   "   65536°

………

3235 km   "   "   "
(Have Hanni figure it out …)?
In any case, stronger than the blazing heat of the sun.[9]
My dear old love, please excuse the fact that I'm always silly. I just arrived in Tiflis[10] (with memories of our honeymoon in the Caucasus). I'm sitting in "Inturist" and eating kebab. Terribly sharp. Better and more genuine than in Moscow in the Darial on Tverskaia.
I have 4 days and 4 nights behind me. Your mattress saved my bones—no comparison with the rental mattresses. So I was lying 4 + 4, almost without standing up; in this way I became almost like an Indian fakir. Have become completely silly and have noticed nothing around me you know—that is the main thing. It is now 9:30 in the evening, and I am incapable of doing anything. I'm happy to have a room (stinks). Maybe there will be hot water tomorrow (for a bath). I just washed the dirt from my head at the barber's. There is a place in the room where the bathtub should be, but there is only a folding screen. Tomorrow I will go to the post office; perhaps will find a love note from you. I hope that you have received my two telegrams. Hopefully, my accommodations will be settled tomorrow. The Caucasians are full of songs of praise and wonder for Abastuman.[11]

June 7, [1935]

Today I got my *putevka*.[12] They were very nice and told me that I would be in a sanitarium until July 1 and from July 1 to August 1 in a convalescent home, where I will have a room to myself, better food, etc. Everything for free and can stay longer. "Subtropiki"[13] bring dividends!
Tomorrow will travel early and should arrive on site in the evening. So, that will be the beginning. Today I walked about here and felt that I really am ill. In Moscow, I had the feeling that I was overworked and tense, and that if I rest a day, everything is finished. But for almost a week I have done nothing and just lie about. Actually, I lack for nothing (except Mutti) and I am so … exhausted. I am placing a great deal of hope on Abastuman, but one must go through that for a lengthier period, and how is that possible?
I want to send you this letter; it is already past 9, and I have to get up at 5 tomorrow. I will go the post office to … [letter is incomplete].

7 El Lissitzky: *Sophie Küppers.* Ca. 1930. Gelatin silver print. Sprengel Museum Hannover. Cat. 88

8 In these letters Lissitzky refers to Küppers as "Mama," "Mutti," "Mamasha," and "Muttilein."
9 As in most other instances, Lissitzky used mathematics here without making sense. The degree of his love is not directly proportional to the square of distance. His formulas randomly indicate that it was in fact much more.
10 A former name for Tbilisi, a capital of Georgia.
11 Abastumani is a famous health resort situated in the mountains of Georgia, 1,250 meters above sea level. In his letters Lissitzky used the spelling Abastuman.
12 A government-subsidized pass to sanitariums, summer camps, and vacation resorts.
13 *Sovetskie subtropiki* (*Soviet Subtropics;* Moscow, 1934) was designed by Lissitzky in collaboration with Küppers; twenty thousand copies were printed.

Abastuman
June 16, 1935

My dearest dear one, my Mutti,

Your first letter just arrived. I am so happy and grateful to you. Just the first lines, not even the content—the sound, the smell, everything brings you closer to me here as if you were sitting, you my old, the same girl—Mutti, wife, comrade, tovarich—sweetheart.

Now the *Album*.[14]

So, you are the tenth Jewess needed for a minyan in the synagogue. Just keep a cool head with that band because really, when I remember the excitement I had with them, I think, "How can a person be so stupid?"

I think that it should be published sooner, but for that to happen, everything must be prepared at the same time. That means that during the time you are working on the dummy, the paper, color, and everything else must already be in storage. Somorov[15] is needed for that. Now we must make sure that

1. The cover is absolutely to be executed in the manner we indicated. I wrote to you day before yesterday about it. I can't think of anything better for футляр [the album case] than bast. That would also be good for the binding, with transparent and opaque material. Put Abramsky to work on it until you have to do montage.[16] I spent too little time with the covers of the previous albums (Red Army, industrialization,[17] Subtropiki) and left it to the last, which was a mistake—first impressions are everything.

2. Take care that the principles used in constructing the dummy are not changed. For that reason, absolutely a nice strong *white* cardboard for the covers (on which the folded "prospectus" is pictured). Like the French model. That will be printed in blue on the outside (lithographically) and then in silver with the respective writing.

3. For the entr'acte, a paper whose color contrasts strongly with that of the main paper, the best would be a nice pearl gray. I have a particular fear of the synagogue concerning this point. The comrade who was supposed to procure the materials was one of the calmer ones. Please speak with him.

3. [*sic*] They should determine more quickly all pictorial elements—maps, diagrams, etc., that we need to consider and put in the contract. In general, your tactics must be to take all the demands that they swamp you with and give them even more,—thus you must force Litvak to work through the "entr'acte scenario" hard and fast.[18] And please write how things stand with the entr'acte's draftsman. But that you are running the entire project through with the "Koto" machine is just too impossible. Better on Bronnaia St. or at Listikov's (one of Hebebrandt's rooms) and Lestikov too. And then take at least 2 days off, completely off. Are you sure that you aren't ruining yourself?

My poor Mama, the hope of traveling to Germany has fallen through. Relationships are getting worse and worse—Hitler is whipping people up. German passports now have the notation "valid for all foreign travel *except* to Russia." Inturist [international tourist] activities are almost forbidden. And you, my poor thing, are the victim. But, I am not losing the certainty that we will all in the next few years come with you out of the country.

But that is exactly why you must now make nice clothes for yourself and procure

14 Refers to the album *Pishchevaia industria: Listy iz alboma* (*Food Industry: Pages from the Album*, Moscow: IZOGIZ, 1936); fifteen hundred copies were printed.
15 B. A. Somorov was a technical editor of *Food Industry*.
16 I. P. Abramsky was a consultant of *Food Industry*.
17 Here Lissitzky refers to his books *Raboche-krest'ianskaia krasnaia armia* (*Workers'-Peasants' Red Army*, Moscow: IZOGIZ, 1934) and *Industriia sotsializma* (*Industry of Socialism*, Moscow: Stroim, 1935).
18 A. M. Litvak wrote the texts that accompanied images in *Food Industry*.

everything that you can. Even a shabby bohemian and dirty lout like me understands that a person like you must wear the very finest in order to feel comfortable. Muttilein, don't have fears about money—our trust is still solvent. It is nice that you exchanged gifts with the Lestikovs (but don't have them make clothes anymore). Let Nusha off now for 2 weeks and then for 2 more in November-December. See that her sister stays and overnights. You must do everything you can to get free from the housework. Get (the devil) Maria Andreevna. Just no housework. I will try to get the house over here. I just have to get some things in order so I can look around. I am still in bed. In the morning my temperature is 36.5 and in the evening 37.5. On top of it, my stomach isn't right, but I sense that will go away. The weather is bad as well, cold and rainy today. I lie alone. Don't speak more than 50 words per day (you think it is healthy for me). There are strangers about. It is a hospital. The doctor knocks; powders will be sent. I'm under repair. I hope something will come of it for us.
Thanks and more thanks for your wonderful and brave letter.
I hug you and the children. Kiss Bubka[19] and Hani, and don't forget Kurti.
Your ever silly
Lis

Abastuman
July 2, 1935

My dear Mutti,
I received your letter of the 25th yesterday evening and just now the one dated the 21st. At night electrical current is insufficient and so we use miserable kerosene lamps. That is why I have decided to write early this morning. But in the morning, I got 3 attacks of sharp bowel pains. Felt terrible and had to lie in bed all day with a hot water bottle, and now things are better and your letter just arrived. First of all, don't get upset about my condition and my scribbling. My temperature is becoming more normal (today it was 36.9, for example). Only my bowels torture me sometimes, but it is nothing organic but rather the chow that I have to get used to. If we have to stay here somewhat longer, I think that it will perhaps be better for you as well. Nevertheless, this beginning not withstanding, I have a feeling that I will recover here. If you have the opportunity, go to *SSSR na stroike* [*USSR in Construction*], ask about my pay and speak with Ezhova[20] about whether they will come to Abastuman this summer as well. If that were the case, we would be well taken care of with you and Bubka as far as apartment and everything are concerned since the people consider them "dear Lord God." I wrote her a few lines with thanks for the accommodations here. I am just writing this to you in consideration of the best arrangement for us *together*. Then I can work again later for both periodicals. You are suffering in Moscow from the heat, you poor person, and here it is almost too cold with much rain. You now have no one, no friend, and that is very hard. We drew our circle of acquaintances too narrow and now we are suffering the consequences. Of course, we are such strange sorts, and similar people are not easy to find to have close contact with. Why don't you call Tretiakova,[21] she is dear. You wrote so nice about Bubka in your last letter that I saw him right in

19 Refers to Jen Lissitzky, Küppers and Lissitzky's son, born in 1930. In these letters, Lissitzky also calls him "Buba," "Bubi," and "Bubilein."
20 Elena Ezhova was one of the editors of *SSSR na stroike* and the wife of Nikolai Ezhov, who became head of the NKVD (the security police; later the KGB) in 1937.
21 Olga Tretiakova was the wife of the writer and critic Sergei Tretiakov, a close friend of Lissitzky's since 1926. Sergei Tretiakov was purged in 1937.

front of me as he smells the big flowers. I will now paint in a sketch book; have already planned something out. I do not have time to write Kurti. My lying down makes everything inconvenient, e.g., when I have finished a letter, it just lies there from morning to evening until the sister goes home after work and takes it with her to the post office. No one is available to get postcards or other things. I hope that I will soon be able to go out. My stomach is better today, but it is still cold. Please send me one of the photos where you are with Bubka. I had a few with me but can't find them now. Now about our holy album. First, congratulations and felicitations upon your success with Narkom [the People's Commissar].[22] I am so pleased about the evaluation of your work and that you don't have to change anything. That is the most unpleasant thing. As many kisses as many pages as you have finished. That is why I am pleased that you are choosing Leistikov; it will not be that much work for him (you have a technical assistant), but whenever something has to be drawn, Leistikov is very exact. Hopefully he is not too swamped with work. Greet him for me.

I am not completely clear why they didn't want to give you Somorov. If he is already engaged, explain the layout to him and ask him to send me a detailed letter with all questions and I will send him detailed instructions in answer. I am afraid, for example, that the first, the paper *without* Somorov, will not be of the necessary quality, etc. I read in the newspaper that our chief editor Ingulov[23] has received an important new post (as chief censor for the entire press). But I hope that he will remain the editor of the album? I will soon send you the little mock-up for the title; I have something that is a bit cleverer than what I had worked out before. Leistikov would be a good one to execute it. Then we also have to consider the ending for "Plenty";[24] and then it is finished. But, to this point, the instructions for maps, diagrams and graphics in general are not available. And then they will say: редакция проделала колоссальную работу!!! [the editorial office has done a colossal job!!!]. One simply has to force the people to give us everything that we should have from the editorial office over the course of 2 days in order to finish our work by 2 August. And now they are demanding it even earlier; that is why ask always for what they have not yet given. Please excuse me that I am writing this to you, but I am not doing it for you, but so that you can tell them from me that I am lying here and await these things in order to consider how best to execute them. But enough about the album, but it has been my experience with previous albums that when they are done they become a good milk cow from which others get the cream, and one has to be careful from the outset that we aren't the last ones attending its birth. Especially for this eventuality you must demand a cow (mechanical) as a premium. But we will certainly get two smoked herrings. Such a fish can then be put on the cover. (Eye with пищевая промышленность [food industry]) Or a cover like this кушайте на здоровье! пищевая промышленность [eat for your health! food industry] with a drawing.

Please excuse the silliness, but when one gets bored … I thank you for your love and wonderful letters. I kiss you for everything and be healthy and brave mama Your Lis

Give my regards and kisses to the boys.

Convey my regards to all.

8 El Lissitzky: Drawing from the artist's letter of July 2, 1935.

Abastuman

July 6, 1935

Dear Mutti,

I am feeling better; yesterday and today I got up and went for a walk and lay down in the woods on a deck chair—the air was wonderful with the scent of resin. Only in the afternoon is there a bit of fever. I now share my room with a comrade, a very nice Georgian, who is here for the 6th time. He is also convalescing; came here with a violent hemorrhage. He's already walking about. It is more cool than warm here—that would be so nice for you. My day goes like this—I get dressed at 10 and work until about 12. I hope to have 6 dummies for the title pages of the individual parts finished tomorrow. I think that it is now more interesting than was the first version. That will give the album, apart from the entr'actes, some small episodes. I have also thought about a possibly simple technical execution. At 3 o'clock we eat lunch, then there is a rest period until 5. Then I draw and write poetry for the picture book for Buba. You see how nice I have it here.

I am only sorry that now that I am forced to have so much free time, I cannot get anything really good to read but must be happy if any sort of printed paper falls into my hands. That is how the days and the time pass. It has already been a month that I have been separated from you. Every morning when I wake up I consider the unsolved moments in the Album. I spent all my time on the titles. I just got finished with the final one. My work method was that after several considerations, after many repetitions of the saying: кадры, кадры, кадры,… Потребление, потребление…Изобилие, изобилие… [cadres, cadres, cadres … Consumption, consumption … Plenty, plenty …] and then the same saying in German, since I now think in gibberish—half Russian, half German—I get into a state where I begin to go out of thought over to something I see, then I must have a pencil in order to scribble; but these scribblings are only partially thoughtlike, until finally *the* form that corresponds to the thing comes out like Bubka out of your little tummy. But with me it isn't always so unambiguous, complete, and filled with its own round life as our Bubi.

I will try to finish pasting and describing everything today and send it to you tomorrow as a registered letter.

July 9, 1935

It was delayed, but I just completed the maquettes and send them to you. I think that the explanations on the backs will make everything fairly clear to you. For the first section сырье [raw material] we will retain a folded page with ocean, river, shore, field just like the dummy that you have (this bound book). For all the other sections, included. In general, I am satisfied with how it came out. I think it is right for this type of album, this subject. I think that each corresponds to its section. The last section of "Plenty" is certainly a good conclusion with a star. When you glue on the star, you must place within it the cutout of Stalin. In the album you must use photos of the *Fiskultur* [sport] parade. There were some very nice ones in the 2 July *Isvestia* by Debabov.[25] I am a little concerned that one should not make a woodcut so that it looks like a wall calendar.

22 Refers to Anastas Ivanovich Mikoian, the commissar of the food industry.
23 S. B. Ingulov was a chief editor of *Food Industry*.
24 Lissitzky refers to the *Food Industry* album as "Plenty," thereby implying that its general theme was about a plenitude of food in the Soviet Union.
25 *Izvestia* is a daily Moscow newspaper. Dmitry Debabov (1901–49) was a Soviet photojournalist.

My dear, I want to send it off today and therefore an end. Kisses, many kisses to you and the dear boys. I hug you

Your Lis

Give my regards to people.

I am feeling better; I get up more. Don't have any heavy thoughts.

Abastuman

July 10, 1935

My dear, I received your telegram and letter in one day. Please don't make yourself upset on my account. The doctor was just here and examined me and said that the music in my lungs is 50% quieter. You can see what sorts of wonders Abastuman works. In any case, it has become easier for me to breathe, less sputum, and I've already been for a walk. It is too bad that it rained here yesterday and today so that I could not develop my walk further. That is why I still can't tell you anything about this region. In any case, September is supposed to be the nicest season, and then you will certainly be here. Then there are supposed to be very nice fruits. Now there is nothing, just a few green onions, radishes, lettuce, and that only rarely. Primitive agriculture in general.

That you are all alone and without any human contact makes me very sad. What sort of stupid life have we ordered up. What you write about Bubi, that he is strong and full of life is a great joy and happiness. Father also wrote, and he is absolutely enchanted by the little one. That Hans convalesces best at home is no surprise. That Kurt is to go to Rabfak[26] also makes me very happy. He should certainly have a *putevka*. I am now concerned that without Nusha things will be even harder for you. I understood that aside from the new help, that Nusha's sister from Chowrins [Khovrino][27] would also be with us. How is it with that? But by the time I get an answer, the month will be over. This is crazy with the post, apart from the fact that it is so far away. The post arrives now in 5 days, now in eight. And I'm never sure that it doesn't get lost. I am especially fearful about the registered letter that contained the mock-ups for the titles.

Dear, everything that you write about your work on the album and your fears and worries are baseless. I know how everything that you do turns out well. I would have said that you are too conscientious, at least in comparison to me—but, I'm being educated to be a real bolshevik by the dear people for whom I work. So, don't break your head so much. We have already created enough that is extraordinary for this album. Now we need only take care that it is executed as we have directed. That the wind has already gone out of them with regard to the material is the very worst. But, one has to put an end to it—what isn't there, isn't there, and an end must be put to it. I know the story: it is supposed to be finished on 20 July—but it won't be "finished" by 20 July 1937 either. Period. Nothing is expected anymore. To date I still don't know whether Samorov will be in charge of the printing? And when it is possible for me to get the dummy. The assistant could do it. Makes no difference the size. I ask that you make sure everything is delivered by the *beginning* of August in such a way that in every section a few pages are not yet filled. That will force them to fill them with something. Otherwise you will never be finished. As far as the entr'actes are concerned: the idea of the "Song of

26 A department for a special workers' education in various educational institutions.
27 A suburb of Moscow, now one of its districts.

the Children" is magnificent, and I am sure that you will succeed best of all with it. You can include beautiful drawings from the children's books (there were children's books at Mrs. Schmidt). Try to get photos from the *Izvestiia* photographer. For the other entr'actes one can find other completed drawings. I would recommend that you look through a year of the periodical Советское Искусство [*Soviet Art*]. Somorov can get this for you and find a few things that are suitable for the individual booklets (Kolkhoz [collective farm], etc.). From the very beginning, I thought that when they blab about "drawings, art" that when it came down to it, there would be no art. That means, "Au, Abramski, Crocodile, where are you?" Furthermore, I am very uneasy about the 1,000 ruble premium. If that is not there already, I will write a letter to Tal. With the cover of the album it is so. I wrongly wrote you to glue plastic with celluloid. There is *opaque celluloid* in different colors and styles. This can be easily glued with transparent celluloid. But you are right: the people are lazy, and one takes work. I gave them the address of a man who is supposed to do experiments with plastic on cardboard. Then one should try to get nitrocellulose lacquer. I'm sure nothing has been done. I also tried to have an experiment done to make a binding out of клеенка [plastic]. And then what is with the bast protective carton?

Muttilein, dearest, excuse me, the wild man, who hits you over the head with so many assignments. I do it for the last time only to learn what is to be expected when we want to finish the matter. Then you will also depart and everything that they want to know can only be done by post, or Litvak can come here himself. They have brought my health to the point that today I don't know when I will return to Moscow. I think that I have actually made a new discovery (after Koch) that this type of worker is the tuberculosis bacillus that infects us, and I now have a deathly fear that you will be infected by them and then we are finished. And the unfinished bast on protective cover for the album will be our coffin. Please tell them that and that they should have sympathy with us.

Now I just hope that Lestikov will help us over the matter and then one should push. Only take care—better more salt and pepper than none.

An end with the album.

So, father wrote to say that guests are coming and that he is already too old and deaf to busy himself with them, and I am not there and you are busy too. Can't help. Don't let yourself be bound if you can't find a real consent with the people. Please accept my point of view—relationship as duty is a painful prejudice for which one must use bedbug powder. And perhaps they are good people. Now I wish you an easy end to the work and hope that you can come here to recover as soon as possible. Kiss our red boys. Tell Bubi that I really will have the picture book finished for him soon.

I thank you for your loving letters and kiss you all over; you know a l l o v e r. Your Lis

P.S. I had such a dream, in which you fled from me to America, but I caught up with you in flight and you gave me a kiss.

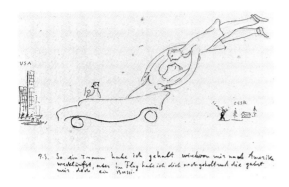

P.S. So ein Traum habe ich gehalt wiederum mir nach Amerika wiederlänft, aber im Flug habe ich dich nach geholt und die gabst mir doch ein Bussi.

9 El Lissitzky: Drawing from the artist's letter of July 10, 1935.

28 Lissitzky went to Gurzuf, a town in Crimea, after he finished the design of *Raboche-krest'ianskaia krasnaia armiia.*

Abastuman
July 16, 1935

My dear little Mutti,

I had just begun to quiet myself about the post, and then your letter arrived. I don't know where to begin—so much is there at once. First, I congratulate you about your success with Narkom. I am very happy that you got yourself into the highest atmosphere; you probably have had the same impression, namely that there they think more simply and directly and that there is more agreement with our views than with the little people with whom one is forced to prepare work. Right that you want to associate with Ingulov. So, on with the album. And I congratulate you that young (of course handsome) men find you young and beautiful. You see, when I tell you repeatedly that you look like a *girl* you never believe me (because I am old). Yes, my love, you just need to be calm, and then you don't look like the mother of 3 bandits, but like Sopherl. I am happy that even handsome young men say this to you. But, that you catch cold in the summer and have the flu is not nice at all. That is most certainly the result of overwork and the wide fluctuations in the weather. As for me, things are considerably better. I get up, take a little walk, and lie in the woods next to the sanitarium where the scent of pine resin is strong. As for Abastuman, I think that I've found the right place. Because what else is Crimea, Yalta; the summer is *hot,* only good in the spring and autumn. But after Gurzuf's experience,[28] I see that the air here is better for me. Borovoe is also only good for a few months because of быт [everyday routine]; it is much more primitive than here and the trip is longer. What is there here? First, I don't feel the altitude; my heart is pretty much in order. Then there is an observatory here, and a worker from there told me that they have 220 completely clear days and nights for observations. That says a great deal for the place. Then again there is never oppressive heat. And the main thing is the number of positive cases. They say here that if you don't croak immediately upon arrival, you will certainly be healed. The problem is—time and we will just have to see. In any case, it is important to me that here you can recuperate well yourself, and nearby you can take baths as needed. The only negative thing is connections to Moscow; but there the fault is the USSR, which comprises a sixth of the world. I write in such detail because you think I made a mistake and that you didn't make certain that I consulted with the doctor. Please don't think about it any more, love. Now back to the album according to the saying "Revenont aux nous moutonts" (sure everything written wrong). The main thing is that it is pleasing, what you have made, and that the errors are of an editorial sort. The positive thing is Narkom (don't forget that Mikoian is not an average Narkom but rather a member of the Politburo) and therefore the content is somewhat secure, politically as well. I don't think that in reality radical changes will result because the material is *exhausted*. I also don't think that they will now succeed in making many new pictures. What is to be added as sections or the realization of what exists is the most important to me; the entire structure must not be destroyed. But, the *main thing* is that it is not our fault, and we don't want to finish our thing later than the 2nd (say the 10th) of August. That is why a final layout of the album must be done immediately with who, how, what. And then they can set the photos that are not yet available into the frames themselves. We must indicate everything else so that everything else follows in writing Moscow-Abastuman at the latest after 10 August. When does Lestikov want to go away?

My only fear now is that this work will delay you crazy and long; then I'll have to come to Moscow to chase you away and finish it. Your idea for the melody with the notes is very good; I would have done it so: a photo on the background printed in a light color (masses at the *Fiskultur* parade or such) and above it the notes so that there is a photo in each point. Or make a folded "tongue" out of several sheets like the panoramas. In any case, the idea is very good. Take the notes from the Internationale. I *definitely* want them to send me the new plan for the book as an index (without a listing of details) but with final title designation for the book, the sections, etc., so that I can compose the most important inscriptions. Finished with the book. In the garden, are things growing yet, and the roses, are they blooming yet? And you want to get a dog; the boys will have a good time. How is Kurti; doesn't seem too bad? Someone is coming on the free day. Rosa Naumovna has to go to Gagri[29] or another spa; there she will certainly find her happiness, but it is too bad that it goes so with Boria. The dear woman gnawed a piece of his heart; she certainly has a good appetite for all her fear of getting fat. Give my regards to them. Bubka and Ganka are well Thank God, what should he lack with such a mother, except perhaps bird milk. O Mamascha, Mamascha, when will we get our bird milk. Stay healthy and always as young as you are. Kiss our children and finish up and come to me again, if I may make that request.

I hug you tight

Your silly-ist Lis

Abastuman

July 20, 1935

Дом отдыха лечкомиссии

[Vacation Resort of the Cure Committee]

Dear Muttilein,

I hope that you received my telegram with the new address, by which you can see that I have moved. A few days ago they told me completely unexpectedly that I had to move. I was very glad and did it immediately. So I am presently not in a hospital, but among healthy people. It is a sort of small park through which runs a little stream and surrounded by 3 buildings.

1—where the restaurant and social rooms are (previously the summer residence of the crown prince).

2—a house where most of the women are with their children (there are 60 guests, of which 24 are children). And

3—a 2-story stone building, the crown prince's winter house is set apart, and there I share a fairly large room with a comrade (an old bolshevik).

It is more civilized than the sanitarium except that all the magnificence was stolen by the Turks who occupied the region during the civil war. Even today one can find peasants in the neighboring mountain villages who have pianos as chests for their personal belongings, and they sleep on top of them—the entire musical part has been ripped out. Here I have a wash stand (умывальник [a washer]) in the room

29 A town in Georgia.

and I can wash myself in the morning (you're laughing!). The quantity of the food is the same, but tastier and served in a more civilized way. More form. I feel psychologically better and have begun to walk, and I think that is better for me, too. On the whole, I think I need active sorts of regions. At the sanitarium, I was always supposed to be lying under several blankets. Here I only lie down after lunch from 3:30 to 5:30, a half an hour completely naked and then in pajamas without a blanket, and I feel how I air out. In the morning, I go into a gorge (climb), take the travel rug, air pillow, and book and evenings I take a walk again. It is beautiful here, except that one must always climb.

So, I have described my life to you in detail. Now my main concern is that you finish more quickly and come here. My neighbor is supposed to leave in mid-August, and it would be wonderful if you could come then. It is my hope that we could keep the room. The mattress that you bought for me is wrapped up in the corner for Bubka. Oh, how wonderful it would be. This damned album! I expect to get another letter from you in the next few days and hear how all the new radical changes affect your plans.

Please begin to prepare for the trip; order clothes (the Chinese silk, etc.) just so that it doesn't hold you up later. I will send this letter off like this because I think that a letter from you will arrive tomorrow, and then I will write more. I am sending a little picture book for Bubka personally by registered letter. Kiss the 3 bandits. And they should kiss you for me. And I squeeze your paw firmly.

Мой миленький товарищ Софи твой домашний дурак Лис
[My dearest comrade Sophie, your domesticated fool, Lis]

Abastuman
July 22, 1935

My dear Muttilein,

Your letter of the 13th is very sad and heavy-hearted. My dear Sophie, it is so hard for you to bear everything that burdens you alone and all the things that you load upon yourself. You write that "every day you experience new blows" and "get loaded with 'nice' surprises." Why don't you write exactly what these are? I cudgel my brain trying to imagine what these new things might be. My dear human being, if it is serious, I have a right to know what it is. If it is dirt, then all you have to do is spit on it. It is also sad that the visits on the outing days are, on the one hand pleasant, but on the other make you upset and sad in different ways. And the foreign letters! But Mutti, Mutti, one cannot say such things. Everything is breaking in me. We aren't so old and we aren't at the ends of our lives that we should think such things. When things get difficult for the heart, one says certain things. But then the heart beats more strongly again and life continues upward. You are a strong person, my good, beautiful Mutti, and certainly things are looking up in our country, and we can always find work that is interesting, and now all you have to do is come here to recover. And it will still be nice. Things will be wonderful again. We cannot wait forever for the album, or they must make the entire thing nice from the beginning. In the meantime we will recover, and when we return we will start from the beginning. They will certainly pay for the trip.

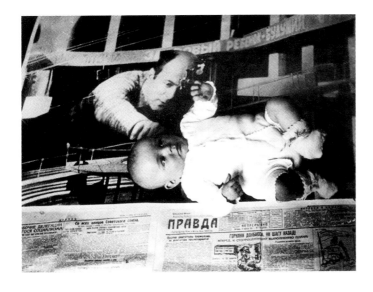

10 El Lissitzky:
Untitled (Jen Lissitzky super-imposed on a photograph of El Lissitzky working on a stage design of *I Want a Child*). 1930. Gelatin silver print. Private Collection. Cat. 95

11 Anonymous:
El Lissitzky and Jen Lissitzky. Ca. 1931. Gelatin silver print. RGALI, Moscow. Cat. 244

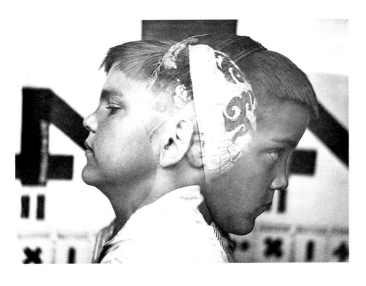

12 El Lissitzky:
Birth Announcement for Jen Lissitzky. 1930. Gelatin silver print. Collection of Robert Shapazian, Los Angeles. Cat. 93

13 El Lissitzky: *Jen Lissitzky.* Ca. 1931. Photomontage. Private Archive. Cat. 98

14 El Lissitsky: *Kurt and Hans Küppers.* 1930. Gelatin silver print. Barry Friedman Ltd. New York. Cat. 91

15 El Lissitzky:
Kurt and Hans Küppers. 1930. Gelatin silver print. Private Archive. Cat. 90

Naturally with Bubka—I don't want to be without the little fellow for too long. If it really becomes impossible (which I can hardly believe), then I will return home. Understand me right: This has nothing to do with me, it is not that I need you as my "bed-nanny" for my pleasure. I cannot imagine that I will live here long-term only for myself and recover and you without vacation, without a free hour. Particularly now that we can afford things and when the boys are big. One can surely let the mother's breast alone a bit (they are certainly well cared for, perhaps better than I am here at the sanitarium) and the littlest one is already so big that he can be brought along. Please understand me, Sophie: I am here with a sick conscience because I am your eternal exploiter. Well yes, it will be very nice for me when you are here with Buba (perhaps it will also be good for you to be here with me for a time). But the first thing is that you must get out of the vise in which you are trapped. I know that I'm an idiot and don't understand what you have to do for yourself.

Now something about money—you have again misunderstood when I asked about our purchases as if it meant that you have to save. To the contrary, we earned so much this year that saving is the last thing we need to do. And during that period, I used very little. Therefore, love, love, I ask you not to worry about money, and in particular, buy whatever you need. So, please, no money worries. Now, how am I? From my previous letter you will see that I am already no longer at the sanitarium. This house is the best in Abastuman and is only for high Party and government functionaries. They are not responsible for the fact that we with our European ways have expectations of a different level, and the main thing, of necessities and possibilities of which one *has a sense* that with our material situation are completely within reach. In any case, I think that my dislike of sanitariums is right because I immediately began to feel different here. My intestines are better, also my temperature and expectoration is less. Only my cough continues to bother me. My breathing is better, so that I can even walk in steep places. All in all, the climate has a strong effect. I sometimes visit the invalids with whom I was together in the sanitarium and see how enervated they are, so depressed they are and without movement. They sit almost the entire day in their room and infect each other with bad moods and irritability against the medical personnel. I am happy that I am no longer there. Please don't worry about me. I will be all right; about the future, I cannot make plans (don't be angry) because there are several possibilities, and if one has to decide, it will actually only be to choose.

I am so happy that Bubi is growing so well and is your happiness. Yesterday, I finally sent him the picture book (please sew it together). I drew it in bed while I was still at the sanitarium. I can't do anything in peace anymore. When I remember how I lay in bed in Switzerland and everything bubbled up in me, made Proun sketches, wrote, created advertisements for Pelikan, and made the *Ism*[30] book, my present life seems somehow sickly and desiccated. And yet I have the feeling that I could still accomplish different things. Now the execution of the new building plan is setting crazy demands. I'm sure they will soon prepare for the 1937 Paris World Exhibition ("Art and Technology").[31]

If only I weren't poisoned. The new doctor asked me whether I hadn't had syphilis and my tuberculosis was a result of that. How do you like that one? We must make certain that our boys are strong and that my "little woman" stays healthy and

30 Pelikan was an office-supply firm in Hanover, Germany; Lissitzky's advertisements for the firm, done in 1924, became famous. He designed *Die Kunstismen. Les Ismes de l'Art. The Isms of Art* with Hans Arp in 1925.
31 In June 1936 Lissitzky was asked to lead a team of artists that would design the interior of the Soviet pavilion for the Paris World's Fair. Organized around the theme "Art and Technology in Contemporary Life" the Soviet pavilion was to demonstrate to the capitalist world the accomplishments of the socialist system. On this and other of Lissitzky's design contributions to Soviet pavilions in the late 1930s, see my *Glaube, Hoffnung-Anpassung: Sowjetische Bilder, 1928–1945* (Essen: Folkwang Museum, 1995), 156–59.

brave. Then we will be able to get some things accomplished. Kiss all three boys, and they should kiss you and not bring you any worries.

I hug you and all my kisses only for you.

Your Lis

Abastuman

July 31, 1935

Dear Mutti,

These past few days I have survived all sorts of things. An instinctive feeling tortured me because I didn't get any news from you. Then I sent the telegram in the morning and in the evening your letter arrived that surpassed my worst projections. You hid Bubi's illness from me, and even more, as I sense reading between the lines. I immediately decided to come home and sent off the second telegram. And just now your answer to my first telegram arrived. It was a great joy that everything is healthy and that you are coming with Bubi and that Gans is going to grandmother. But I am unsure whether this actually corresponds to reality. You are correct that correspondence at such long distance tends to abstraction. Particularly because something new rains down upon you every day, and here one day is like the next. I can well imagine that my letters are not to the point, because when I write I imagine one thing, and by the time it arrives things are completely different.

I am writing you this quickly at the post office because a letter should go off quickly. What has happened to Bubilein—we had him inoculated against scarlet fever and diphtheria. Or did the shot contain water? Does he really have no complications or ill consequences? Poor Mutti, what you have not had to contend with in one year with the children; you are a heroic person. What is going on with Kurt there? At 18 he is already an independent person. We will always do for him what we consider useful, but if he wants to get his own life in order, then he should take the responsibility for it upon himself and leave us alone with his troubles. I will write you tomorrow in greater detail.

Love, see that you finish the album quickly, if possible, so that you can get out of Moscow. I hope that it will do you good, and just the prospect of quieting you here holds me here. Otherwise, I would have wanted to come to you tomorrow so that I might unburden and help you.

Kiss our boys. I so much want to see миленький [dearest] Buba and hug you and thank you for all the effort and torment that you have had to bear, on my account as well. I kiss you deeply.

Your Lis

Abastuman
August 1, 1935

Dear dear Mutti,

For the past few days there was a real storm on the sea so that it rolled until finally the sun reappeared. Your letter with the news of Buba's illness, not so much this news but the entire coloration of the letter, was like a thrust into my heart, and the difficulties that I have left you to deal with alone stood before me like an accusation. I actually wanted to leave here and come to you without sending a telegram. But I had already sent you a telegram before the letter came, and I was expecting an answer. The day I got your letter, the *putevka* arrived for the month of August, again free of charge. Then in one day I got 2 telegrams from you in answer to my two and then your letters one right after another, the last one the best that you have written me in years. How I thank you for everything, my love. The sun, you my sun, stand high in the heavens and give everyone happiness. But to the point (so that you don't laugh at me).

1. The album—it would be best to liquidate it. In order to complete it the way one wants to do it oneself, one has to be in Moscow the whole time, and I absolutely don't want that for you. Therefore, only the entire conception is ours, and the execution should be done by whoever is there. But when I write this, I don't know the situation and by the time the letter arrives, everything is changed again. That is why I am telegraphing now, and I ask that you always telegraph me because then one can be clear about the actual situation. Please don't be worried about the money; we're not yet in a position where we must sell our souls to the devil. We have enough stored up, and you stop counting the expenses. I know your criteria, and I will continue to earn what is needed along with you. Therefore:

2. Please get your wardrobe together as soon as possible. You know that I find you most beautiful without all the fig leafs, but I want to see you well dressed like you always were. I want to be proud of you, your taste. And I particularly want that you feel good in a new dress. Again—we now have money, and please don't be sparing. Just be sure that it doesn't hold you up. You may not leave later than the 25th of this month.

3. The trip—I think that your plan to come via Sevastopol-Batumi is perhaps a bit more complicated than direct via Tiflis. There is now supposed to be a sleeper through to Tiflis. The trip through Batumi also takes longer. Perhaps you could return via Batumi. From here there is a road over a pass on which there is no bus traffic, only private automobiles. It takes 4 hours to Kutaisi (from there it is not far to Sukhumi and Batumi), then you don't need an indirect route via Tiflis. So, when they are helping you with a ticket for the sleeper or class direct to Tiflis, it would be easier than with changes, in which case one always has to buy new tickets.

4. Buba—Naturally you must bring him here; he is already a big fellow. Here there are a lot of little children, and he will be able to play with them all day. If you have to go to a health resort for 2 weeks, he can stay with me; I have nothing to do and can well take care of him. I think it will be good for all 3 of us if we can be alone with the little one. Once I am back at work in Moscow, I will see so little of the child, and soon the little one will become a boy, etc.

5. Doctor—you must ascertain what sort of a cure is the right one for you. The main thing is to get the right diagnosis. For example, Tskhaltubo is supposed to do wonders with its radioactive baths, but they say that if one's kidneys are not in order that one may not take them. I will make inquiries, and you go to a good doctor who can tell you what isn't in order and what is best for you. Please do it right away. And then the main thing—don't give yourself the assignment of completing everything before you leave. One must flee from Moscow as from a prison—let everything lie. You will see that it is not at all dangerous. Good that Ruva[32] and Lelia will be living at our place. Will leave money for them so no concerns about the house. And to the devil with everything else. You must be here with Buba by 1 September at the latest. With Hani I understand that if he's not going to Germany, then to Kurti's friend. So, that's in order, too. Kurti should also have a vacation with a trip?

6. The house—just wrote to Alabian,[33] but regardless, don't let it be a point of delay. We will figure something out for the winter. To summarize—to the devil with the album; to the devil with all "important" and "unimportant" matters. Get your wardrobe together, pack the suitcases, take the little cavalier under your arm—and departure! Mutti, the hours, days, and years are beginning to slip away ever faster; and the dumbest thing is when one starts to look back. That is why we want to harness our strength and make tomorrow today. I expect you on 1 September. In the next letter I will write you in detail about the trip and what to bring, etc. My condition is generally better. On the whole, with my "colossal" constitution, as you know, my organism is tough enough that I'm not so easy to defeat. I feel stronger; only my cough is sometimes worse, sometimes better, but less in any case. Temperature also better. I write this so that you need not worry about me. Life is monotonous here. The people are always changing; sometimes they have only a month. There are many children with their mothers. I'm living with a fellow who reminds me a little of Aunt Nina, but more positive. The people here are so isolated. A sick Gruzinian [Georgian] writer is also living in Abastuman, with whom I occasionally get together; seems like a good fellow, but one doesn't come into real contact with people.

I will try to get stronger this month so that I can receive you in such a way as will make you happy and take you on my arm and that you can have peace so that you become strong again. I will try to draw the promised picture book for you, but I am afraid to give my fantasies full reign because then a sturdy castle would be necessary to contain this little picture.

So, my dear Mami, I will wait and wait.

I live with the taste of your skin which I have kissed, which I kiss, and which I will kiss until I draw my last breath.

So, kiss our Bubushka and the children

Your silly Lis

32 Ruvim Lissitzky was El Lissitzky's brother.
33 Probably the architect Karo Alabian, who graduated from the VKhUTEMAS architecture department in 1929 and became first secretary of the Union of Soviet Architects in 1933.

Abastuman
August 10, 1935

Dear Mutti,

I received your letter of 31 July in which you write about the telegram about my trip back to Moscow. The post is so stupid and like a card game mixes up all events. In any case, I now see that you have had more than enough on your hands with all 3 boys.

What all has Kurti had to go through? And where should he go to from Moscow? O, my poor thing.

And on top of it, the weather where you are is still so bad, and I can imagine the mud on our street. I await news from you about Hani's departure. You have labored so hard that you need at least a half year's vacation.

What am I to do with you? Please take 3 to 4 thousand rubles with you. For that you must certainly use the account of the Construction exhibition.[34] The best thing would be to have them issue a portion (2000) as credit directly at the bank (one can draw on it in any city). You will get 2 slips of paper. Place each in a different place. If one is stolen, they can't get anything without the other. Have 1000 rubles transferred to my address and take the other 1000 with you. Then you must leave enough with someone in Moscow to take care of household expenses and the boys for about a month and a half. Just don't worry about money; we will earn when we get back.

I read in the newspaper that a new building for the German school (Hani) has been finished in the Kropotkinskaia at the place where our house (by the architects) is to be built. Then I read that the book about "Hubert" was just published in *Ogonek*.[35] Try to get a copy. Also bring a "Subtropiki"—people here know it and praise it. That can be your business card.

For about a week, the weather here has been changeable—cool and with occasional rain, but the sun shines every so often. Frolov, my roommate, has left, and he promised to call you in Moscow.

I'm working on a picture book for you—my dear God, I'm afraid what sort of trouble I will get into with you for it. Highly heretical. I think I will call it "The Quintessence of Nonsense" in 3 parts, with a dedication, prologue, and epilogue. Soon we will find out where we can live together; whether in a *Dom Otdykha* [vacation home] or here in a *gostinitsa* [hotel].

And each day I wait for you and wait. And now I kiss you and the little boy and the big ones.

Hug you,
Your Lis

34 Lissitzky was head of the Construction Exhibition from 1931 on.
35 *Ogonek* was a major illustrated magazine published in Moscow.

Abastuman

August 29, 1935

My dear Mutti,

Your letter dated 18 August just arrived. You will probably read my letter on about 6 September—almost 20 days from letter to answer. That is why it is so hard. Your previous letter of 12 August was the most beautiful you have written me and this one is so hard. I try to understand everything and imagine. You have had an extraordinarily difficult summer with the children, with work, with everything, and on top of that (as always) no help from me—and worries, too. Nothing allows you to get away, and I fear that 15 September might not work out as well. When I read your letter I wanted to come home immediately, but then I had the thought that then you would never get away. You must not think that I am bored waiting for you—I wait and wait for you not for my amusement but so that you may recuperate sooner, and if it becomes necessary for me to go home so that you may come here, I will certainly do it.

Mutti dear, it is always hard for me when I have to make clear to you things that I always thought were settled between us.

I know that when everything is so hard for you that you begin to think about various things you would never believe in a calmer situation.

There are in your letters such bitter lines about Ezhova. You write, "you always find me ridiculous and jealous on this point." My dear Sophie, you I have found to be the least ridiculous about any point. I can only be proud of your jealousy because it is supposed to be a proof of love. But if you believe anything from me, believe what I say to you: From the moment we met, I cannot recall a single time when a woman was as intellectually interesting to me as you or when any conversation with her placed her above you. There has not been a single time when a woman attracted me erotically. And I have been long periods without you. I sit here and let our 12 years go by me and I cannot remember that I have ever been untrue to you, not only physically but in my thoughts as well. And this is not because I am some sort of holy man, but rather because, put primitively, you fill me and satisfy completely all my human desires. And this with my views that if another woman really had attracted me, I would not have considered it a sin. I just would never have done anything without your knowledge. I am not blind to other women's positive characteristics. I can see that Mrs. X has a nicer nose than you have—but I love yours and on the whole you are more beautiful to me than all others. I think that when you make the biggest reproaches and torture me and yourself the most, that deep down you don't believe what you are saying. Because then you wouldn't trust me, and you wouldn't have lived with me for 12 years. That is why this story that you are writing is so sad because of you. I can't imagine what Litvak blabbered about. I met the woman 3 to 5 times and talked with her always in the company of several people. I also don't know where she recommends me everywhere as a special favorite. When did I become M'sieur Pompadour. Appears to be my fault somehow if I have brought you to such a state, but that it is the talk of the town is, I think, a bit exaggerated. I think it would be better for me to decline working on *USSR in Construction* because it would always make you uncomfortable. But let us make an agreement, my dear love, that if you notice something that doesn't seem right to you that you tell me calmly and immediately and that we make clean with it. I know that you can't help it that you have such moments, and I, I can't help it that your mistrust of me makes me so upset. Because I love you, and it insults me and particularly because by putting yourself on the same level as some other woman you do to yourself what I never do in my thoughts, putting you on the same level with someone else. Mutti, believe, believe me. Can you find any way that I have ever lied to you?

Let us have done with this.

You seem to be generally satisfied with the work. You have done it from the beginning completely by yourself. I am glad that Lestikov is doing something on the thing. It is a shame that I have no idea how the album looks now, but I will find patience. It is perhaps a good thing that you want to fly, if only it is a good airplane and pilot. I don't know how it can be arranged with us. Here the Dom Otdykha will be open until the end of September, so if you come on the 20th, little time will remain and then I think it will turn cold, which it is now already in the evening and morning. My *putevka* will run out in a few days. Tomorrow I am supposed to get word from Alpert[36] in Tiflis; perhaps I must go to Tiflis. I think that perhaps I should see about staying here another half month and then pick you up in Tiflis. And then we should find an accommodation on the coast somewhere between Batumi and Sukhumi. There it will be warm, ocean for you and Buba and fruit harvest (Subtropiki). I want to do the nicest thing for you, but you chose a bungler for a husband, my poor wife, good for only one thing—skirt chasing. It seems to be our fate that things are still up in the air with the boys! Perhaps everything will work out for the best at the last moment.

I beseech the heavens that the 15th will really stay the 15th.

I hope that when this letter arrives you will have an easier moment and that my true kiss doesn't insult you and that you will give me a nice little kiss as well.

I kiss our Buba and he should calm you when things are hard for you.

Kiss and greet the big boys for me.

I hug you

Your Lis

P.S. I received your telegram of Ludmila's death. Poor woman. Was it the neck? It is surely a blow for her helpless husband and for Lelia. It is surely not good if she is completely dependent on Lisa's company. I just received a telegraphic transfer at the post office of 1000 rubles for the album. Thank you. That is for you.

36 Max Alpert (1899–1980), a Soviet photo-journalist, took pictures for various issues of *USSR in Construction* and *At the Construction of MTS and Sovkhozy.*

Tiflis

September 3, 1935

ул. Руставели Гостиница Ориант

[Rustaveli Street, Hotel Oriant]

Dear, dear Muttilein,

I have left Abastuman. My *putevka* ran out, and I would have had to turn to Ezhova, and I didn't want to do that anymore (they themselves aren't coming to the Caucasus), and I particularly didn't want to because of your last letters. I decided to go to Tiflis, not just in connection with work, but also to be able to correspond with you more easily and clarify whether you are coming, to pick you up here and maybe better go to the sea or to a spa that the doctor will prescribe, or if everything is out of the question, which I dare not imagine, to go home immediately. I cannot leave you so long alone with all your sorrows. My health is such that I can breathe more easily, produce less sputum, and the temperature is more normal. I think that I can return to Moscow.

Our problem is the apartment. I telegraphed you that your news concerning exhibition work with Mikoian I would gladly accept in case of the apartment. I am prepared to commit myself to everything that I can. I think that you would also like this better because then you can go on working together with people whom you know and who know you.

Вut Я думаю и думаю [I think and think] (do you remember Bubushka) that you first come to recuperate.

I say this to you—I am prepared to come to you any time, but you don't need me now, but recuperation; that is clear from every line in your letter. For that I have the following alternative. Yesterday Alpert and I visited Beria;[37] he received us very cordially and suggested I should also make an album for Georgia's jubilee. He remembered that I was the artist who was at Abastuman (also because of Subtropiki) and stated, "If you do a good job for us, we will put you up in Abastuman for a year." That is important, not just because of Abastuman, but also in connection with a longer stay in the South. I write this to show you that we are independent of the Protection that is unsympathetic to you, and we can get it ourselves here.[38] You know that I always try to have many alternatives—there is one here too. I telegraphed you and hope to have an answer by tomorrow at the latest. At present I am helping to set up USSR N° plan in connection with the procurement of the materials for the album.[39] I have no absolute commitments, but I do not want to let N° for the periodical drop completely, insofar as I have come in contact with the leading people locally. It is only an issue of the time that I dedicate to the matter here, 5 days or a month. So, I await your answer. Here I have better lodgings (a bathroom with a toilet fit for humans), my digestion is better, and I eat wonderful fruit every day. What I would only give to have you here already. Now comes the beautiful season when it will be less hot and fruit harvest as well. I think that the sea will be better for you and Buba than 1300 m. I hope that our letters reach us faster and make understanding easier.

I sent an exposition about the work to Lazlo. There I didn't develop any creative ideas but rather an organizational plan for the construction of model work. What you write me about Brosterman, he is simply shameless. In Komsomolskaia

37 Lavrenty Beriia replaced Ezhov as a head of the NKVD in 1938.
38 At the time of this comment Lissitzky did not yet know that Ezhov would become a head of NKVD and that his wife would therefore become more than just an editor at *SSSR na stroike*.
39 Refers most likely to a book version of the album *Pischevaia industriia*.

Pravda[40] there was an essay about the exhibition and … I am also drawn to make some recommendations. But I have little appetite to eat everything. I am prepared to let *Pischevaia industria [Food Industry]* process me into sausage just so that my wife get a boudoir and my children can eat until full.

Muttilein, my dear human being, you know that I'm no good at making jokes, but I am always good to you in spite of all the craziness, and I want to do what you say because I am more and more convinced of your wisdom and trust my own "cleverness" less and less. And I love you more and more when you become jealous and you get the little horn on your forehead[41] (I didn't create it), but it doesn't suit you. In any case, it is hard for me to live without you, and I tolerate it only with the thought that it is better for you without me.

So, Mutti, leave the album; they should write us further now that the contact is easier. Just come soon. Alpert told me that there is now a sleeper and a boy got him a ticket in очередь [queue] in 2 days for only 25 rubles. Flying is also complicated; one must sleep at the airdrome in Moscow to be ready for the departure at 5 in the morning. Then overnight again, then change to another plane that sometimes isn't there. See how it is better.

I only have concerns about Kurti, that you aren't able to put him up somewhere by then. I understand that it is finished with AMO [automobile factory]. I hope you can put Hani up close to Danzig again.

One thing is clear to me—without a revolution you will never get out of the house. I think I should come and abduct you from Skhodnia.

I await your telegram.

My dear person, don't be so angry with me and love me just a little, my heart still needs a little air—don't be stingy.

It is everything, not the right words; I have never understood how to create the right language for you.

But my hugs correspond completely to my love for you, you my only beloved Muttilein.

I kiss you, your heart

Your silly Lis

Kisses and greetings to the boys.

40 Komsomol'skaia *Pravda* is a major daily newspaper published in Moscow.
41 In Russian, as in certain other languages, the phrase to "get the little horn on one's forehead" implies that one has been cuckolded.

1890

Lazar Markovich Lissitzky born in Smolensk region. Grows up in Vitebsk and Smolensk.

1909

After failing admittance to the Saint Petersburg Academy of Arts, goes to Germany and enters the Technical Institute of Darmstadt. Studies architecture and drawing.

1912

Walks more than twelve hundred miles across Italy, drawing and studying. Visits Paris.

1914

Graduates from the Technical Institute of Darmstadt. Returns to Russia at the outbreak of World War I.

1915

Enters Riga Polytechnic Institute, which is moved to Moscow during the war.

1917

After the October Revolution designs the first banner of VTSIK (the All-Union Central Executive Committee). Works in the IZO Narkompros (the Section of Visual Arts of the People's Commissariat of Enlightenment).

1 Anonymous: *El Lissitzky,* Vitebsk. 1919–20. Gelatin silver print. Private Archive. Cat. 231

1919

Goes to Vitebsk to head the Workshops of Graphic and Printing Arts, and architecture at the Artistic-Technical Institute (Khudozhestvenno-Prakticheski Institut) established by Marc Chagall. Designs propagandistic posters and other projects (some with Kazimir Malevich) in abstract style. Produces first Suprematist drawings and paintings.

1920

For his Suprematist works coins the neologism "Proun" (an acronym for Proekt Utverzhdenia Novogo, or Project for the Affirmation of the New). Works for the Political Directorate of the Western Front (Politupravlenie zapadnogo fronta), which makes the poster *Beat the Whites with the Red Wedge* (*Klinom krasnym bei belykh*). Becomes a member of INKhUK (the Institute of Artistic Culture). Makes Suprematist designs of figurines for Aleksei Kruchenykh's Futurist opera *Victory over the Sun* (*Pobeda nad solntsem*).

1921

Leaves Vitebsk for Moscow to teach at VKhUTEMAS (the Higher State Artistic-Technical Workshops) on monumental painting and architecture. Leaves for Berlin and associates with Berlin circle of Russian intelligentsia, including Victor Shklovsky, Nikolai Aseev, Boris Pasternak, Andrei Belyi, and Lili Brik. Begins illustrations for Ilia Ehrenburg's book *6 Tales with Easy Endings* (*Shest povestei o legkikh kontsakh*), in which he uses photographic imagery for the first time. In the Soviet Union, Lenin inaugurates the New Economic Policy (NEP), which reintroduces market economy.

2 Anonymous: *El Lissitzky.* Bauhaus. 1923. Gelatin silver print. Private Archive. Cat. 232

3 Anonymous: *El Lissitzky.* Locarno. 1924. Gelatin silver print. Russian State Archive for Literature and Art, Moscow. Cat. 234

1922

With Ilia Ehrenburg sets up a periodical *Veshch*. Takes part in the organization of the First Russian Art Exhibition (Erste Russische Kunstausstellung) held in the autumn at the Galerie Van Diemen in Berlin. Erenburg's *6 Tales with Easy Endings*, with Lissitzky's illustrations, is printed. Regularly visits the studio shared by László Moholy-Nagy and Kurt Schwitters in Berlin. There meets Raoul Hausmann, Hannah Höch, and Hans Richter. With Moholy-Nagy discusses the technique of photogram. Participates in the First International Congress of Progressive Artists, held in Düsseldorf. Goes to Hanover and receives support from Aleksander Dorner and Eckard von Sydow, both members of Kestner Society. Meets Sophie Küppers, artistic director of the Kestner Society. Makes cover designs for the magazines *Broom* and *Wendingen*.

1923

Designs Vladimir Mayakovsky's book of poems *For the Voice* (*Dlia golosa*). Receives first solo exhibition at the Kestner Society. His first *Kestner Portfolio Proun* (*Kestnermappe*) is printed. Lectures and writes about modern Russian art. Collaborates with Vilmos Huszar on a photogram published in *Merz*. Becomes sick with tuberculosis.

1924

Travels to Switzerland for cure. As part of a collaboration with Schwitters on *Merz*, coedits the issue titled *Nasci*. Works for the firm of Günther Wagner on advertisements for Pelikan ink and other products. Makes a series of photographic self-portraits, including the one known as Constructor. Translates Malevich's texts, including "Lenin," and adds Lenin's figure to a tribune designed by Ilia Chashnik in 1920 in Vitebsk. With Hans Arp prepares *The Isms of Art*. Conceives *Wolkenbügel* (*Cloud Stirrup*) for Moscow.

1925

Leaves Switzerland after he is harassed by the Swiss authorities. Returns to Moscow to practice architecture. Becomes member of ASNOVA (Association of New Architects) and designs a water-sports and yacht club for a sports stadium as well as other architectural projects. Shortly after, resumes work in graphic design and photography that henceforth parallels his architectural designs.

1926

Returns to Germany to install a *Room for Constructivist Art* at the Dresden International Art Exhibition (Internationale Kunstausstellung) and the *Abstract Cabinet* (*Das Abstrakte Kabinett*) at the Provinzialmuseum Hannover. Resumes his teaching at VKhUTEMAS as an instructor of interior and furniture design. Designs photographic frieze he calls *Record* to be installed at a sports stadium. Designs sets for Sergei Tretiakov's play *I Want a Child* (*Khochu rebenka*), to be staged at the Meyerhold Theater.

1927

Sophie Küppers arrives in Moscow and marries Lissitzky. They settle in a room in a communal apartment. Designs the All-Union Printing Trades Exhibition (Vsesouznaia poligraficheskaia vystavka). Establishes first contacts with Soviet photographers and practitioners of photomontage. Coins the term *fotopis* (photo writing or photo scribing), which he juxtaposes to the photogram.

1928

First Five Year Plan initiates a program of industrialization and forced collectivization of agriculture. Lissitzky joins the graphic design section of the October (Oktiabr) group. Invited to be general designer of the Soviet Pavilion of the International Press Exhibition Pressa (Internationale Presse-Ausstellung Pressa) in Cologne. Travels to Cologne to install the preliminary designs of a large group of Soviet artists. Visits Bauhaus. Travels to Paris and photographs the city with Ehrenburg's camera. Receives a commission to design *Neues Bauen in der Welt: Russland, Amerika, Frankreich*, three volumes on contemporary architecture. Participates in architectural competitions held in the Soviet Union. Submits proposals for the *Pravda* headquarters and the House of Industry, neither of which is realized.

1929

Invited to be a designer of Film and Photo Exhibition (Internationale Ausstellung des Deutschen Werkbunds Film und Foto). Assigns Küppers to select films for enlargement. Meets Dziga Vertov. Vertov's film *Man with a Movie Camera* (*Chelovek s kinoapparatom*) is released. Publishes a short article on fotopis in *Soviet Photo* (*Sovetskoe foto*). Designs poster for the Russian Exhibition in Kunstgewerbemuseum, Zurich. Takes job as an architect with the Central Park of Culture and Rest, known as Gorky Park, founded in 1928 in Moscow.

1930

Participates in the first general exhibition of October group, which opens in Gorky Park. Travels to Germany with Küppers to design Soviet pavilions at the International Hygiene Exhibition (Internationale Hygiene-Ausstellung) in Dresden and the International Fur Trade Exhibition (Internationale Pelz-Fachausstellung) in Leipzig. Returns to Moscow with Küppers's two sons, Hans and Kurt. Jen Lissitzky is born. Vertov's film *Enthusiasm* (*Entuziazm*) is released.

1931

Becomes chief artist of the Permanent Construction Exhibition (Stroitelnaia vystavka).

1932

The Central Committee of the Communist Party decrees the abolition of all artistic associations. MOSKh (the Moscow branch of the Union of Soviet Artists) is established. Lissitzky becomes a designer of the monthly propaganda magazine *USSR in Construction* (*SSSR na stroike*), in collaboration with major Soviet photojournalists. They often visit Lissitzky at his house in Skhodnia, located about sixty kilometers from Moscow.

1933

Designs *USSR Building Socialism* (*SSSR stroit sotsializm*) and makes photomontage illustrations for Ehrenburg's *My Paris* (*Moi Parizh*). Vertov's film *Three Songs of Lenin* (*Tri pesni o Lenine*) is released. Second Five Year Plan begins.

4 Josef Albers: *El Lissitzky.* Bauhaus. 1928. Gelatin silver print. Private Archive. Cat. 236

5 Mikhail Prekhner: *El Lissitzky*. 1934. Gelatin silver print. Collection fredo's. Cat. 248

1934

Begins to collaborate with Küppers on issues of *USSR in Construction*. Designs *Workers'-Peasants' Red Army* (*Raboche-krestianskaia krasnaia armia*) and *Soviet Subtropics* (*Sovetskie subtropiki*) with Küppers. Begins work on the magazine *At the Construction of MTS and of Sovkhozy* (*Na stroike MTS i sovkhozov*). Becomes chief artist of the All-Union Agricultural Exhibition (Vsesouznaia selskokhoziaistvennaia vystavka). After a conflict with its administration, refuses to work on the project. Makes designs for the Soviet pavilion of the International Aviation Exhibition in Paris.

1935

Designs *Industry of Socialism* (*Industria sotsializma*). Continues to work with Küppers on issues of *USSR in Construction*. Spends three months at Georgian health resort in Abastumani. From there collaborates with Küppers on the design of the album *Food Industry* (*Pishchevaia industria*).

1936

Leads a team of artists who make drawings for the interior design of the Soviet pavilion for the Paris World's Fair.

1937

World's Fair opens. Agrees to be responsible for the interior design of the main pavilion of the All-Union Agricultural Exhibition. Chooses to execute the main pavilion's frieze in painting, relinquishing photomontage, the main technique used in his earlier exhibition designs. With Küppers designs four-volume issue of *USSR in Construction* dedicated to the Stalin Constitution. Tretiakov is arrested and killed shortly thereafter.

1938

Third Five Year Plan begins. Plans exhibition on the state of Soviet heavy industry for the New York World's Fair. Assembles a team of artists to execute drawings and maquettes for the Soviet pavilion in New York. Gustav Klutsis arrested and killed shortly thereafter.

1939

Designs *USSR: An Album Illustrating the State Organization and National Economy of the USSR* for New York World's Fair, which opens that year. Vsevolod Meyerhold arrested.

1940

Prepares illustrations for Ehrenburg's novel *Fall of Paris* (*Padenie Parizha*).

1941

Makes designs for Soviet pavilion at the Belgrade International Exhibition, which is canceled owing to the outbreak of war. Works on the cover for the book *Mayakovsky* and for covers of the screen scripts for *Lenin in October* (*Lenin v Oktiabre*), *Deputy of Baltic* (*Deputat Baltiki*), and other films. Designs the poster *Produce More Tanks* (*Davaite pobolshe tankov*) and several antifascist posters. Dies on December 30.

Moholy-Nagy, László. *Malerei Fotografie Film.* Bauhaus Book 8. Munich: Albert Langen Verlag, 1925; 2d expanded ed., 1927. Published in English as *Painting, Photography, Film.* Trans. Janet Seligman. Cambridge: MIT Press, 1969.

Lissitzky-Küppers, Sophie, ed. *El Lissitzky: Life, Letters, Texts.* Greenwich: New York Graphic Society, 1968.

Lissitzky, El. *Russia: An Architecture for World Revolution.* Trans. Eric Dluhosch. Cambridge: MIT Press, 1970. Originally published as *Rusland: Die Rekonstruktion der Architektur in der Sowjetunion.* Vienna: Verlag Anton Schroll, 1930.

Birnholz, Alan Curtis. "El Lissitzky." Ph.D. diss., Yale University, 1973.

El Lissitzky. Cologne: Galerie Gmurzynska, 1976.

El Lissitzky, 1890–1941. Oxford: Museum of Modern Art, 1977.

Lissitzky-Küppers, Sophie, and Jen Lissitzky, eds. *El Lissitzky, Proun und Wolkenbügel: Schriften, Briefe, Dokumente.* Dresden: VEB Verlag der Kunst, 1977.

Eskildsen, Ute, and Jan-Christopher Horak, eds. *Film und Foto der zwanziger Jahre: Eine Betrachtung der Internationalen Werkbundausstellung "Film und Foto," 1929.* Stuttgart: Hatje, 1979.

Futter, Werner, and Hubertus Gassner, eds. *Sergei Tret'iakov: Selbstgemachte Tiere.* Cologne: Verlag der Buchhandlung Walther König, 1980.

Scharfe, J., ed. *El Lissitzky: Maler, Architekt, Typograf, Fotograf.* Halle: Staatliche Galerie, 1982.

Lodder, Christina. *Russian Constructivism.* New Haven: Yale University Press, 1983.

Buchloh, Benjamin H. D. "From Faktura to Factography." *October,* no. 30 (Fall 1984): 83–119.

Michelson, Annette, ed. *Dziga, Dziga. Kino-Eye: The Writings of Dziga Vertov.* Trans. Kevin O'Brien. Berkeley: University of California Press, 1984.

Nisbet, Peter, ed. *El Lissitzky, 1890–1941.* Cambridge: Harvard University Art Museums, Busch-Reisinger Museum, 1987.

Petric, Vlada. *Constructivism in Film: The Man with the Movie Camera. A Cinematic Analysis.* Cambridge: Cambridge University Press, 1987.

Bois, Yve-Alain. "El Lissitzky: Radical Reversibility." *Art in America* 76, no. 4 (April 1988): 160–81.

El Lissitzky: 1890–1941. Hanover: Sprengel Museum, 1988.

Taylor, Richard, and Jan Christie, eds. *The Film Factory: Russian and Soviet Cinema in Documents, 1896–1939.* London: Routledge, 1988.

Phillips, Christopher, ed. *Photography in the Modern Era: European Documents and Critical Writings, 1913–1940.* New York: Metropolitan Museum of Art and *Aperture,* 1989.

Stites, Richard. *Revolutionary Dreams: Utopian Vision and Experimental Life in the Russian Revolution.* New York: Oxford University Press, 1989.

Andrews, Richard, and Milena Kalinovska. *Art into Life: Russian Constructivism 1914–1932.* New York: Rizzoli, 1990.

El Lissitzky: Architect, Painter, Photographer, Typographer, 1890–1941. Eindhoven: Municipal Van Abbemuseum, 1990.

El Lissitzky: Experiments in Photography. New York: Houk Friedman, 1990.

L. M. Lisitskii, 1890–1941. Moscow: Tretiakov Gallery, 1990.

Gassner, Hubertus, and Roland Nachtigaller. *Gustav Klucis: Retrospective.* Kassel: Museum Fredericianum, 1991.

Morris Hambourg, Maria, and Christopher Phillips. *The New Vision: Photography between the World Wars.* New York: Metropolitan Museum of Art, 1991.

Elliott, David, ed. *Photography in Russia, 1840–1940.* London: Thames and Hudson, 1992.

Teitelbaum, Matthew, ed. *Montage and Modern Life, 1919–1942.* Cambridge: MIT Press, 1992.

Antonowa, Irina, and Jorn Merkert, eds. *Berlin-Moskau, 1900–1950.* Munich: Prestel Verlag, 1995.

Tupitsyn, Margarita. *Glaube, Hoffnung, Anpassung: Sowjetische Bilder, 1928–1945.* Essen: Folkwang Museum, 1995.

Kruchenykh, Aleksei. *Nash vykhod.* Moscow: RA, 1996.

Tupitsyn, Margarita. *The Soviet Photograph, 1924–1937.* New Haven: Yale University Press, 1996.

Khardzhiev, N. I. *Stat'i ob avantgarde.* 2 vols. Moscow: RA, 1997.

Margolin, Victor. *The Struggle for Utopia: Rodchenko, Lissitzky, Moholy-Nagy, 1917–1946.* Chicago: University of Chicago Press, 1997.

Dabrowski, Magdalena, Liah Dickerman, and Peter Galasi. *Aleksandr Rodchenko.* New York: Museum of Modern Art, 1998.

Catalogue of the Exhibition

The catalogue is generally chronological.

Abbreviations:
RGALI = Russian State Archive of Art and
           Literature, Moscow
ORGTG = Department of Manuscripts,
            State Tretiakov Gallery, Moscow

I. Works by El Lissitzky

Photography and Design Sketches

1 (Plate 3)
Maquette for an illustration for *6 Tales with
Easy Endings* (*6 povestei o legkikh kontsakh*),
a novel by Ilia Ehrenburg, 1921–22.
Photo collage, ink, pencil on cardboard.
29.2 x 2.9 cm.
Private Collection.

2 (Plate 4)
Maquette for an illustration for *6 Tales with
Easy Endings,* a novel by Ilia Ehrenburg, 1921–22.
Photo collage, pencil, gouache, ink on cardboard.
33 x 24.3 cm.
State Tretiakov Gallery, Moscow.

3 (Plate 5)
Black Sphere. Illustration for *6 Tales with
Easy Endings,* a novel by Ilia Ehrenburg, 1921–22.
Gelatin silver print. 23 x 17 cm.
Private Archive.

4 (Plate 6)
Proun B 111 (Self-Portrait), 1922.
Photo collage. 11 x 17 cm.
Private Collection. Courtesy Galerie Gmurzynska,
Cologne.

5
Untitled (page from Käte Steinitz guest book,
Hanover), 1923.
Graphite pencil. 27 x 33 cm.
Sprengel Museum Hannover.

6 (Plate 37)
Lenin Tribune, with Ilia Chashnik, 1920–24.
Gelatin silver print. 22 x 16.3 cm.
Private Archive.

7 (Plate 8)
Untitled (Lissitzky and Huszar), 1923.
Photogram. 17.6 x 23.7 cm.
The Art Institute of Chicago, Mary L. and
Leigh B. Block Collection, 1992.100. ©1999.
The Art Institute of Chicago, Chicago.
All Rights Reserved.

8 (Plate 49)
For the Voice (Dlia golosa), a poem by
Vladimir Mayakovsky, 1923.
Gelatin silver print. 13 x 10 cm.
RGALI, f. 2361, op. 1, ed. khr. 3, l. 9.

9 (Plate 17)
Untitled, ca. 1924.
Gelatin silver print with text. 16 x 11 cm.
Collection Thomas Walther, New York.

10 (Plate 7)
In the Studio, ca. 1923.
Gelatin silver print. 10.9 x 8.3 cm.
Metropolitan Museum of Art, Ford Motor Company
Collection, Gift of Ford Motor Company and
John C. Waddell, 1987, 1987.1100.62. ©1999.
The Metropolitan Museum of Art, New York.

11 (Plate 45)
Untitled (Composition with Spoon), ca. 1923–27.
Photogram. 23.3 x 29.1 cm.
Collection WAVE PBK, Cologne.

12 (Plate 22)
Hans Arp, 1924.
Gelatin silver print with text. "Fotopis portrait
of Schwalbendada Hans Arp, 1924."
Page from the album compiled by
Aleksei Kruchenykh. 22 x 33.8 cm.
RGALI, f. 1072, op. 2, ed. khr. 357, ll. 87–88.

13 (Plate 23)
Hans Arp, 1924.
Gelatin silver print. 18 x 12.9 cm.
Galerie Berinson, Berlin.

14 (Plate 9)
Maquette for the book *Prounen*, ca. 1924.
Seventeen pages. Gelatin silver prints, lithographs,
and collages on paper. 28 x 21.2 cm.
RGALI, f. 2361, op. 1, ed. khr. 2, ll. 22–44.

15 (Plate 24)
Pelikan Ink, 1924.
Photogram. 21.1 x 14.8 cm.
Galerie Berinson, Berlin.

16 (Plate 25)
Pelikan Ink, 1924.
Photogram. 21.5 x 15.1 cm.
Collection Manfred Heiting, Amsterdam.

17 (Plate 26)
Pelikan Ink, 1924.
Photogram. 17.9 x 12.9 cm.
RGALI, f. 2361, op. 1, ed. khr. 5, l. 18.

18 (Plate 27)
Pelikan Ink, Typewriter Ribbon, Carbon Paper, 1924.
Gelatin silver print. 11.4 x 8.3 cm.
RGALI, f. 2361, op. 1, ed. khr. 5, l. 22.

19 (Plate 28)
Pelikan Carbon Paper, 1924.
Photogram. 17.8 x 12.9 cm.
RGALI, f. 2361, op. 1, ed. khr. 5, l. 24.

20 (Plate 29)
Pelikan Carbon Paper, 1924.
Photogram. 17.9 x 13 cm.
RGALI, f. 2361, op. 1, ed. khr. 5, l. 21.

21 (Plate 30)
Pelikan Carbon Paper, 1924.
Photogram. 17.9 x 12.9 cm.
RGALI, f. 2361, op. 1, ed. khr. 5, l. 19.

22 (Plate 31)
Pelikan Carbon Paper, 1924.
Photogram. 17.2 x 13 cm.
RGALI, f. 2361, op. 1, ed. khr. 5, l. 20.

23 (Plate 32)
*Design for Pelikan (Advertising for Typewriter
Carbon Paper)*, 1924.
Gelatin silver print. 15.7 x 11 cm.
RGALI, f. 2361, ed. khr. 5, l. 23.

24 (Plate 33)
Pelikan Carbon Paper, 1924.
Photogram. 12.8 x 12.9 cm.
RGALI, f. 2361, op. 1, ed. khr. 5, l. 17.

25 (Plate 34)
Pelikan Sealing Wax, 1924.
Gelatin silver print, gouache. 18 x 24 cm.
RGALI, f. 2361, op. 1, ed. khr. 5, l. 4.

26 (not illustrated)
Pelican Ink, 1924.
Gelatin silver print. 27.3 x 21.2 cm.
RGALI, f. 2361, op. 1, ed. khr. 5, l. 4.

27 (Plate 18)
Kurt Schwitters, ca. 1924.
Modern print from original glass negative.
17.8 x 12.9 cm.
Sprengel Museum Hannover. Permanent Loan.
Niedersächsische Sparkassenstiftung.

28 (Plate 19)
Kurt Schwitters, ca. 1924.
Modern print from original glass negative.
17.8 x 12.9 cm.
Sprengel Museum Hannover. Permanent Loan.
Niedersächsische Sparkassenstiftung.

29 (Plate 20)
Kurt Schwitters, ca. 1924.
Gelatin silver print. 11.1 x 10 cm.
Collection Thomas Walther, New York.

30 (Plate 10)
Untitled (Hand with a Compass), 1924.
Gelatin silver print. 14.6 x 20.5 cm.
Sprengel Museum Hannover. Permanent Loan.
Collection Ann and Jürgen Wilde, Zülpich.

31 (Plate 11)
Self-Portrait, 1924.
Gelatin silver print. 16.8 x 12.1 cm.
Barry Friedman Ltd., New York.

32 (Plate 12)
Self-Portrait, 1924.
Modern print from original glass negative.
17.8 x 12.9 cm.
Sprengel Museum Hannover. Permanent Loan.
Niedersächsische Sparkassenstiftung.

33 (Plate 13)
Self-Portrait (Constructor), 1924.
Gelatin silver print (negative). 12.6 x 14.4 cm.
Galerie Berinson, Berlin.

34 (Plate 14)
Self-Portrait (Constructor), 1924.
Gelatin silver print, collage. 19.3 x 21.2 cm.
State Tretiakov Gallery,
Inv. ORGTG, b. 76, ed. khr. 11, l. 1.

35 (Plate 16)
Self-Portrait, 1924,
Gelatin silver print. 17.3 x 12.1 cm.
Collection Gilman Paper Company, New York.

36 (Plate 61)
Der Wolkenbügel (*Cloud Stirrup*), 1924 – 25.
Photomontage, retouched. 40 x 55.5 cm.
RGALI, f. 2361, op. 1, ed. khr. 6, l. 12.

37 (Drutt, fig. 11)
Design for *Room for Constructivist Art*
(*Raum für konstruktivistische Kunst*) at the
International Art Exhibition in Dresden, 1926.
Gelatin silver print. 16.6 x 11.7 cm.
Private Archive.

38 (frontispiece)
Design for the *Abstract Cabinet* (*Das Abstrakte
Kabinett*) in the Provinzialmuseum, Hannover,
1927.
Gouache, collage. 39.9 x 52.3 cm.
Sprengel Museum Hannover.

39 (Plate 43)
Untitled (Pliers and Wire), ca. 1927.
Photogram (positive). 23 x 29 cm.
Galerie Berinson, Berlin.

40 (Plate 44)
Untitled (Pliers and Wire), ca. 1927.
Photogram (negative). 23 x 29 cm.
Galerie Berinson, Berlin.

41 (Plate 39)
Record (Runner), 1926.
Photomontage. Gelatin silver print. 25 x 17.8 cm.
Collection Thomas Walther, New York.

42 (Plate 40)
Runner in the City, 1926.
Photo collage. 13.1 x 12.8 cm.
Metropolitan Museum of Art, Ford Motor Company
Collection. Gift of Ford Motor Company and
John C. Waddell, 1987, 1987.1100.47. ©1999.
The Metropolitan Museum of Art, New York.

43 (Plate 41)
Record (Runner), 1926.
Photo collage. 12 x 21.4 cm.
Galerie Berinson, Berlin.

44 (Plate 38)
Untitled (Superimposed Portrait), 1926–30.
Photomontage. Gelatin silver print. 16.1 x 11.8 cm.
Museum of Modern Art, New York.
Gift of Shirley C. Burden and David H. McAlpin
by exchange. ©1999, Museum of Modern Art,
New York.

45 (Plate 42)
Footballer, 1926.
Gelatin silver print. 13.3 x 10.7 cm.
Alexander Kaplen, New York.

46 (Plate 51)
Guide for the All-Union Printing Trades Exhibition
(*Vsesouznaia Poligraficheskaia Vystavka*), with
Solomon Telingater, 1927.
Gelatin silver print, retouched. 14.6 x 10.4 cm.
Private Archive.

47 (Plate 52)
Guide for the All-Union Printing Trades Exhibition,
with Solomon Telingater, 1927.
Gelatin silver print. 9 x 10.8 cm.
Private Archive.

48 (Plate 47.1)
Untitled, ca. 1927.
Cyanotype. 18.3 x 13.1 cm.
RGALI, f. 2361, op. 1, ed. khr. 21, l. 12.

49 (Plate 47.2)
Untitled, ca. 1927.
Cyanotype. 17.9 x 12. cm.
RGALI, f. 2361, op. 1, ed. khr. 21, l. 11.

50 (Plate 47.3)
Untitled, ca. 1927.
Cyanotype. 10.1 x 13.1 cm.
RGALI, f. 2361, op. 1, ed. khr. 21, l. 10.

51 (Plate 58)
Untitled. Detail from the Soviet pavilion
of the International Press Exhibition Pressa
(Internationale Presse-Ausstellung Pressa),
Cologne, 1928.
Gelatin silver print. 11.5 x 8.6 cm.
Private Archive.

52 (Plate 57)
Installation view of El Lissitzky's *Jubiläumsschau
eines Dorfes* (*Anniversary Show of a Village*),
designed for Pressa and preinstalled in the
State Universal Store (GUM), Moscow, 1928.
Photomontage. Gelatin silver print.
16.1 x 11.8 cm.
RGALI, f. 2361, op. 1, ed. khr. 12, l. 38.

53 (Plate 48)
Untitled, n.d.
Gouache on paper. 21.5 x 16 cm.
RGALI, f. 1334, op. 2, ed. khr. 311, l. 1.

54 (Plate 54)
Cover design for the brochure of the Soviet
pavilion at Pressa, 1928.
Gouache on paper, collage. 28.4 x 22 cm.
RGALI, f. 2361, op. 1, ed. khr. 11, l. 7 – 8.

55 (Plate 55)
Catalogue for the Soviet pavilion at Pressa, 1928.
Gelatin silver print, photo collage, ink.
14.9 x 10.9 cm.
Art Gallery of New South Wales, Australia.

56 (Plate 50)
Design for a window mobile for a bookstore
of the Land and Factory Publishing House, 1928.
Photo collage, gouache, ink, pencil on cardboard.
36.4 x 53.1 cm.
State Tretiakov Gallery, Inv. RS-1907.

57 (Plate 53)
Maquette for the cover of the complete edition
of Lev Tolstoy's novels, 1928.
Photo collage. 23.9 x 16 cm.
RGALI, f. 2361, op. 1, ed. khr. 11, l. 6.

58 (Plate 59)
Flagpole for the Soviet pavilion at Pressa, 1928.
Gouache, ink, photo collage on paper.
70.8 x 52.8 cm.
State Tretiakov Gallery, Inv. RS-1842.

59 (Plate 46)
Attributed to El Lissitzky; believed to be
Grigory Miller, *Untitled* (What Is Svetopis
[Chto takoe svetopis]), ca. 1928.
Photogram. 8.7 x 12.7 cm.
Collection Gilman Paper Company, New York.

60 (Tupitsyn, fig. 12)
Self-Portrait, Pressa, 1928.
Photomontage. Gelatin silver print. 8.3 x 9 cm.
Private Archive.

61 (Plate 60)
Untitled (page from the Bode family guest book,
Hanover), 1928.
Photo collage, graphite pencil. 26 x 21.5 cm.
Sprengel Museum Hannover. Private Collection.
On Loan.

62 (Plate 62)
Eiffel Tower, 1928.
Gelatin silver print. 5.8 x 8.6 cm.
Galerie Gmurzynska, Cologne.

63 (Plate 63)
Eiffel Tower, 1928.
Gelatin silver print. 6 x 8.7 cm.
Private Archive.

64 (Plate 64)
Eiffel Tower, 1928.
Gelatin silver print. 13.7 x 9.2 cm.
Galerie Gmurzynska, Cologne.

65 (Plate 65)
Eiffel Tower, 1928.
Gelatin silver print. 13.7 x 9.2 cm.
Galerie Gmurzynska, Cologne.

66 (Plate 66.1)
Eiffel Tower, 1928.
Contact gelatin silver print. 3.6 x 4.6 cm.
Private Archive.

67 (Plate 66.2)
Eiffel Tower, 1928.
Contact gelatin silver print. 3 x 4.4 cm.
Private Archive.

68 (Plate 66.3)
Eiffel Tower, 1928.
Contact gelatin silver print. 3.3 x 4.7 cm.
Private Archive.

69 (Plate 66.4)
Eiffel Tower, 1928.
Contact gelatin silver print. 3.2 x 4.6 cm.
Private Archive.

70 (Plate 66.5)
Eiffel Tower, 1928.
Contact gelatin silver print. 3.3 x 4.6 cm.
Private Archive.

71 (Plate 67)
Eiffel Tower, 1928.
Gelatin silver print. 9.8 x 13.1 cm.
Private Archive.

72 (not illustrated)
Eiffel Tower, 1928.
Gelatin silver print. 13.8 x 8.9 cm.
Galerie Gmurzynska, Cologne.

73 (not illustrated)
Rue de Rivoli, Paris, 1928.
Contact gelatin silver print. 3.5 x 9 cm.
Private Archive.

74 (not illustrated)
Paris, 1928.
Contact gelatin silver print. 3.8 x 9.2 cm.
Private Archive.

75 (not illustrated)
Paris, 1928.
Contact gelatin silver print. 3.4 x 4.7 cm.
Private Archive.

76 (Letters, fig. 2)
Sophie Küppers in the House of Le Corbusier,
Paris, 1928.
Gelatin silver print. 17. 8 x 23.7 cm.
Private Archive.

77 (Plate 68)
Untitled, ca. 1928.
Photogram. 29.1 x 23.5 cm.
RGALI, f. 2361, op. 1, ed. khr. 21, l. 9.

78 (Plate 83)
Soldier near the Shabolovskaia Radio Tower, 1929.
Gelatin silver print. 22.3 x 16.8 cm.
RGALI, f. 1334, op. 2, ed. khr. 312, l. 4.

79 (Plate 75)
Poster design for the Russian Exhibition
(Russische Ausstellung) in the Kunstgewerbe-
museum, Zürich, 1929.
Gelatin silver print. 23.5 x 22.5 cm.
Staatliche Galerie Moritzburg Halle, Landeskunst-
museum Sachsen-Anhalt, Photography Collection.

80 (Plate 74)
Maquette for "Kinoglaz," an unpublished book
by Dziga Vertov, 1929.
Photomontage, retouched. 11.8 x 15.2 cm.
Collection Manfred Heiting, Amsterdam.

81 (Plate 80)
Cover design for *Russia,* vol. 1 of *New Building in
the World (Neues Bauen in der Welt)*, a book by
El Lissitzky, 1929–30.
Photomontage. Gelatin silver print. 26.8 x 19.7 cm.
Collection Thomas Walther, New York.

82 (Plate 81)
Cover design for *America,* vol. 2 of *New Building in
the World (Neues Bauen in der Welt),* a book

by Richard J. Neutra, 1929–30.
Photomontage. Gelatin silver print. 25.5 x 19 cm.
Collection Thomas Walther, New York.

83 (Plate 82)
Cover design for *France*, vol. 3 of *New Building in
the World (Neues Bauen in der Welt)*, a book
by Roger Ginzburger, 1929–30.
Photomontage. Gelatin silver print. 28 x 21.1 cm.
Barry Friedman Ltd. New York.

84 (Plate 84)
Untitled (detail from the Soviet pavilion of the
International Hygiene Exhibition), Dresden, 1930.
Gelatin silver print. 27.2 x 21 cm.
Collection Robert Shapazian, Los Angeles.

85 (Plate 86)
Untitled (detail from the Soviet pavilion of the
International Hygiene Exhibition), 1930.
Photomontage. Gelatin silver print. 16.8 x 29.5 cm.
Private Archive.

86 (not illustrated)
Untitled (detail from the Soviet pavilion of the
International Hygiene Exhibition), 1930.
Photomontage. Gelatin silver print. 15 x 19.8 cm.
Barry Friedman Ltd., New York.

87 (Plate 87)
Untitled (page from Alexander Dorner's guest
book, Hanover), 1930.
Photo collage with text. 22.1 x 17.5 cm.
Sprengel Museum Hannover.

88 (Letters, fig. 7)
Sophie Küppers, ca. 1930.
Gelatin silver print. 18 x 13 cm.
Sprengel Museum Hannover.

89 (Tupitsyn, fig. 20)
Kurt and Hans Küppers, 1930.
Gelatin silver print. 13.3 x 18.1 cm.
Private Archive.

90 (Letters, fig. 15)
Kurt and Hans Küppers, 1930.
Gelatin silver print. 20.6 x 12.9 cm.
Private Archive.

91 (Letters, fig. 14)
Kurt and Hans Küppers, 1930.
Gelatin silver print. 12.1 x 16. 8 cm.
Barry Friedman Ltd. New York.

92 (Plate 89)
Untitled (Lenin), 1930.
Photomontage. Gelatin silver print. 25.9 x 21 cm.
Private Archive.

93 (Letters, fig. 12)
Birth Announcement for Jen Lissitzky, 1930.
Gelatin silver print. 13.5 x 8.9 cm.
Collection Robert Shapazian, Los Angeles.

94 (not illustrated)
Birth Announcement for Jen Lissitzky, 1930.
Gelatin silver print. 20.3 x 13.7 cm.
Private Archive.

95 (Letters, fig.10)
Untitled (Jen Lissitzky superimposed on
a photograph of El Lissitzky working on a stage
design of *I Want a Child,* a play by Sergei Tretiakov),
1930.
Gelatin silver print. 17.8 x 23.7 cm.
Private Collection.

96 (Plate 91)
Design for *USSR in Construction (SSSR na
stroike)*, 1930.
Photomontage. Gelatin silver print. 24 x 16.7 cm.
RGALI, f. 1334, op. 2, ed. khr. 312, l. 5.

97 (Plate 92)
Design for *USSR in Construction*, 1930.
Photomontage. Gelatin silver print. 29 x 21 cm.
RGALI. f. 2361, op. 1, ed. khr. 21, l. 7.

98 (Letters, fig. 13)
Jen Lissitzky, ca. 1931.
Photomontage. 17.1 x 17. 4 cm.
Private Archive.

99 (Plate 90)
Untitled, n.d.
Photomontage. 42.5 x 52 cm.
RGALI, f. 2361, op. 1, ed. khr. 15, ll. 10–12.

100 (Plate 93)
Design of a double page for *USSR in Construction*,
no. 10, 1932.
Photomontage. Gelatin silver print. 6.6 x 10.5 cm.
Priska Pasquer, Photographic Consulting, Cologne.

101 (Plate 94)
Design for *USSR in Construction*, no. 10, 1932.
Photomontage. Gelatin silver print. 8.2 x 10.1 cm.
Howard Schickler Fine Art, New York.

102 (Plate 97)
Architectural design for the field for mass activities
in Recreational Park in Sverdlovsk, 1932.
Photo collage, pencil on cardboard. 46 x 58 cm.
Private Archive.

103 (Plate 70)
Design for illustrations for *My Paris (Moi Parizh)*,
a book by Ilia Ehrenburg, ca. 1933.
Photomontage. Gelatin silver print. 13 x 12.7 cm.
RGALI, f. 2361, op.1, ed. khr. 18, l. 6.

104 (Plate 71)
Design for cover and illustrations for *My Paris,*
a book by Ilia Ehrenburg, ca. 1933.
Gelatin silver print. 17.1 x 5.3 cm.
RGALI, f. 2361, op. 1, ed. khr. 18, l. 5.

105 (not illustrated)
Design for illustrations for *My Paris,* a book by
Ilia Ehrenburg, ca. 1933.
Gelatin silver print. 17.9 x 23.9 cm.
RGALI, f. 2361, op.1, ed. khr. 18, l. 7.

106 (Plate 95)
Cover design for *USSR in Construction*, no. 10,
1936.
Photomontage. Gelatin silver print with text.
17.5 x 11.5 cm.
RGALI, f. 2361, op.1, ed. khr. 15, l. 2.

107 (Plate 96)
Design for *USSR in Construction*, no. 10, 1934.
Photomontage. Gelatin silver print. 21 x 15.1 cm.
RGALI, f. 1334, op. 2, ed. khr. 312, l. 2.

108 (Plate 114)
Design of a title page for *USSR in Construction*,
nos. 9–12, 1937.
Photomontage. Gelatin silver print, hand-colored.
60.5 x 43.3 cm.
Private Archive.

109 (Plate 115)
Maquette for *USSR in Construction*, nos. 9–12,
1937.
Ten gelatin silver prints, collage on paper.
Fourteen pages, each 25 x 17 cm.
Private Archive.

110 (Plate 116)
Design for *USSR in Construction*, nos. 9–12, 1937.
Photomontage. Gelatin silver print. 21.5 x 30.1 cm.
Priska Pasquer, Photographic Art Consulting,
Cologne.

111 (Plate 117)
Design for *USSR in Construction*, nos. 9–12, 1937.
Photomontage. Gelatin silver print. 17.4 x 27. 2 cm.
Museum Folkwang, Essen.

112 (Tupitsyn, fig. 29.1)
Design for *USSR in Construction*, nos. 9–12, 1937.
Photomontage. Gelatin silver print. 21. x 27.4 cm.
Priska Pasquer, Photographic Art Consulting,
Cologne.

113 (Tupitsyn, fig. 29.2)
Design for *USSR in Construction*, nos. 9–12, 1937.
Photomontage. Gelatin silver print, 17.4 x 23.7 cm.
Statens Konstmuseer, Moderna Museet, Stockholm.

114 (Tupitsyn, fig. 29.3)
Design for *USSR in Construction*, nos. 9–12, 1937.
Photomontage. Gelatin silver print. 17.5 x 23.8 cm.
Priska Pasquer, Photographic Art Consulting,
Cologne.

115 (Tupitsyn, fig. 29.4)
Design for *USSR in Construction*, nos. 9–12, 1937.
Photomontage. Gelatin silver print. 22.2 x 30 cm.
Priska Pasquer, Photographic Art Consulting,
Cologne.

116 (not illustrated)
Design for *USSR in Construction*, nos. 9–12, 1937.
Photomontage. Gelatin silver print. 20.9 x 28.7 cm.
Priska Pasquer, Photographic Art Consulting,
Cologne.

117 (not illustrated)
Design for *USSR in Construction*, nos. 9–12, 1937.
Photomontage. Gelatin silver print. 17.9 x 24.5 cm.
Priska Pasquer, Photographic Art Consulting,
Cologne.

118 (not illustrated)
Design for *USSR in Construction*, nos. 9–12, 1937.
Photomontage. Gelatin silver print. 20.9 x 28.8 cm.
Priska Pasquer, Photographic Art Consulting,
Cologne.

119 (not illustrated)
Design for *USSR in Construction*, nos. 9–12, 1937.
Photomontage. Gelatin silver print. 18.0 x 28.5 cm.
Priska Pasquer, Photographic Art Consulting,
Cologne.

120 (Plate 119)
All Power to the Soviets, 1937.
Photo collage. 49.8 x 67.3 cm.
Museum Folkwang, Essen.

121 (not illustrated)
Cover design for *USSR in Construction*, nos. 2–3,
1940.
Photomontage. Gelatin silver print. 18.1 x 23.8 cm.
Priska Pasquer, Photographic Art Consulting,
Cologne.

Printed Matter

122 (Plates 2.1–2.2)
Kestner Portfolio. *Proun* (1919–23).
Lithography. Plate 3: 60 x 44 cm;
plate 6: 44 x 60 cm.
Sprengel Museum Hannover.

123 (Drutt, figs. 4.1–4.4)
Cover and illustrations for the book *6 Tales with
Easy Endings*, Gelikon Publishing House, Berlin,
1922.
20.2 x 13.8 cm.
Stedelijk Van Abbemuseum, Eindhoven.

124 (Drutt, fig. 3)
Cover and typography for the magazine *Veshch-
Gegenstand-Object*, vols. 1–2, Berlin, 1922.
31 x 23. 9 cm.
Collection Ann and Jürgen Wilde, Zülpich.

125 (Plate 1)
The New (*Novyi*) from figurine portfolio for
Victory over the Sun (*Pobeda nad solntsem*),
a libretto by Aleksei Kruchenykh, 1920–23.
Lithography. Plate 10: 53.4 x 45.5 cm.
Sprengel Museum Hannover.

126 (Drutt, fig. 7)
4 i Lamp (Heliokonstruktion 125 Volt) (*4 i Lampe*
[Heliokonstruktion 125 Volt]), with Vilmos Huszar.
Merz, no. 6. Merzverlag, Hanover, 1923.
Kunsthaus, Zurich.

127 (Plate 15)
Self-Portrait (Constructor), ca. 1924.
Halftone photo lithograph. 36 x 48 cm.
Private Archive. This image was reversed during
its original printing.

128 (Plate 35)
Pelikan Drawing Ink, 1924.
Lithography. 32.5 x 44.5 cm.
Museum für Kunst und Gewerbe, Hamburg.

129 (Drutt, figs. 10.1–10.2)
*Die Kunstismen. Les Ismes de l'Art. The Isms of
Art, 1924–1914*, with Hans Arp, 1925.
26.3 x 41.2 cm.
Stedelijk Van Abbemuseum, Eindhoven.

130 (Plate 36)
Cover for *VKhUTEMAS Architecture (Arkhitektura
VKhUTEMAS)*. VKhUTEMAS, Moscow, 1927.
Letterpress. 24.2 x 17.4 cm.
Collection of Larry Zeman and Howard Garfinkel,
Productive Arts, Brooklyn Heights, Ohio.

131 (Tupitsyn, fig. 7)
Page with *Self-Portrait* (Constructor), from the
magazine *Gebrauchsgraphik* (*Production Graphics*),
December 1928, Berlin-New York. From the album
compiled by Aleksei Kruchenykh.
30.5 x 22.2 cm.
RGALI, f. 1334, op. 2, ed. khr. 313, l. 1.

132 (not illustrated)
Cover for the brochure for the Soviet pavilion
at Pressa, 1928.
21.1 x 15.3 cm.
Die Deutsche Bibliothek, Deutsches Buch und
Schriftmuseum der Deutschen Bücherei, Leipzig.

133 (Tupitsyn, fig. 14)
Page from *Sovetskoe Foto* (*Soviet Photo*), no. 10,
1929, with photograms and the article "Fotopis"
by El Lissitzky.
25 x 17.4 cm.
Larry Zeman and Howard Garfinkel, Productive
Arts, Brooklyn Heights, Ohio.

134 (Plate 56)
Foldout from the catalogue for the Soviet pavilion
at Pressa, 1928.
Letterpress. 20.2 x 231 cm.
Collection David King, London.

135 (Plate 21)
Cover for the book *Notes of a Poet* (*Zapiski poeta*),
by Ilia Selvinski, IZOGIZ, Moscow, 1928.
17.4 x 12.7 cm.
Galerie Schlégl-Nicole Schlégl, Zürich.

136 (Plate 73)
Cover for the catalogue of the Japanese Cinema
Exhibition (Iaponskoe kino), Gosznak, Moscow,
1929.
Letterpress. 14.7 x 21.3 cm.
Stedelijk Van Abbemuseum, Eindhoven.

137 (not illustrated)
Poster for the Russian Exhibition at
Kunstgewerbemuseum, Zürich, 1929.
Lithography. Proof. 127 x 90 cm.
Barry Friedman Ltd., New York.

138 (Plate 76)
Poster for the Russian Exhibition at
Kunstgewerbemuseum, Zürich, 1929.
Lithography. 127 x 90 cm.
Schule für Gestaltung, Plakatsammlung, Basel.

139 (Plate 80)
Cover for *Russia*, vol. 1 of *New Building in the
World*, 1930.
Letterpress. 29 x 23 cm.
Collection Ann and Jürgen Wilde, Zülpich.

140 (Plate 81)
Cover for *America*, vol. 2 of *New Building in the
World*, 1930.

Letterpress. 29 x 23 cm.
Instituto Valenciano de Arte Moderno, Generalitat Valencia.

141 (Plate 82)
Cover for *France,* vol. 3 of *New Building in the World,* 1930.
Letterpress. 29 x 23 cm.
Collection Ann and Jürgen Wilde, Zülpich.

142 (Plate 85)
Cover for the catalogue of the Soviet pavilion at the International Hygiene Exhibition, Dresden, 1930.
Letterpress. 29.2 x 20.8 cm.
Bibliothek des Deutschen Hygiene-Museums, Dresden.

143 (Plate 89)
Cover for the catalogue of the Soviet pavilion at the International Fur Trade Exhibition, Leipzig, 1930.
Letterpress. 29.5 x 20.7 cm.
Die Deutsche Bibliothek, Deutsches Buch und Schriftmuseum der Deutschen Bücherei, Leipzig.

144 (Letters, fig. 5)
Page from *Izofront: Class Struggle on the Front of Visual Arts (Izofront: Klassovaia borba na fronte prostranstvennykh iskusstv)* with photographs by El Lissitzky and Jan Tschichold, publication of October Group, IZOGIZ, Moscow, 1931.
17.2 x 13 cm.
Larry Zeman and Howard Garfinkel, Productive Arts, Brooklyn Heights, Ohio.

145 (Plate 72)
Cover for the magazine *Brigada khudozhnikov* (Artists' Brigade), no. 4, 1931.
Letterpress. 31.2 x 22 cm.
Larry Zeman and Howard Garfinkel, Productive Arts, Brooklyn Heights, Ohio.

146 (Plate 98)
USSR in Construction, no. 10, 1932.
Lithography and gravure. 42 x 29.7 cm.
Plan of the issue with Max Alpert, devoted to the construction of Dneiper Dam.
Photography: Max Alpert and Arkady Shaikhet.
German edition.
Larry Zeman and Howard Garfinkel, Productive Arts, Brooklyn Heights, Ohio.

147 (Plate 99)
USSR in Construction, no. 2, 1933.
Lithography and gravure. 42 x 30 cm.
Plan of the issue with Semen Fridliand, devoted to the fifteenth anniversary of the Red Army.
Photography: Alpert, Georgy Zelma, Fridliand, Nikolai Shtertser, Union Photo (Souzfoto).
French edition.
Larry Zeman and Howard Garfinkel, Productive Arts, Brooklyn Heights, Ohio.

148 (Plate 102)
USSR in Construction, no. 9, 1933.
Lithography and gravure. 42 x 30 cm.
Devoted to the Soviet Arctic.
Photography: Anonymous.
English edition.
Larry Zeman and Howard Garfinkel, Productive Arts, Brooklyn Heights, Ohio.

149 (Plate 100)
USSR Building Socialism (SSSR stroit sotsialism).
IZOGIZ, Moscow, 1933.
Lithography. 34.5 x 26.5 cm.
Larry Zeman and Howard Garfinkel, Productive Arts, Brooklyn Heights, Ohio.

150 (Plate 69)
Cover and illustrations for the book *My Paris.*
IZOGIZ, Moscow, 1933.
16.7 x 19.5 cm.
Larry Zeman and Howard Garfinkel, Productive Arts, Brooklyn Heights, Ohio.

151 (Plate 103)
USSR in Construction, no. 2, 1934, with Sophie Küppers. Lithography and gravure. 42 x 30 cm.
Devoted to the four bolshevik victories: (1) Epron; (2) the Moscow – Kara Kum – Moscow Automobile Run; (3) the Pamir Expedition; (4) the flight of the Stratospheric aircraft *USSR.*
Photography: Union Photo and Press Cliché.
Russian edition.
Larry Zeman and Howard Garfinkel, Productive Arts, Brooklyn Heights, Ohio.

152 (Plate 104)
Workers'-Peasants' Red Army (Raboche-krestianskaia krasnaia armia). IZOGIZ, Moscow, 1934.
Lithography. 30 x 35.5 cm.
Larry Zeman and Howard Garfinkel, Productive Arts, Brooklyn Heights, Ohio.

153 (Plate 105)
USSR in Construction, no. 6, 1934, with Sophie Küppers.
Lithography and gravure. 42 x 30 cm.
Devoted to Soviet science.
Photography: Georgy Petrusov.
English edition.
Larry Zeman and Howard Garfinkel, Productive Arts, Brooklyn Heights, Ohio.

154 (Plate 106)
USSR in Construction, no. 10, 1934, with Sophie Küppers.
Lithography and gravure. 42 x 30 cm.
Devoted to the epic of the Cheluskin exploration.
Photography: Pavel Novitsky, Ivan Shagin, Shaikhet.
English edition.
Larry Zeman and Howard Garfinkel, Productive Arts, Brooklyn Heights, Ohio.

155 (Plate 101)
Soviet Subtropics (Sovetskie subtropiki), with Sophie Küppers, Newspaper and Magazine Union, Moscow, 1934.
Lithography. 30 x 23 cm.
Photography: Zelma, Shaikhet, E. Mikulina, Fridliand, Shagin, Union Photo.
Larry Zeman and Howard Garfinkel, Productive Arts, Brooklyn Heights, Ohio.

156 (Plate 107)
At the Construction of MTS and of Sovkhozy (Na stroike MTS i Sovkhozov), no. 4, 1934.
Lithography and gravure. 36.4 x 26.2 cm.

Photography: Anatoly Skurikhin, Shaikhet.
Larry Zeman and Howard Garfinkel, Productive Arts, Brooklyn Heights, Ohio.

157 (Plate 108)
At the Construction of MTS and of Sovkhozy, no. 2, 1935.
Lithography and gravure. 36.4 x 26.2 cm.
Photography: Mikhail Prekhner, Dmitry Debabov, Petrusov.
Larry Zeman and Howard Garfinkel, Productive Arts, Brooklyn Heights, Ohio.

158 (Plate 109)
Industry of Socialism (Industria sotsializma), Stroim, Moscow, 1935.
Seven separately bound volumes in a case.
35.1 x 25.8 cm.
Larry Zeman and Howard Garfinkel, Productive Arts, Brooklyn Heights, Ohio.

159 (not illustrated)
USSR in Construction, no. 5, 1935, with Sophie Küppers.
Lithography and gravure. 42 x 29.7 cm.
Devoted to the fifteenth anniversary of the Azerbaidjan oil industry.
Photography: Alpert and Petrusov.
Russian edition.
Larry Zeman and Howard Garfinkel, Productive Arts, Brooklyn Heights, Ohio.

160 (Plate 112)
USSR in Construction, nos. 4 – 5, 1936.
Lithography and gravure. 42 x 29.7 cm.
Devoted to the fifteenth anniversary of Soviet Georgia.
Photography: Alpert, Shagin, and others.
Russian edition.
Larry Zeman and Howard Garfinkel, Productive Arts, Brooklyn Heights, Ohio.

161 (not illustrated)
USSR in Construction, no. 10, 1936, with Sophie Küppers.
Lithography and gravure. 42 x 29. 7 cm.
Devoted to Kabardino-Balkarian autonomous region.
Photography: Petrusov, Yury Eremin, Prekhner.
English edition.
Larry Zeman and Howard Garfinkel, Productive Arts, Brooklyn Heights, Ohio.

162 (Plate 110)
Food Industry (Pishchevaia industria), with Sophie Küppers, 1936.
Lithography. 50.8 x 40.6 cm.
Fifty-eight lithographs with a booklet in a portfolio.
Photography: Vladimir Gruntal, Shtertser, Shaikhet, Skurikhin, and others.
Museum Folkwang, Essen.

163 (Plate 111)
USSR in Construction, no. 1, 1937, with Sophie Küppers.
Lithography and gravure. 42 x 29. 7 cm.
Devoted to the Workers' and Peasants' Red Navy.
Photography: Petrusov, Nikolai Petrov, Yakov Khalip, and others.
Russian edition.

Larry Zeman and Howard Garfinkel, Productive Arts, Brooklyn Heights, Ohio.

164 (Plate 113)
USSR in Construction, no. 3, 1937, with Sophie Küppers.
Lithography and gravure. 42 x 29 cm.
Devoted to the people of the Ordzhonikidze territory (northern Caucasus).
Photography: Alpert, Eremin, and others.
English edition.
Larry Zeman and Howard Garfinkel, Productive Arts, Brooklyn Heights, Ohio.

165 (Plate 118)
USSR in Construction, nos. 9–12, 1937, with Sophie Küppers.
Lithography and gravure. 42 x 29.7 cm.
Devoted to Stalin's Constitution.
Photography: Alpert, Alperin, Mikhail Grachev, Gostev, Debabov, Boris Kudoiarov, Elizar Langman, Mark Markov, Mikulina, Petrusov, Petrov, Prekhner, Fridliand, Khalip, Shagin, Shaikhet, Abram Shterenberg, and others.
English edition.
Larry Zeman and Howard Garfinkel, Productive Arts, Brooklyn Heights, Ohio.

166 (Plate 120)
USSR in Construction, nos. 5–6, 1938, with Sophie Küppers.
Lithography and gravure. 42 x 30 cm.
Devoted to Far Eastern territory.
Photography: Prekhner, Shaikhet.
Russian edition.
Larry Zeman and Howard Garfinkel, Productive Arts, Brooklyn Heights, Ohio.

167 (Plate 121)
USSR in Construction, no. 6, 1939, with Sophie Küppers.
Lithography and gravure. 42 x 30 cm.
Devoted to the Korobov family.
Photography: Petrusov, Alpert, Langman, Fridliand, Khalip.
Russian edition.
Larry Zeman and Howard Garfinkel, Productive Arts, Brooklyn Heights, Ohio.

168 (back cover)
USSR: An Album Illustrating the State Organization and National Economy of the USSR, with Aleksandr Grigorovich and Mikhail V. Nikolaev, 1939.
24.2 x 34.6 cm.
Scientific Publishing Institute of Pictorial Statistics, Moscow.
Larry Zeman and Howard Garfinkel, Productive Arts, Brooklyn Heights, Ohio.

169 (Plate 123)
USSR in Construction, no. 1, 1940, with Sophie Küppers.
Lithography and gravure. 42 x 30 cm.
Devoted to the Stalin Grand Canal of Fergana.
Photography: Alpert.
English edition.
Larry Zeman and Howard Garfinkel, Productive Arts, Brooklyn Heights, Ohio.

170 (Plate 124)
USSR in Construction, nos. 2–3, 1940.
Lithography and gravure. 39.5 x 30 cm.
Devoted to the western Ukraine and western Belorussia.
Photography: Petrusov, Kolli, Mikhail Ozerski, TASS.
German edition.
Larry Zeman and Howard Garfinkel, Productive Arts, Brooklyn Heights, Ohio.

171 (Plate 125)
USSR in Construction, no. 10, 1940, with Sophie Küppers.
Lithography and gravure. 42 x 30 cm.
Devoted to Bessarabia and northern Bukovina.
Photography: Petrusov, TASS.
German edition.
Larry Zeman and Howard Garfinkel, Productive Arts, Brooklyn Heights, Ohio.

172 (Plate 122)
USSR in Construction, no. 11, 1940, with Sophie Küppers.
Lithography and gravure. 42 x 30 cm.
Devoted to the construction of the warfleet.
Photography: Petrusov, Alpert, Prekhner.
Russian edition.
Larry Zeman and Howard Garfinkel, Productive Arts, Brooklyn Heights, Ohio.

173 (not illustrated)
USSR in Construction, no. 3, 1941, with Sophie Küppers.
Lithography and gravure. 42 x 30 cm.
Devoted to inventors in the Soviet Union.
Photography: Prekhner, Press Cliché, TASS.
Russian edition.
Larry Zeman and Howard Garfinkel, Productive Arts, Brooklyn Heights, Ohio.

174 (Plate 126)
Produce More Tanks (Davaite pobolshe tankov), with Nikolai Troshin, 1942.
Lithography. 89.2 x 58.8 cm.
Staatliche Galerie Moritzburg, Halle, Landeskunstmuseum Sachsen-Anhalt, Photography Collection.

II. Works by Other Artists

Experimental Photography and Design

175 (Archive, fig. 1.1)
Man Ray, *5ᵉ rayogramme*, from the album *Champs délicieux*, 1922.
20.5 x 15.8 cm. Copy print.
Private Archive.

176 (Archive, fig. 1.2)
Man Ray, *6ᵉ rayogramme*, from the album *Champs délicieux*, 1922.
21.2 x 16.7 cm. Copy print.
Private Archive.

177 (Archive, fig. 1.3)
Man Ray, *7ᵉ rayogramme*, from the album *Champs délicieux*, 1922.
20.4 x 15.9 cm. Copy print.
Private Archive.

178 (Archive, fig. 1.4)
Man Ray, *9ᵉ rayogramme*, from the album *Champs délicieux*, 1922.
20 x 15.5 cm. Copy print.
Private Archive.

179 (Archive, fig. 1.5)
Man Ray, *12ᵉ rayogramme*, from the album *Champs délicieux*, 1922.
20.4 x 15.8 cm. Copy print.
Private Archive.

180 (Archive, fig. 2)
Attributed to Georgy Zimin, *Untitled,* ca. 1927.
Photogram. 17.2 x 12.9 cm.
Page from the album compiled by Aleksei Kruchenykh.
RGALI, f. 1334, op. 1, ed. khr. 1094, l. 3.

181 (Archive, fig.3)
Georgy Zimin, *Untitled,* ca. 1927.
Photogram. 18 x 22.5 cm.
Page from the album compiled by Aleksei Kruchenykh.
RGALI, f. 1334, op. 1, ed. khr. 1094, l. 39.

182 (not illustrated)
Attributed to Georgy Zimin, *Untitled,* ca. 1927.
Photogram. 18 x 22.7 cm.
Page from the album compiled by Aleksei Kruchenykh.
RGALI, f. 1334, op.1, ed. khr. 1094, l. 84.

183 (Archive, fig. 6)
Gustav Klutsis and Sergei Senkin, dust jacket for the book *In Memory of Fallen Leaders (Pamiati pogibshikh vozhdei)*, 1927.
Lithography. 42.9 x 59.1 cm.
Howard Schickler Fine Art, New York.

184 (not illustrated)
Sergei Senkin and Gustav Klutsis, *Untitled*, ca. 1927.
Gelatin silver print, cyanotype. 18 x 21 cm.
Page from the album compiled by Aleksei Kruchenykh.
RGALI, f. 1334, op. 1, ed. khr. 1094, ll. 7–10.

185 (Archive, fig. 4)
Sergei Senkin, *Through Fabric (Cherez materiu)*,
1927.
Cyanotype. 21.5 x 33 cm.
Page from the album compiled by
Aleksei Kruchenykh.
RGALI, f. 1334, op. 1, ed. khr. 1092, l. 50.

186 (Archive, fig. 5)
Attributed to Sergei Senkin, *Untitled*, ca. 1927.
Cyanotype. 17.4 x 11.7 cm.
RGALI, f. 1334, op. 1 ed. khr. 1094, l. 14.

187 (Plate 46.1)
Grigory Miller, Cover for the book
What Is Svetopis, by A. Predvoditelev.
Letterpress. 17 x 12. 6 cm.
Private Collection.

188 (Plate 79.1)
Boris Ignatovich, *Untitled*, 1929.
Gelatin silver print (printed in the 1960s).
19 x 28.3 cm.
Private Collection.

189 (not illustrated)
Franz Roh and Jan Tschichold, *Foto-Auge*, 1929.
Letterpress. 29. 2 x 21 cm.
Kunst- und Museumsbibliothek der Stadt Köln,
Cologne.

Pressa, Cologne, 1928

190 (Tupitsyn, fig. 10)
Anonymous, installation of the photofrieze at
the Soviet pavilion at Pressa, 1928.
Gelatin silver print. 16.2 x 20.5 cm.
RGALI, f. 2361, op. 1, ed. khr. 12, l. 62.

191 (Tupitsyn, fig. 11)
Anonymous, installation of the Soviet pavilion
at Pressa, 1928.
Gelatin silver print. 23.3 x 15.8 cm.
RGALI, f. 2361, op. 1, ed. khr. 12, l. 51.

192 (not illustrated)
Scholz [?], public viewing of the Soviet pavilion
at Pressa, 1928.
Gelatin silver print. 17 x 22.7 cm.
RGALI, f. 2361, op. 1, ed. khr. 12, l. 42.

193 (Archive, fig. 8)
Sergei Senkin, *Varia Organizes Pioneers*
(*Varia organizuet pionerov*, left), 1926, and
My Frieze from the Cologne Exhibition Pressa
(*Moi friz kelnskoy vystavki Pressy*), 1928.
Gelatin silver prints mounted on paper.
11.5 x 9.2 cm. and 8.9 x 3.9 cm.
Page from the album compiled by
Aleksei Kruchenykh.
RGALI, f. 1334, op. 1, ed. khr. 288, ll. 253–254.

194 (Archive, fig. 9)
Sergei Senkin, *Untitled* (left), 1927, and
Self-Portrait (right), 1928.
Gelatin silver prints mounted on paper.
12.2 x 17.4 cm. and 9.8 x 6 cm.
Page from the album compiled by
Aleksei Kruchenykh.
RGALI, f. 1334, op. 1, ed. khr. 288, ll. 250–51.

195 (Tupitsyn, fig. 9)
Gustav Klutsis, view of Pressa designs
preinstalled in GUM, Moscow, 1928.
Gelatin silver print. 16.6 x 11.2 cm.
Private Collection.

196 (Archive, fig. 7)
Gustav Klutsis, view of Valentina Kulagina's
Stand for the Soviet Village preinstalled in GUM,
Moscow, 1928.
Gelatin silver print. 17.3 x 11.2 cm.
Priska Pasquer, Photographic Consulting, Cologne.

197 (Tupitsyn, fig. 13)
Scholz [?], *El Lissitzky, Sergei Senkin, Nikolai Simon
at Pressa*, Cologne, 1928.
Gelatin silver print. 17.8 x 23.7 cm.
Private Archive.

Internationale Ausstellung
des Deutschen Werkbunds Film und Foto

198 (Pohlmann, fig. 2)
Anonymous, installation view of the Soviet section
at the International Film and Photo Exhibition,
photo section, 1929.
Gelatin silver print. 10.2 x 12.3 cm.
RGALI, f. 2361, op. 1, ed. khr. 7, l. 2.

199 (Pohlmann, fig. 3)
Anonymous. Installation view of the Soviet section
at Film and Photo Exhibition, film section, 1929.
Gelatin silver print. 11.2 x 15.1 cm.
RGALI, f. 2361, op. 1, ed. khr. 7, l. 3.

Dziga Vertov

200 (Archive, fig. 10)
Dziga Vertov [?], advertisement for *Sixth Part of the
World (Shestaia chast sveta)*, a film by Dziga Vertov,
1926.
Gelatin silver print. 21.5 x 15.5 cm.
RGALI, f. 2091, op. 1, ed. khr. 1, l. 4.

201 (Archive, fig. 11.1)
Dziga Vertov [?], German advertisement for
*Man with a Movie Camera (Chelovek s kinoappa-
ratom)*, a film by Dziga Vertov, 1929.
Gelatin silver print. 21.5 x 15.2 cm.
RGALI, f. 2091, op. 1, ed. khr. 1, l. 2.

202 (Archive, fig. 11.2)
Dziga Vertov [?], German advertisement for
Enthusiasm (Entuziazm), a film by Dziga Vertov,
1930–31.
Gelatin silver print. 21.7 x 15.3 cm.
RGALI, f. 2091, op. 1, ed. khr. 46, l. 5.

203 (Archive, fig. 12.1)
Still from the film *Man with a Movie Camera*, 1929.
28.7 x 40.1 cm.
Collection Thomas Walther, New York.

204 (Archive, fig. 12.2)
Still from the film *Man with a Movie Camera*. 1929.
Gelatin silver print. 21.5 x 15.5 cm.
RGALI, f. 1923, op. 2, ed. khr. 2687, l. 30.

205 (Archive, fig. 12.3)
Still from the film *Man with a Movie Camera*, 1929.
Gelatin silver print. 16.7 x 16 cm.
RGALI, f. 1923, op. 2, ed. khr. 2687, l. 28.

206 (Archive, fig. 12.4)
Still from the film *Man with a Movie Camera*, 1929.
Gelatin silver print. 11 x 17 cm.
RGALI, f. 1923, op. 2, ed. khr. 2687, l. 20.

207 (not illustrated)
Still from the film *Man with a Movie Camera*, 1929.
Gelatin silver print. 11.8 x 17.2 cm.
RGALI, f. 1923, op. 2, ed. khr. 2687, l. 13.

208 (not illustrated)
Still from the film *Man with a Movie Camera*, 1929.
Gelatin silver print. 8.7 x 11.3 cm.
RGALI, f. 1923, op. 2, ed. khr. 2687, l. 12.

209 (not illustrated)
Still from the film *Man with a Movie Camera*, 1929.
Gelatin silver print. 25 x 34.4 cm.
RGALI, f. 2986, op. 1, ed. khr. 59, l. 26.

210 (not illustrated)
Still from the film *Man with a Movie Camera*, 1929.
Gelatin silver print. 25.2 x 34.4 cm.
RGALI, f. 2986, op. 1, ed. khr. 59, l. 30.

211 (Plate 74.1)
Still from *Man with a Movie Camera*. 1929.
Sequence 22, adopted from "Kino glaz," 1924.
Gelatin silver print. 29 x 36.5 cm.
Collection Manfred Heiting, Amsterdam.

212 (not illustrated)
Subtitles from the film *Man with a Movie Camera*,
1929.
Offset. 11.5 x 15.7 cm.
RGALI, f. 2091, op. 1, ed. khr. 31, ll. 1–7.

213 (Archive, fig. 13.1)
Still from the film *Three Songs of Lenin
(Tri pesni o Lenine)*, a film by Dziga Vertov,
1933–34.
Gelatin silver print. 23.6 x 17.5 cm.
RGALI, f. 2091, op. 1, ed. khr. 52, l. 1.

214 (Archive, fig. 13.2)
Still from the film *Three Songs of Lenin*,
by Dziga Vertov, 1933–34.
Gelatin silver print. 9.5 x 12.9 cm.
RGALI, f. 2986, op. 1, ed. khr. 54, l. 25.

215 (Archive, fig. 13.3)
Still from the film *Three Songs of Lenin*, 1933–34.
Gelatin silver print. 16.1 x 21.5 cm.
RGALI, f. 2091, op. 1, ed. khr. 52, l. 5.

216 (Archive, fig. 13.4)
Still from the film *Three Songs of Lenin*, 1933–34.
Gelatin silver print. 16.1 x 21.3 cm.
RGALI, f. 2091, op. 1, ed. khr. 52, l. 3.

217 (Archive, fig. 13.5)
Still from the film *Three Songs of Lenin*, 1933–34.
Gelatin silver print. 16.4 x 21.5 cm.
RGALI, f. 2091, op. 1, ed. khr. 52, l. 17.

218 (not illustrated)
Still from the film *Three Songs of Lenin,* 1933 – 34.
Gelatin silver print. 16.2 x 21.5 cm.
RGALI, f. 2091, op. 1, ed. khr. 52, l. 21.

219 (not illustrated)
Still from the film *Three Songs of Lenin,* 1933 – 34.
Gelatin silver print. 16 x 21.2 cm.
RGALI, f. 2091, op. 1, ed. khr. 52, l. 15.

220 (not illustrated)
Still from the film *Three Songs of Lenin,* 1933 – 34.
Gelatin silver print. 15.9 x 21 cm.
RGALI, f. 2091, op. 1, ed. khr. 52, l. 18.

221 (not illustrated)
Still from the film *Three Songs of Lenin,* 1933 – 34.
Gelatin silver print. 15.9 x 21 cm.
RGALI, f. 2091, op. 1, ed. khr. 52, l. 19.

222 (not illustrated)
Still from the film *Three Songs of Lenin,* 1933 – 34.
Gelatin silver print. 15.9 x 21 cm.
RGALI, f. 2091, op. 1, ed. khr. 52, l. 14.

223 (not illustrated)
Subtitles from the film *Three Songs of Lenin,*
1933 – 34.
Offset. Each 10.9 x 6.2 cm.
RGALI, f. 2091, op. 1, ed. khr. 51, ll. 1 – 10.

224 (Archive, fig. 13.6)
Anonymous, Red Army soldiers march to the movie
theater to view *Three Songs of Lenin*, 1934.
Gelatin silver print. 16 x 21.2 cm.
RGALI, f. 2091, op. 1, ed. khr. 57, l. 11.

225 (not illustrated)
Anonymous, Red Army soldiers march to the movie
theater to view *Three Songs of Lenin*, 1934.
Gelatin silver print, 16 x 21.2 cm.
RGALI, f. 2091, op. 1, ed. khr. 57, l. 10.

226 (Tupitsyn, fig. 16)
Umbo (Otto Umbehr), *Dziga Vertov*, Berlin, 1929.
Gelatin silver print. 6 x 23.8 cm.
RGALI, f. 2091, op. 2, ed. khr. 574, l. 11.

227 (not illustrated)
Anonymous, *Dziga Vertov*, ca. 1929.
Gelatin silver print. 11 x 15.9 cm.
RGALI, f. 2091, op. 2, ed. khr. 580, l. 21.

228 (not illustrated)
Anonymous, *Dziga Vertov*, ca. 1930.
Gelatin silver print. 16.3 x 6.7 cm.
RGALI, f. 2091, op. 2, ed. khr. 580, l. 13.

229 (Tupitsyn, fig. 19)
Elizaveta Svilova, *Dziga Vertov and Sophie Küp-
pers's Son,* ca. 1930 – 31.
Gelatin silver print. 15 x 9.6 cm.
Priska Pasquer, Photographic Consulting, Cologne.

230 (Tupitsyn, fig. 22)
Elizaveta Svilova, *El Lissitzky,
Dziga Vertov, Sophie Küppers, and Ruvim Lissitzky
in Skhodnia,* 1932.
Gelatin silver print. 12 x 18.1 cm.
Private Archive.

Portraits of El Lissitzky

231 (Chronology, fig. 1)
Anonymous, *El Lissitzky*, Vitebsk, 1919 – 20.
Gelatin silver print. 15.6 x 4.7 cm.
Private Archive.

232 (Chronology, fig. 2)
Anonymous, *El Lissitzky,* Bauhaus, 1923.
Gelatin silver print. 10.3 x 7.9 cm.
Private Archive.

233 (not illustrated)
Anonymous, *El Lissitzky,* Berlin, 1924.
Gelatin silver print. 5.9 x 4 cm.
RGALI, f. 2361, op. 1, ed. khr. 72, l. 3.

234 (Chronology, fig. 3)
Anonymous, *El Lissitzky,* Locarno, 1924.
Gelatin silver print. 13.7 x 8.3 cm.
RGALI, f. 2361, op. 1, ed. khr. 72, l. 3.

235 (not illustrated)
Anonymous, *El Lissitzky,* Bauhaus, 1928.
Gelatin silver print. 11.7 x 17 cm.
RGALI, f. 2361, op. 1, ed. khr. 72, l. 5.

236 (Chronology, fig. 4)
Josef Albers, *El Lissitzky*, Bauhaus, 1928.
Gelatin silver print. 16.7 x 11.5 cm.
Private Archive.

237 (not illustrated)
Josef Albers, *El Lissitzky*, Bauhaus, 1928.
Gelatin silver print. 17.4 x 11 cm.
Private Archive.

238 (Tupitsyn, fig. 3)
Anonymous, El Lissitzky working on a stage
design of Sergei Tretiakov's play *I Want a Child*
in the Meyerhold Theater, 1926 – 28.
Gelatin silver prints. 8.6 x 12.8 cm.
Private Archive.

239 (Tupitsyn, fig. 4)
Anonymous, El Lissitzky working on a stage
design of Sergei Tretiakov's play *I Want a Child*
in the Meyerhold Theater, 1926 – 28.
Gelatin silver print. 8.4 x 9.5 cm.
Private Archive.

240 (not illustrated)
Anonymous, El Lissitzky working on a stage
design of Sergei Tretiakov's play *I Want a Child*
in the Meyerhold Theater, 1926 – 28.
Gelatin silver print. 8.9 x 13.9 cm.
Private Archive.

241 (not illustrated)
Anonymous, El Lissitzky working on a stage
design of Sergei Tretiakov's play *I Want a Child*
in the Meyerhold Theater, 1926 – 28.
Gelatin silver print. 8.8 x 13.9 cm.
Private Archive.

242 (Tupitsyn, fig. 5)
Josef Albers, *El Lissitzky*, Bauhaus, 1928 – 30.
Photomontage. 41.8 x 29.7 cm.
Metropolitan Museum of Art, New York, Ford Motor

Company Collection, Gift of Ford Motor Company
and John C. Waddell, 1987. 100.464. ©1999.
The Metropolitan Museum of Art, New York.

243 (not illustrated)
Gustav Klutsis, *El Lissitzky*, ca. 1931.
Gelatin silver print. 7.4 x 14.1 cm.
RGALI, f. 1334, op. 2, ed. khr. 313, l. 3.

244 (Letters, fig. 11)
Anonymous, *El Lissitzky and Jen Lissitzky*,
ca. 1931.
Gelatin silver print. 8.5 x 11.4 cm.
RGALI, f. 1334, op. 2, ed. khr. 313, l. 5.

245 (Letters, fig. 6)
Max Alpert, *El Lissitzky*, Dnieper Dam, 1932.
Gelatin silver print. 7.9 x 12.8 cm.
Private Archive.

246 (Letters, fig. 3)
Max Alpert, *El Lissitzky, Sophie Küppers and
Unidentified Person,* Skhodnia, ca. 1932.
Gelatin silver print. 9.7 x 14.5 cm.
RGALI, f. 2361, op. 1, ed. khr. 73, l. 9.

247 (Tupitsyn, fig. 26)
Georgy Zelma, El Lissitzky working on the album
Workers'-Peasants' Red Army, 1934.
Gelatin silver print. 15.7 x 22.7 cm.
Private Collection.

248 (Chronology, fig. 5)
Mikhail Prekhner, *El Lissitzky*, 1934.
Gelatin silver print. 23.1 x 14.8 cm.
Collection fredo's.

249 (not illustrated)
Mikhail Prekhner, *El Lissitzky*, 1934.
Gelatin silver print. 17.7 x 22.2 cm.
Collection Dorothee Altenburg, Cologne.

250 (Letters, fig. 1)
Mikhail Prekhner, *El Lissitzky*, 1934.
Gelatin silver print. 39 x 24.6 cm.
RGALI, f. 2361, op. 1, ed. khr. 72, l. 8.

Photographs Associated with and Used in El Lissitzky's Photographic Designs for Mass-Media Publications

251 (Plate 92.1)
Dmitry Debabov, *Smokestacks*, 1929.
Gelatin silver print. 43.2 x 30.2 cm.
Howard Schickler Fine Art, New York.

252 (Tupitsyn, fig. 25)
Anonymous, Georgy Zelma photographing a scene staged by El Lissitzky for an issue of *USSR in Construction* devoted to the fifteenth anniversary of the Red Army. Mezhrabpom (International Workers Aid) Film Studio, ca. 1932.
Gelatin silver print. 12 x 16.9 cm.
Howard Schickler Fine Art, New York.

253 (not illustrated)
Levedev and M. P. Gorbunov [?], *Soviet Pamir (Tadzhikistan)*, 1933.
Gelatin silver print. 21.2 x 14.3 cm.
Sveriges Television, International Historical Press Photo Collection, Stockholm, XAH 471.

254 (not illustrated)
Levedev and M. P. Gorbunov [?], *Soviet Pamir (Tadzhikistan)*, 1933.
Gelatin silver print. 21.1 x 14.3 cm.
Sveriges Television, International Historical Press Photo Collection, Stockholm, XAH 472.

255 (not illustrated)
Anonymous, *Roof of the World: German-Russian Joint Pamir Expedition*, 1933.
Gelatin silver print. 20.5 x 16.5 cm.
Sveriges Television, International Historical Press Photo Collection, Stockholm, XAH 473.

256 (Archive, fig. 19)
Anonymous, *Roof of the World: German-Russian Joint Pamir Expedition*, 1933.
Gelatin silver print. 20.5 x 16.5 cm.
Sveriges Television, International Historical Press Photo Collection, Stockholm, XAH 474.

257 (Archive, fig. 20)
Kislov [?], *The Soviet Stratospheric Balloon "USSR" Breaks the Record,* 1933.
Gelatin silver print. 17.5 x 12 cm.
Sveriges Television, International Historical Press Photo Collection, Stockholm, XAH 470.

258 (not illustrated)
Roman Karmen, *To the Second Soviet Stratospheric Flight*, 1934.
Gelatin silver print. 15 x 21 cm.
Sveriges Television, International Historical Press Photo Collection, Stockholm, XAH 469.

259 (not illustrated)
Kuibyshev [?], *The Heroes of Stratospheric Flight Report*, 1933.
Gelatin silver print. 16.7 x 21.9 cm.
Sveriges Television, International Historical Press Photo Collection, Stockholm, XAH 468.

260 (Archive, fig. 21)
Eduard Tisse, *9500 Kilometers on Soviet Roads (The Moscow – Kara Kum – Moscow Automobile Run)*, 1933.
Gelatin silver print. 14.7 x 21 cm.
Sveriges Television, International Historical Press Photo Collection, Stockholm, XAH 467.

261 (not illustrated)
Abram Shterenberg, *The Moscow – Kara Kum – Moscow Automobile Run*, 1933.
Gelatin silver print. 21.3 x 15.2 cm.
Sveriges Television, International Historical Press Photo Collection, Stockholm, XAH 466.

262 (Archive, fig. 15)
Georgy Petrusov, *Socialist Treaty for Competition*, 1934.
Gelatin silver print. 28.3 x 49 cm.
Collection fredo's.

263 (Archive, fig. 16)
Georgy Petrusov, *Untitled*, 1934.
Gelatin silver print. 33.9 x 49 cm.
Private Archive.

264 (Tupitsyn, fig. 24)
Anonymous, Max Alpert and Georgy Petrusov at the offices of *USSR in Construction*, ca. 1934.
Gelatin silver print. 21.7 x 29.3 cm.
Howard Schickler Fine Art, New York.

265 (not illustrated)
Ivan Shagin, *A Participant in the Cross-Country Horseback Ride, Ashkhabad-Moscow*, ca. 1936.
Gelatin silver print. 37 x 27.7 cm.
Private Archive.

266 (not illustrated)
Georgy Petrusov, *Untitled*, ca. 1937.
Gelatin silver print. 19.8 x 29 cm.
Priska Pasquer, Photographic Consulting, Cologne.

267 (Archive, fig. 18)
Georgy Petrusov, *Untitled* (the Korobov family), ca. 1939.
Gelatin silver print. 45 x 29 cm.
Private Archive.

268 (not illustrated)
Ivan Shagin, *Untitled*, 1930s.
Gelatin silver print. 38.7 x 27.6 cm.
Private Archive.

269 (Archive, fig. 14)
Ivan Shagin, *Nina Kamneva, Who Set a World Record in a Delayed Parachute Jump*, 1930s.
Gelatin silver print. 38.7 x 28 cm.
Private Archive.

270 (Archive, fig. 17)
Ivan Shagin, *Untitled*, 1930s.
Gelatin silver print. 45.4 x 30 cm.
Private Archive.

271 (not illustrated)
Anonymous, *Untitled*, 1930s.
Gelatin silver print. 27 x 38.6 cm.
Private Archive.

III. Documents

272 (not illustrated)
An official questionnaire filled out by El Lissitzky, August 25, 1930.
29.4 x 21 cm.
RGALI, f. 2361, op. 1, ed. khr. 58, ll. 4 – 5.

273 (not illustrated)
A letter of recommendation given to El Lissitzky by E. Melinadze, editor of *USSR in Construction*, June 7, 1941.
18.3 x 18.9 cm.
RGALI, f. 2361, op. 1., ed. khr. 61, l. 20.

274 (not illustrated)
Advertising leaflet for a German edition of *USSR in Construction*, no. 10, 1932, with a text: "the first copy smelling bloody paint," 1932.
Paper, ink, color pencil.
RGALI, f. 2361, op. 1, ed. khr. 3, l. 21.